F/50

D0444415

REVISED SECOND EDITION

REVISED SECOND EDITION

BY DAVE DEWITT

Research Assistance by Mary Jane Wilan

Gulf Publishing Company
Houston, Texas

Copyright © 1989, 1994 by David A. DeWitt. All rights including reproduction by photographic or electronic process and translation into other languages are fully reserved under the International Copyright Union, the Universal Copyright Convention, and the Pan-American Copyright Convention. Reproduction or use of this book in whole or in part in any manner without written permission of the publisher is strictly prohibited.

Gulf Publishing Company
Book Division
P. O. Box 2608 ☐ Houston, Texas 77252-2608

10 9 8 7 6 5 4 3 2 1

Library of Congress Cataloging-in-Publication Data

DeWitt, Dave.
    New Mexico / by Dave DeWitt ; research assistance by Mary Jane Wilan. — 2nd ed.
        p.   cm. — (The Texas monthly guidebooks)
    Includes index.
    ISBN 0-87719-238-3
    1. New Mexico—Guidebooks. I. Wilan, Mary Jane. II. Title.
III. Series.
F794.3.D49   1993
917.8904'53—dc20   93-9007
                                                              CIP

Texas Monthly is a registered trademark of Mediatex Communications Corporation.

Printed in the United States of America.

Contents

Acknowledgments

Muchas gracias to the dedicated workers at the state's various chambers of commerce, many of whom provided detailed and occasionally privileged information in return for anonymity.

I would also like to thank my wife, Mary Jane Wilan, who loyally sacrificed a summer vacation for a book deadline, and various friends who contributed information and advice to this project: Doug and Jeanette Geist, Jeff and Nancy Gerlach, Diane Reveal, Joseph Sanchez, Wayne Scheiner, Dave and Barbara Schrader, Robert Simon, Robert Spiegel, and Susan Stiger.

Introduction

On my first visit to New Mexico, I felt I was coming home to a place I had never been before. In fact, my infatuation with this state was so intense that I made my permanent home here within three months of that first trip. My fascination with the land and culture here has only grown over the course of the subsequent fifteen years during which I have been discovering New Mexico. In 1979, frustrated because I could find no current travel guides to the state, I wrote and self-published *Discover New Mexico*, which was a modest attempt to collect in one volume all the important attractions in the state. In the introduction to that book, I noted: "Nearly every kind of landscape in the world is here—we lack only a seashore—and there is much diversity in the cities and towns themselves. We have cowtowns, farm towns, mining towns, oil towns, resort towns, ghost towns, mountain villages, Indian pueblos, a huge metropolis within ten miles of soaring eagles, and the oldest capital in the United States. Much of New Mexico's distinctiveness is owed to its tri-cultural heritage: Indian, Hispanic, and Anglo populations existing together in harmony, respect, and cooperation."

Then, as now, the primary difficulty in appreciating the land and culture of New Mexico has been the physical size of the state. New Mexico's 121,666 square miles make it the fifth largest state, after Alaska, Texas, California, and Montana, so in writing this present volume I began with the premise that any exploration of a state larger than many countries needed a systematic approach.

Because of its rectangular shape and the fact it's roughly bisected by two interstate highways, the state is often described in terms of quadrants; so it seemed logical to divide this guidebook into four parts, one for each quadrant. For the mapmakers in the audience, my scheme divides New Mexico north and south by a line at 35 degrees north latitude and east and west by a line at 106 degrees, 30 minutes west longitude. Each quadrant has a designated lead-off city which can be used as a base of operations for a driving tour of the quadrant. These cities are the four largest in New Mexico and all have excellent visitor accommodations. After discussing the lead-off city in each quadrant, we take a city-by-city loop tour that returns close to the lead-off city. Along the way there is a distinct tendency to get sidetracked by geology, nature, history, and tall tales, but eventually we get to the lodging and dining recommendations. Although it was not possible for me to shop in every gallery, eat in every restaurant, or sleep in every motel listed in this guidebook, I didn't miss it by too much. I have visited nearly every town and attraction listed, and I've dined at perhaps one-third of the restaurants in this book. In order to recommend places I could not personally visit, I relied on the opinions of experts whose identities I cannot reveal.

A perfect guidebook does not exist. This one is designed to provide clear and accurate information about New Mexico's most interesting and popular attractions, but does not purport to be the ultimate historical reference or geographical atlas. Also, life goes on and things change as books are written and published. Although it is unlikely that the mountains will move, shops and restaurants open and close, telephone numbers and addresses change, and travel conditions are in a constant state of flux. Hence it is always a good idea to phone the more distant attractions before taking a long trip to visit them.

Guidebook writers live in constant fear that they've left out some big attraction, and that is why I'm now apologizing in advance for omitting someone's favorite rock formation or restaurant.

Dave DeWitt
Albuquerque

Recommended Reading

To supplement this guidebook, here are a few publications that I feel capture the land, culture, and ambience of New Mexico. In addition to these nonfiction works, readers should experience the novels of New Mexico authors Rudolfo Anaya, Richard Bradford, Tony Hillerman, Oliver La Farge, and John Nichols.

Albuquerque Monthly. Albuquerque: Starlight Publishing.

Bahti, Tom. *Southwestern Indian Tribes.* Las Vegas, NV: KC Publications, 1968.

Beck, Warren. *New Mexico: A History of Four Centuries.* Norman: University of Oklahoma Press, 1962.

Chilton, Lance, et. al. *New Mexico: A New Guide to the Colorful State.* Albuquerque; University of New Mexico Press, 1984.

Dent, Huntley. *The Feast of Santa Fe: Cooking of the American Southwest.* New York: Simon and Schuster, 1985.

DeWitt, Dave. *Discover New Mexico.* Albuquerque: Sunbelt Press, 1979.

Kues, Barry S. *Fossils of New Mexico.* Albuquerque: University of New Mexico Press, 1982.

Looney, Ralph. *Haunted Highways: The Ghost Towns of New Mexico.* Albuquerque: University of New Mexico Press, 1979.

New Mexico Magazine. Montoya Bldg. 1101 S. Francis, Santa Fe 87503 (827-0220) $18 yr.

Pearce, T.M. *New Mexico Place Names: A Geographical Dictionary.* Albuquerque; University of New Mexico Press, 1965.

Penfield, Thomas. *A Guide to Treasure in New Mexico.* Deming: H.G. Carson Enterprises, 1974.

Sherman, John. *Santa Fe: A Pictorial History*. Norfolk, VA: The Donning Company, 1984.

Simmons, Marc. *Witchcraft in the Southwest: Spanish and Indian Supernaturalism in the Southwest*. Lincoln, NE: Bison Books, 1980.

Simmons, Marc. *Ranchers, Ramblers, and Renegades*. Santa Fe: Ancient City Press, 1984.

Tuska, Jon. *Billy the Kid: A Bio-Bibliography*. Greenwood, 1983.

Waters, Frank. *The Masked Gods: Navaho and Pueblo Ceremonialism*. Athens, Ohio: Ohio University Press, 1950.

Chile Pepper Magazine. Albuquerque: Out West Publishing. P. O. Box 4278, Albuquerque, NM 87196.

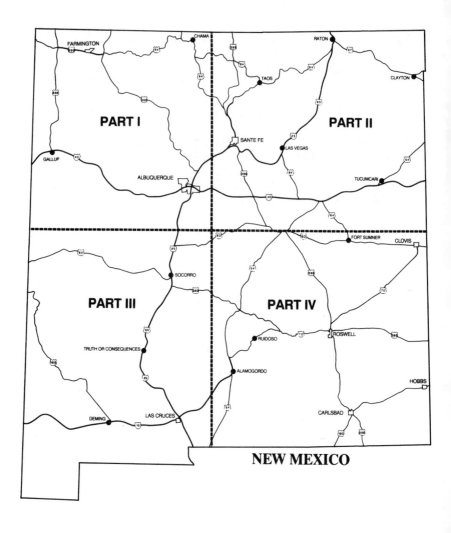

NEW MEXICO

PART I

Albuquerque and the Northwest Quadrant

ALBUQUERQUE

Residents of Albuquerque enjoy a rich and diverse natural setting. Geographically speaking, Albuquerque is situated atop the Rio Grande Rift Valley in central New Mexico, between the Sandia Mountains and the volcanoes on the west mesa, and is sliced in two by the Rio Grande, the fifth longest river in North America, which travels 1640 miles from Colorado to the Gulf of Mexico.

The Sandias rise 5000 feet above Albuquerque and remain preserved as Cibola National Forest and the Sandia Wilderness Area. Because the mountains are so close to the city, golden eagles, black bears, and mountain sheep range within fifteen miles of downtown. The side of these mountains facing the city is the steepest, while the eastern side is gently sloped and extensively forested. The effect is much the same as if one stepped on a loose patio brick, causing one end to tilt at a fifteen-degree angle. The five volcanoes on the west mesa are dormant, last erupting about 250,000 years ago. In the 1930s, fraternity brothers from the University of New Mexico delighted in hauling truck loads of old tires to Vulcan Cone and setting them on fire in hopes that people would think that the volcanoes were erupting.

Preserving the major features of Albuquerque's natural setting has been a top priority with city residents. The city has one of the most ambitious open space programs in the Southwest and has acquired and preserved more than 20,000 acres of land. In addition to the land, Albuquerque has developed an extensive system of museums, parks, nature centers, and open spaces to make sure that the public appreciates the abundance of natural beauty within a major city and understands the delicate balance necessary to maintain it.

However, despite its beautiful setting and its status as a metropolis of half a million people in the center of a vast state with a small rural population, the Duke City has often been forgotten by tourists and criticized by residents of other cities in New Mexico for its size and its supposed emphasis on sprawling growth, freeways, and commerce rather than on history or the arts. But the real Albuquerque is a city that cares about all aspects of its historical, cultural, and natural environments.

The city was named in honor of Don Francisco Fernandez de la Cueva Enriquez, Eighth Duke of Alburquerque (the extra "r" was dropped in the late 1700s) and Viceroy of New Spain. The name Albuquerque is said to be a corruption of "albus quercus," or "white oak" in Latin. The Dukedom of Albuquerque still exists, and visits by the current Spanish duke are always the height of the social season in this city.

Families from nearby Bernalillo founded Albuquerque in 1706 on the spot where Old Town Plaza is today. One of the first buildings was the San Felipe de Neri Church (constructed in 1706, rebuilt in 1793), which is an interesting blend of Spanish colonial, gothic, and Pueblo revival architectural styles. It is open to the public for visits and prayers. Albuquerque soon became a major trade center along the Camino Real de Tierra Adentro (Royal Road of the Interior), the main road—also called the Chihuahua Trail—from Mexico City to El Paso del Norte to Santa Fe.

During the Indian wars and the Civil War in New Mexico, Albuquerque became a regional supply center and its warehouses supplied the forts being built all over the Southwest. The railroad arrived in Albuquerque in 1881 and transformed the city into the trade center of the entire territory. Another settlement two miles east of the Old Town Plaza—where the central business district now stands—was dubbed "New Town." Wool, livestock, alfalfa, and lumber created most of Albuquerque's turn-of-the-century economic activity.

One unlikely boom industry was that of health care, as Albuquerque's low humidity attracted people suffering from pulmonary ailments. Promotional publications called "booster booklets" touted the climate: "Without exception, Albuquerque has the finest climate the year round to be found in the United States," claimed a 1908 publication, which went on to assert, "Albuquerque, by scientific observation is the driest and most healthful spot in the Territory."

Other exaggerations claimed that the highest temperature ever recorded in Albuquerque was 95 degrees (try 104) and the lowest, twenty degrees (actually, minus twenty degrees on rare occasions). One publication stated flatly: "No snow," which simply is not true. The city usually receives two or three minor snowstorms each year, often during the late winter and early spring, which usually melt quickly.

The publicity citing Albuquerque's climate attracted thousands of "consumptives," and a number of hospitals and sanatoriums sprang up to treat them. The Presbyterian National Tubercular Sanitarium was built for $50,000 in the early 1900s and was transformed into Presbyterian Hospital, which today is a leader in the Southwest for treatment of heart disease. Another Albuquerque hospital, Lovelace Medical Center, eventually played a great role in this country's space program. To this day Albuquerque retains an excellent reputation as a health care center.

Albuquerque's population exploded after WW II, from about 40,000 to more than ten times that in just forty years.

Part of the reason for such growth was Route 66, the major highway linking the West Coast with the Midwest and East. A standard Albuquerque joke tells of travelers who got tired of driving west along Route 66 and simply settled in Albuquerque.

The installation of Kirtland Air Force Base and Sandia National Laboratories brought not only people, but also the high technology industry to the city. Today, Albuquerque is part of a network of high tech labs and businesses stretching from Los Alamos to Alamogordo, linked together by a fiber optics communications network. Called the Rio Grande Research Corridor, the network includes national laboratories, major universities, high tech companies, military bases, radio telescopes, and missile ranges.

Two major interstate highways, I-40 east and west, and I-25 north and south, intersect at Albuquerque. The city is roughly divided into the following sections: Old Town/Downtown, Uptown, the Northeast Heights, the West Mesa, and the North and South Valleys. The Uptown area contains the largest shopping malls — Coronado and Winrock Centers — and is a part of the northeast heights on the flanks of the Sandia Mountains to the east of downtown. West Mesa is the site of the city's most recent explosion of new housing and businesses. The North Valley is mostly rural and contains many large haciendas, while the less privileged South Valley in many places resembles funky Mexican border towns, such as Juarez.

★ ★

TOURIST INFORMATION

ALBUQUERQUE CONVENTION AND VISITORS BUREAU
P.O. Box 26866, Albuquerque, NM 87125 (243-3696 or 800-284-2282)

★ ★

NATURE IN THE CITY

NEW MEXICO MUSEUM OF NATURAL HISTORY
The best way to understand the geography and setting of Albuquerque is to visit the New Mexico Museum of Natural History, near Old Town, which traces the 4.6-billion-year geology, paleontology, botany, and zoology of the region. In the spacious central atrium, a pterodactyl-like creature known as Quetzalcoatlus glides close to the sixty-foot ceiling. The Naturalist Center literally buzzes with activity as children observe a working beehive and study museum specimens beneath a video microscope.

The museum, located at 1801 Mountain Road NW, features an ingenious display that depicts the hundreds of millions of years when New Mexico had a seashore. Other imaginative exhibits include a trip inside an erupting volcano and a visit to an Ice Age cave. Be sure to take a trip on the "Evolator," a Disney-like trip back in time to the Age of Dinosaurs.

Dinosaurs, always a favorite of young naturalists, are featured extensively with models and the familiar skeletons. Over the years, the Museum has presented shows featuring dinosaurian art and realistic robotic mechanical dinosaurs. The permanent exhibit about dinosaurs is called "The Age of Giants," and it relates not only the paleontological story of these huge creatures, but also addresses the mysteries of their disappearance and whether or not they were warm-blooded.

The gift shop offers the best selection of books on natural history available in Albuquerque. The museum, open 9 a.m.–5 p.m. every day of the year, is a two-minute walk from Old Town at 1801 Mountain Road NW, Albuquerque, NM 87104, 841-8837. Admission is adults $4, seniors $3, and children $1.

THE RIO GRANDE BOSQUE

At times, the Rio Grande — or Rio Bravo as it's often called — lives up to its name and really does seem grand and wild. During the spring runoff of melting mountain snows, the river and the lakes along it swell to the point of flooding. But in the late summer and fall, when most of the Rio Grande is diverted for irrigation, the river is nearly dry. Humorist Will Rogers, after seeing the Rio Grande in this condition, quipped that it was the first river he'd ever seen that needed irrigating.

A series of dams controls the flow of the Rio Grande, and despite the protests of nature lovers who believe all dams are evil, they serve another important purpose beyond irrigation: flood control. In 1874, the flooding Rio Grande escaped its banks and created a lake of 24 square miles that stretched from Albuquerque to Bernalillo. Ten years later, floodwaters racing at 100,000 cubic feet per second destroyed every bridge on the river from Taos, 125 miles north, to below Albuquerque.

Nowadays, the Rio Grande is completely managed south of Cochiti Dam, about forty miles north of Albuquerque, and agencies such as the Middle Rio Grande Conservancy District provide irrigation water to thousands of North and South Valley residents through a complicated series of levees, drains, and 219 miles of *acequias*, or ditches. Albuquerque columnist V. B. Price, son of the late actor Vincent Price, has called the acequia environment "an invaluable cultural and recreational resource" for Albuquerque. The acequias are part of an amazing series of oases along the Rio Grande: the riparian *bosques* (riparian means riverside; bosque is Spanish for forest), which consist of cottonwood and many other varieties of tree. There are such bosques along the San Juan and Pecos rivers, but by far the most impressive one is the 92-mile-long series of bosques straddling the Rio Grande from Cochiti Lake through Albuquerque to just south of Belen.

Some experts believe this bosque to be the largest cottonwood forest in the world, and despite the fact that less than one percent of New Mexico's land area is composed of bosque, about eighty percent of the region's animal species live there. The Rio Grande Bosque is home to 277 species of birds alone, about sixty percent of the total for the state. These fragile regions are, like the mountain tops, oases of moisture and life in the dry northern Chihuahua desert.

But all is not well in the bosque. Most of the cottonwoods predate the dams, and new trees are prevented from germinating because the river no longer floods in the spring. Thus the cottonwoods are being taken over by foreign invaders: French tamarisks, Chinese elms, and Russian olives. A recent study suggested periodic controlled flooding of the bosque to allow new cottonwoods to grow. Albuquerque, determined to preserve its natural resources and beauty, has forbidden development along the bosque. Thus a driver might be surrounded by concrete and glass in the heart of the city one moment and by trees in the middle of a thick forest the next. When crossing some of the bridges, no signs of human habitation can be seen for a few seconds, and it is difficult to believe one is in the center of a large city. Fortunately for the visitor, there are many ways to explore Albuquerque's bosque.

RIO GRANDE VALLEY STATE PARK
Dedicated in 1986, this 6000-acre park stretches for 25 miles on both sides of the river as it runs through Albuquerque and offers hiking, nature-watching, bicycling, horse trails, and fishing. The park is most easily accessible from the Rio Bravo, Central Avenue, and Corrales bridges which have nearby parking areas. Adjacent to the Central Avenue bridge is **Tingley Beach,** which is not a beach at all but rather several shallow ponds that are stocked with fish. The locals joke about this beach in the desert, but back in the days when Route 66 was the only road through town, the Beach Motel at Tingley Beach was one of the best places to stay. For more information on Rio Grande Valley State Park write Albuquerque Open Space Division, P.O. Box 1293, Albuquerque, NM 87103.

RIO GRANDE NATURE CENTER STATE PARK
Located in the bosque where Candelaria Road dead-ends at the river, the Rio Grande Nature Center offers 270 acres of riverside forest and meadows, plus a cattail marsh alongside a three-acre pond. The site is a winter refuge for migratory waterfowl such as snow geese and sandhill cranes. Two miles of nature trails provide glimpses of raccoons, beavers, pheasants, roadrunners, and maybe a coyote or two. There is also a visitor center and library with 21 self-guided interpretive exhibits offering insight into the natural, historical, and social implications of the Rio Grande. The Center is housed in an unusual structure that is half above ground and half below and provides a good opportunity to study pond life.

The Rio Grande Nature Center is open daily 10 to 5 except major holidays, and admission is $1 adults, children 50¢. Located at 2901 Candelaria Rd. NW, Albuquerque, NM 87107, 344-7240.

RIO GRANDE ZOOLOGICAL PARK

What other location could there be for a zoo in Albuquerque except the bosque? Beneath towering century-old cottonwoods, more than 1000 animals representing more than 300 species comprise what many zookeepers consider to be one of the best zoos in the country. The Rio Grande Zoological Park, founded in 1927, has grown into sixty acres of modern, mostly cageless exhibits on 10th Street in downtown Albuquerque.

The zoo's major bird exhibit, Jungle Habitat, is a walk-through tropical jungle designed to simulate a rain forest. About forty species of birds live amidst the palms, vines, and other jungle plants.

Ape Country is a series of outdoor environments for gorillas, siamangs, and orang-utans. Rock formations surround the grass-covered enclosures where the apes swing on massive, wooden jungle-gym-like structures while the public watches from across dry moats.

Another impressive exhibit is Cat Walk, which features not only all of the big cats, but also some less known but equally fascinating carnivores: meerkats, racoon dogs, lesser pandas, and fennec foxes. The cheetah section of Cat Walk is designed after the New Mexico desert landscape, with cliff formations and sandstone outcroppings.

The Reptile House is a technologically advanced facility with special controls designed to help maintain a simulated natural environment for each species. Be sure not to miss the zoo's collection of rare reptiles such as the dwarf caiman, the San Esteban chuckwalla, and the Round Island skink. The Rio Grande Zoo also has one of the largest collection of hoofed animals in the country, featuring exotics such as the bongo and sable antelopes. One of the zoo's most popular recent attractions is a pair of rare white tigers. Snack bars are located throughout the zoo, and the Ventana Gift Shop offers animal-oriented merchandise. Parking is free, but there is an admission charge of $4.25 for adults and $2.25 for children ages 3–15 and seniors. Hours are 9 to 5 every day except for closings on Thanksgiving, Christmas, and New Year's Day. The Rio Grande Zoological Park, 903 10th Street SW, Albuquerque, NM 87102 (843-7413).

PETROGLYPH NATIONAL MONUMENT

There are certain parts of New Mexico where petroglyphs—Indian rock carvings—are concentrated in huge numbers. Although anthropologists' opinions differ as to the meaning and importance of the petroglyphs, the abundance of these images at specific sites seems to link them to the proximity of volcanic rock and to beautiful vistas. At the site of Petroglyph National Monument, ancient ancestors of the modern Pueblo Indians could marvel over the view of the lush, green Rio Grande Valley with a backdrop of the spectacular watermelon-colored Sandias. Perhaps such a vista somehow inspired creation of the 10,500 petroglyphs here; after all, many of the carvings depict the animals and birds of the region. Another theory holds that this spot was sacred to the Anasazi, who carved religious symbols such as kachina dancers into the rocks in the 1300s. Albuquerque is very concerned about protecting nearby petroglyphs that are threatened by development close to the boundaries of the monument. Four interpretive trails guide the visitor through the park, which is open seven days a week from 8 a.m.–5 p.m. (winter) and 9 a.m.–6 p.m. (summer). Admission is $1.00 per car, and the park is located west of Coors Road on Unser Boulevard. For more information on the monument, call 897-8814 or write Friends of the Albuquerque Petroglyphs, P.O. Box 75277, Albuquerque, NM 87013. For more information on petroglyphs, see the listing for Three Rivers Petroglyph Site.

SANDIA CREST AND THE SANDIA PEAK AERIAL TRAMWAY
To the east of Albuquerque is the mountain range known as the Sandias. The name means "watermelon" in Spanish and is an allusion to the red color of the mountains at sunset. Atop the southernmost peak is a forest of radio and television antennas whose signals reach most of the state. It is the only high mountain top in New Mexico accessible by car to sightseers—the others are for mountain climbers only.

There are actually two tops to the Sandias: Sandia Crest, accessible by car, and Sandia Peak, reached by a tramway. The drive to Sandia Crest is easy since the road is paved all the way. Take I-40 about fifteen miles east of Albuquerque and take the NM Hwy. 14 exit. Follow that road north and watch for the Sandia Crest signs leading to NM Hwy. 165 and NM Hwy. 536. At the end of what seems like endless loops is the Crest, elevation 10,678 feet, with nature trails through the Cibola National Forest and the Sandia Crest Restaurant and Gift Shop.

The tram ride to Sandia Peak is an exciting and educational experience not to be missed. The world's longest tramway (2.7 miles) transports visitors from the city to the wilderness. Specifically, the tram reaches the top of Sandia Peak, elevation 10,378 feet. During the day, a spectacular vista comprising 11,000 square miles can be seen; at night, the violet glow of sprawling Albuquerque creates a very romantic atmosphere. The tram trip to the top of Sandia Peak reveals a cross section of the geography of New Mexico and as the tram rises higher, the life zones found on the mountain begin to resemble regions much farther north. Basically, every one thousand foot increase in elevation is the equivalent to a south-north distance of about three hundred miles. Thus a trip from the Rio Grande Valley to Sandia Crest is the equivalent of a trip from Albuquerque to Alaska.

The environmental conditions on Sandia Peak are a combination of the Hudsonian and Arctic-Alpine life zones and are extremely severe. The winter is hopeless for life—animals are hibernating beneath many feet of snow. Temperatures at the tops of the highest peaks can drop as low as 100 degrees F. below zero—"Siberia in the Southwest," is how one pundit described New Mexico mountain tops.

According to the New Mexico Museum of Natural History, relic plant and animal populations from the Ice Age still survive on isolated mountain tops, separated from northern populations. Such lofty areas, called paleorefugias by ecologists, are sites where ancient species, long vanished from the surrounding landscape, continue to survive because of adaptation. About one-third of the plant species on top of peaks in the Rocky Mountains also occur above the Arctic Circle. Many species of Arctic animals live atop New Mexico peaks such as Sandia Peak. The white-tailed ptarmigan—the quail-like bird everyone remembers from Walt Disney nature specials—is a perfect example of a bird that has survived for millennia in New Mexico's mini-arctic. The ptarmigan changes color according to the seasons and is nearly invisible against the snow in its winter white phase.

Animal life in these altitudes must adapt to restricted vegetation, a significant decrease in available oxygen, and very high winds. Consequently, the bird and mammal populations of the highest peaks vary according to season. During the summer, golden eagles soar over the peaks in search of marmots and chipmunks while elk graze—and, in some cases, overgraze—the vegetation. Rocky Mountain bighorn sheep balance precariously on steep cliffs and mountain lions hunt mule deer. In the frigid winter, the larger animals migrate to the lower, warmer zones while the small mammals and birds hibernate or find refuge in snow-free rock crevices—microclimates that are warmed by even the oblique rays of the weak winter sun.

During the winter, the Tram is utilized mostly for access to Sandia Peak Ski Area. Skiers regularly carry their skis with them on the tram. During the summer, aficionados of hang gliding transport their gliders atop the tram car and then fearlessly leap off the cliffs and, soaring like golden eagles, ride the thermals down to the valley.

Regardless of the season, be sure to take a sweater or a jacket with you on the tram. Even in the hottest days of the summer, the temperatures may be 25 degrees cooler at the Peak, and if the wind is blowing, the wind-chill factor can make the visit quite uncomfortable for someone wearing only shorts and a T-shirt.

Fortunately, in addition to nature and spectacular scenery, there is the **High Finance** restaurant and bar waiting for you at the top. Access to the Tram is by way of either Tramway Road exits on I-25 north or I-40 east and then follow the signs to the Tram. Open daily 9 a.m.–10 p.m. (summer) and 9 a.m.–9 p.m. (winter). Ticket prices are $10.50 for adults, $8 for children and seniors. For details, contact: Sandia Peak Tram Co., #10 Tramway Loop NE, Albuquerque, NM 87122, 298-8518. For High Finance Restaurant reservations, call 243-9742. The restaurant serves lunch and dinner daily and offers discounts on tram rides with dinner.

★ ★
HISTORIC SIGHTSEEING

THE ALBUQUERQUE MUSEUM
Here is the best place to begin an exploration of the history of Albuquerque and the surrounding region. The Albuquerque Museum has assembled the largest collection of Spanish colonial artifacts in the United States and utilizes this collection as a centerpiece for a permanent exhibit entitled "Four Centuries: a History of Albuquerque." This stunning presentation traces the history of the city from the Spanish *conquistadors* through the hardships of colonial life to the frontier days of what has been called "the wildest West." The museum has collected original arms and armor used during the Spanish conquest, religious objects created by the early settlers, domestic goods brought over the Santa Fe Trail, and Civil War artifacts. To top off the Four Centuries exhibit, the Gem Theatre shows a multi-image slide show called "Albuquerque: the Crossroads."

The Museum's art collection is impressive, including works by many famous artists of the Southwest, such as Georgia O'Keefe and Wilson Hurley. The photographic archives are extensive and include historic views of early Albuquerque as well as photographic art by renowned nineteenth century photographers Edward S. Curtis, Ben Wittick, John Hillers, and others. Hours are 9 a.m.–5 p.m. Tues.–Sun. Free admission. The Albuquerque Museum,

2000 Mountain Rd. NW, Albuquerque, NM 87104 (242-4600).

INDIAN PUEBLO CULTURAL CENTER
A counterpoint to the Albuquerque Museum, the Cultural Center features a permanent exhibit that explains the history of the region from the point of view of New Mexico's nineteen Indian pueblos. While the permanent exhibit occupies the lower level, the upper level is devoted to changing exhibits of paintings, ceramics, and sculpture by Native American artists.

During the spring and summer, dances and live demonstrations are held in the Center's performance area, which is surrounded by murals painted by Indian artists. The dances often feature the famous Voladores dancers, who begin their dances by jumping off a tall pole—hence their name, "flying ones." Artists and craftsmen give demonstrations to visitors on how to work silver for jewelry and clay for the renowned Pueblo pottery.

The gift shop features weavings, authentic pottery, sandpaintings, hand-carved kachina dolls, and traditional and contemporary Zuni, Hopi, and Navajo jewelry. The restaurant, of course, specializes in Native American dishes of the Southwest such as green chile stew and fry bread. Admission is $2.50 adults, $1.50 seniors, $1 for students. The Center is open daily, 9 a.m. to 5:30 p.m. The Indian Pueblo Cultural Center is located just off I-40 at 2401 12th Street NW, Albuquerque, NM 87102, 843-7270.

MAXWELL MUSEUM OF ANTHROPOLOGY
The University of New Mexico has one of the best anthropology departments in the United States and this museum on the campus gives the department an opportunity to prove it. A permanent exhibit tells the story of man's 10,000 years—or more—in the Southwest, while changing exhibits often feature folk art and artifacts from cultures worldwide.

The gift shop has an excellent collection of books on Southwestern anthropology and archaeology as well as jewelry, pottery, and baskets. The Maxwell Museum is open Monday through Friday 9 a.m.–4 p.m., Saturdays 10 a.m.–4 p.m., Sundays noon–4 p.m. Admission is free. It's located just off University Blvd. two blocks north of Central Ave. (277-4404).

NATIONAL ATOMIC MUSEUM
Visitors will get a charge out of this small but interesting museum. It opened in 1969 on Kirtland Air Force Base and features the world's most complete nuclear weapons collection—all disarmed. Prominently featured in the museum is the Manhattan Project, the top secret, highly complex, and scientifically sophisticated engi-

neering effort centered in New Mexico that produced and tested the first atomic bomb in then-remote Los Alamos. Other displays show off replicas of famous A-bombs "Little Boy" and "Fat Man," and visitors can watch a 53-minute documentary film on the Manhattan Project titled "Ten Seconds That Shook the World," which is shown three times daily at 10:30 a.m., 2 p.m. and 3 p.m. On display outside the museum are missiles, a B-52 bomber, and a F-105D fighter-bomber.

The National Atomic Museum is accessible through the Gibson and Wyoming gates of Kirtland Air Force Base and admission is free. Open daily 9 a.m.–5 p.m. except major holidays. Ask for a visitor's pass and directions at the gate or call 845-6670. Remember that because the base is the location of Sandia National Laboratory, Kirtland is highly secured; so don't wander into restricted areas.

★ ★

HISTORIC BUILDINGS

FORGOTTEN ALBUQUERQUE

Unfortunately, one of the most interesting and historic buildings in Albuquerque, Castle Huning on W. Central Avenue, was razed in the spring of 1955. Bainbridge Bunting, former professor of art at the University of New Mexico wrote in 1960: "This structure constituted a milestone in the history of the Southwest. The loss of this handsome old mansion is irreparable and no amount of progress in the form of motel, filling station, or supermarket built upon the vacated site can compensate for its destruction."

Completed in 1883, Castle Huning was the home of Franz Huning, one of Albuquerque's most famous early businessmen. It was built with five-foot-thick sod walls and finished on the outside with paneling which imitated the stone work of German castles. It was destroyed because of one overriding factor: the lack of public funds to purchase and restore it.

Another disastrous blow to Albuquerque's architectural history occurred in 1970, when the Alvarado Hotel fell victim to the wrecker's ball. This magnificent structure, which was built at a cost of $200,000, was considered to be the "finest railroad hotel on earth" and was hotel magnate Fred Harvey's finest lodging creation when it opened in 1902. Located along the railroad tracks facing First Street, the Alvarado featured 88 guest rooms, a gigantic dining room, Spanish-tiled roofs, many patios with cascading fountains, and beautiful "Harvey Girls," who were the hostesses and served "all you could eat" meals for one dollar.

Many celebrities stayed at the Alvarado: Rudolph Valentino, Albert Einstein, Charles Lindbergh, Joan Crawford, Katherine Hepburn, and Jack Benny, to name just a few. U.S. Presidents selecting the Alvarado included William H. Taft (who allegedly got stuck in his bathtub), Herbert Hoover, Woodrow Wilson, Frankin D. Roosevelt, and Theodore Roosevelt, who once vanished from a reception at the hotel and was thought to have been kidnapped. The Secret Service men guarding him were in a state of panic until they learned that President Roosevelt had escaped the speeches of local politicos by having lunch at Isleta Pueblo with Isleta Governor Pablo Abeita.

In 1922, the Alvarado was enlarged to accommodate the growing demand for lodging and the hotel was a site for society balls and for displays by Indian craftsmen. In 1969 it was placed on the National Register of Historic Structures, just in time to witness the desertion of downtown Albuquerque for the Heights. The owner of Alvarado, the Santa Fe Railway, attempted to sell it for $1.5 million despite the fact that most real estate people believed that price to be more than double what the property was worth. Rather than donate the building to the city, the Santa Fe Railway began demolition. The destruction of the Alvarado Hotel (and Castle Huning) continues to haunt Albuquerqueans. Believe it or not, there have been several downtown restoration movements which would entail building an exact replica of the Alvarado! Until that unlikely event happens, there is only one hotel which even faintly recalls the ambience of the Alvarado: the restored La Posada. However, there are other interesting buildings which have been preserved. One is the **KiMo Theater,** 423 Central NW (see NIGHTLIFE), which is a beautifully restored example of the architectural style known as Pueblo Deco. The Native American mosaic-type designs which completely cover the exterior are quite a sight and inside, many concerts and plays entertain Albuquerqueans.

Another historic building is the **Ernie Pyle Home and Library,** 900 Girard SE. It features memorabilia of the famous Pulitzer Prize–winning war correspondent and is now a branch of the Albuquerque Public Library system. The home is open Tuesday through Saturday from 9 to 5:30, Tuesday and Thursday evenings until 8. Admission is free. Call 265-2065 for more information.

The National Register of Historic Buildings lists these other Albuquerque buildings: the ornate **Occidental Life Building,** 119 3rd Street NW, **Hodgin Hall** at the University of New Mexico, the **Rosewald Building,** 320 Central SW, the **Antonio Vigil House,** 413 Romero NW, and the **Salvador Armijo House** (now the Maria Teresa Restaurant), 618 Rio Grande NW.

For architecture enthusiasts, the **University of New Mexico** on Central Avenue between University and Girard provides the most enjoyable experience. The master plan for the University was set in 1901 when its president, Dr. William Tight, determined that the proper look for the future was the Spanish and Pueblo styles. Except for temporary quonset huts used after World War II, the University has maintained a consistent appearance, with modern architects giving their contemporary versions of the Spanish-Pueblo style. The central campus, complete with plaza, pond and modern sculpture, is automobile-free and is quite striking.

OTHER MUSEUMS
The University of New Mexico campus has its share of museums and galleries (see listings below and for the Maxwell Museum, above). The **Geology Museum** and **Meteoric Museum** in Northrup Hall feature small but interesting displays ranging from dinosaur bones unearthed in New Mexico to moon rocks. They're open Monday through Friday 8 a.m.–5 p.m., closed from noon–1 p.m. daily. Admission is free; call 277-4204 for more information. Another UNM museum is the **Museum of Southwest Biology,** in the Potter wing of Castetter Hall, which displays examples of flora and fauna of the Southwest (277-3411). This is a research museum and tours are by appointment only.

Two smaller museums are the **Spanish History Museum,** 2221 Lead SE, which has exhibits and photographs depicting the Hispanic history of the region (268-9981) and is open from 1 p.m.–5 p.m. daily (winter), 10 a.m.–5 p.m. (summer).

The smallest museum of all is the **Tinkertown Museum,** located on the east side of the Sandia mountains in Sandia Park, off NM Hwy. 14 on NM Hwy. 536 (281-5233). This miniature Old West town carved in wood showcases some six thousand different objects in 26 tiny buildings. Admission is $2 for adults and $.50 for children under sixteen. Open April through December 9 a.m.–6 p.m. daily.

★ ★
ARTS AND CRAFTS

Although Albuquerque does not have the reputation of Santa Fe or Taos for being a legendary center of the arts, the city has its share of excellent museums, art galleries, and craft shops. Perhaps the best collection of works of art in Albuquerque is on display at the Albuquerque Museum, and after the art lover has examined that collection, there are quite a few more places to visit.

MUSEUMS

UNIVERSITY ART MUSEUM
Located at the Fine Arts Center on Cornell Street NE just north of
Central Avenue, the University Art Museum specializes in chang-
ing exhibitions of nineteenth and twentieth century American and
European art. The permanent collection includes photography,
Spanish Colonial, and early twentieth century American art. The
University Art Museum is open all year around Tues.–Fri. 9 a.m.–
4 p.m., Tuesday evening 5 p.m.–9 p.m., and Sunday 1 p.m.–4 p.m.
Closed Saturday, Monday, and holidays. Admission is free and
more information is available by calling 277-4001.

JONSON GALLERY
Also on the UNM campus, this gallery is housed in the home of the
late Modernist painter Raymond Jonson. Its focus is, of course, the
work of Jonson, but also includes that of the Transcendentalists
and other contemporary artists. Admission is free and hours are
9 a.m.–4 p.m. Tues.–Fri., and Tuesday evening 5 p.m.–9 p.m., or
by appointment on weekends for group tours. Located at 1909 Las
Lomas NE (277-4967).

THE TAMARIND INSTITUTE
This unique operation is both a gallery and a workshop that
specializes in one artistic form: the lithograph. It is an important
regional resource and at one time was one of the very few such
workshops in the country. Open 9 a.m.–5 p.m. Mon.–Fri. and by
appointment, Tamarind is located just off the UNM campus at 108
Cornell SE (277-3901).

THE FINE ARTS GALLERY AT THE NEW MEXICO STATE FAIR
Home of the State Fair Juried Exhibit held in September, in which
the state's best artists and craftspersons compete for awards, the
Fine Arts Gallery presents regular exhibits throughout the year that
are sponsored by city businesses and art patrons. Recent exhibits
have included traditional New Mexico art, photographic art, contemporary works, and the finest in Western art. The Fine Arts
Gallery is located by entering the State Fair fairgrounds through
gate 4 off San Pedro NE and turning left on Main Street. For more
information call (265-1791, ext. 228), or write P.O. Box 8546,
Albuquerque, NM 87198.

PRIVATE GALLERIES

WEEMS GALLERIES
Owner Mary Ann Weems believes that since New Mexico has more
artists and craftspersons per capita than any other state, her gallery
should show off as much of the best work as possible. Her philosophy is to offer original art and crafts for the same prices paid elsewhere for prints and reproductions. Not buying art while in New
Mexico, jokes Mary Ann, is "like not buying pineapples when
you're in Hawaii."
There are two locations: in the Eastdale Shopping Center, at
2801 W. Eubank at intersection with Candelaria NE (293-6133),
hours Mon.–Sat. 10 a.m.–6 p.m.; and 129 Winrock Center
(881-3794), hours Mon.–Fri. 10 a.m.–9 p.m., Sat. 10 a.m.–6 p.m.,
and Sun. noon–5 p.m.

ANDREWS PUEBLO POTTERY
The name of this gallery is slightly misleading since it offers quite
a bit more than pottery. In addition to prehistoric, historic, and
contemporary pottery, Andrews has a fine collection of original
graphics and paintings by Southwestern artists as well as kachinas,
fetishes, and baskets. The gallery is located in Old Town at 400 San
Felipe NW, 243-0414. Open 7 days a week, 10 a.m.–6 p.m.

AMAPOLA GALLERY
In terms of display space and numbers of artists represented, the
Amapola is perhaps the largest in the state. It's a fourteen-year-
old cooperative gallery featuring the works of 46 artists who
are predominantly Southwestern in style—though there is contemporary art here as well. The Amapola is noted for its water
colors and unusual crafts. Hours are Mon.–Sat. 10 a.m.–5 p.m.
and Sun. 11 a.m.–5 p.m.; located at 2045 S. Plaza NW in Old
Town (242-4311).
Other recommended galleries include: **Mariposa Gallery,** open
10 a.m.–5 p.m. Mon–Sat. and noon–5 p.m. on Sundays at 113
Romero NW in Old Town (842-9097), **Brandywine Galleries, Ltd.,**
120 Morningside Dr. SE (255-0266); **Weyrich Gallery,** 2935-D
Louisiana NE (883-7410), and **Navajo Gallery,** which exclusively
features the art of famous Navajo artist R.C. Gorman, 323 Romero
NW (843-7666).

★ ★
LODGING

A note on rates: since room rates vary as much as fifty percent
because of season, promotions, and whims, any published dollar
amounts would almost certainly be in error. We suggest visitors
write or call the hotels directly to obtain information on rates.

LA POSADA DE ALBUQUERQUE
Built in 1939 by Conrad Hilton, La Posada de Albuquerque served
as the Hilton Inn until the newer Hilton was built on University
Avenue. La Posada was purchased by the Somerset hotel chain and
completely remodeled in 1984 to preserve its original features,
which include beautiful tile work, carved wooden appointments,
and a charming lobby bar. La Posada's 114 rooms are within a
block of the Convention Center and within five minutes of the zoo,
Old Town, and the University. History buffs will appreciate the
fact that the hotel is listed on the National Register of Historic
Places. It's located at 125 2nd Street NW at Copper, 242-9090 or
1-800-445-8667.

ALBUQUERQUE HILTON
The "new" Hilton, one of the state's largest hotels, has already been
renovated to improve its Southwestern appearance, a trend with all
major chains which operate in New Mexico. Indian rugs, kachinas,
pottery, and art decorate this spacious 253-room hotel. Other
amenities include heated indoor and outdoor pools, two tennis
courts, a whirlpool, and a sauna. Two of the three restaurants in
the Hilton, the Rancher's Club and Casa Chaco, are recommended
under "Dining."
     It is centrally located at 1901 University NE near the "Big I" inter-
change where I-40 intersects with I-25, or call 884-2500 or
1-800-821-1901.

THE BEST WESTERN FRED HARVEY HOTEL
The Fred Harvey is most convenient hotel to the recently enlarged
and renovated Albuquerque International Airport—a mere nine
hundred feet away, a shorter distance than the length of many
airport terminals. Traveling businesspersons love it, as do visitors who fly into town and make the Fred Harvey their home
base for automobile trips around the state. The Southwestern-
style, fourteen-story hotel offers 270 guest rooms, twelve suites,

tennis courts, sauna, a huge swimming pool, and two restaurants (see "Lil's" under "Dining"). The rooms are large at the Fred Harvey, about four hundred square feet, and are completely soundproofed against noise from the airport or adjoining rooms. The view of Albuquerque, the Rio Grande, and Sandia Mountains is great from the Fred Harvey Rooms, as is the aircraft-spotting. Exotic military aircraft land all the time at Kirtland Air Force Base, which uses the same runways as the commercial airplanes. There are complete convention facilities, including numerous meeting rooms, available. The Fred Harvey is located at 2910 Yale Blvd. SE, 843-7000 or (800) 227-1117.

ALBUQUERQUE MARRIOTT

Another large high-rise hotel, the sixteen-floor Marriott, is Albuquerque's most luxurious—and expensive—hotel. Although located alongside I-40, all of the Marriott's more than four hundred rooms are cleverly situated so that their windows face the Sandia Mountains rather than the tractor trailers on the freeway. The Marriott prides itself on its health facilities, which include a large outdoor-indoor pool, a hydrotherapy pool, a complete health club, and saunas for men and women. For kids, there's a complete video game arcade. Compulsive shoppers and moviegoers will love the fact that the Marriott is located within two blocks of two major malls with hundreds of shops and movie theatres with a total of fifteen screens, at 2101 Louisiana Blvd. NE, 881-6800 or 1-800-228-9290.

HOLIDAY INN JOURNAL CENTER

Although there is not an Aztec stepped pyramid within a thousand miles of Albuquerque, designers of this hotel decided to build one. The architecture may be unusual for the region, but the hotel is very elegant, featuring a ten-story atrium complete with waterfall. It has 315 guestrooms, including Presidential and deluxe suites, and its list of amenities is impressive: a year-round indoor/outdoor pool, fitness center and health club, glass-enclosed elevators, and the largest convention complex of any Albuquerque hotel. The restaurant here, **The Gallery,** offers fine dining with continental and New Southwest specialties. The Holiday Inn Journal Center, usually referred to as "The Pyramid," is located at exit 232 off I-25 north (Paseo del Norte). For information and reservations call 821-3333 or 1-800-HOLIDAY.

HYATT REGENCY ALBUQUERQUE

Located in the tallest office complex in the state, the Hyatt Regency is quickly gaining the reputation of being one of New

Mexico's finer hotels. It features 395 guest rooms and suites, an outdoor swimming pool, an indoor athletic club, and a small shopping mall offering New Mexican crafts and foods. There are two lounges which locals and visitors make frequent use of, plus an excellent restaurant (McGrath's). The Hyatt Regency is located downtown at 330 Tijeras Ave. NW. For reservations, call 842-1234 or (800) 233-1234.

SHERATON OLD TOWN
Its ads brag about the fact it won a coveted "Mobil 4-Star Rating" for its amenities, but more important for visitors is the Sheraton's location, one that is convenient for exploring Old Town's museums, galleries, and shops. The hotel is adjacent to Old Town, and is only one block from the Albuquerque and Natural History Museums, and just a couple of minutes from the Rio Grande Nature Center, the Zoo, and glorious Tingley Beach. The Sheraton, 800 Rio Grande NW, 843-6300 or 1-800-325-3535 nationwide or in New Mexico 1-800-237-2133.

The list of hotels above is by no means complete. Bed and breakfast enthusiasts should inquire about **Casita Chamisa,** 850 Chamisal Rd. NW (897-4644), which is located near the Rio Grande Bosque and has both an enclosed pool and archaeological site on the grounds. Another recommended B&B is the **Pine Cone Inn** in Sandia Park on the east side of the Sandias (281-1384).

ECLECTIC LODGING NEAR ALBUQUERQUE

Albuquerque's recommended lodging varies enormously: **Elaine's,** a mountain B&B in Cedar Crest (800-821-3092); **Adobe & Roses,** an adobe hacienda in the North Valley (898-0654); **La Cueva Lodge,** a mountain retreat in Jemez Springs (829-3814); **La Mimosa,** an adobe guesthouse among cottonwoods in Corrales (898-1354); **The Mauger Estate,** an 1897 Queen Anne Victorian guesthouse near Old Town (242-8755); and **The Corrales Inn,** gracious rooms surrounding a courtyard (897-4422).

★ ★
DINING

Albuquerque has hundreds of restaurants offering every cuisine imaginable. One distinguishing feature of the native food in Albuquerque and the rest of the state is the reliance on chile peppers to add the needed heat. More than any other state in the Union, New Mexico depends upon red and green chile in its cuisine, which was adapted from Mexican but is more properly referred to as "New Mexican." For details on chile peppers and New Mexican cuisine, see the Las Cruces listing. Recommended restaurants in Albuquerque, grouped by type of cuisine, follow.

NEW MEXICAN

El Patio owner Dave Sandoval, a former cameraman who shot movie film of missiles exploding for Sandia National Labs, now enjoys a less dangerous career of serving the most authentic New Mexican cuisine possible. To accomplish that feat, he depends upon his father-in-law, Tom Baca, who creates fantastic red chile sauce, *carne adovada*, and *posole* with *chile caribe*. Of course, both El Patio locations offer dining outdoors on the—uh, terrace; 142 Harvard SE (268-4245). Beer and wine only; open 11 a.m.–9:30 p.m., Mon.–Sun.

Another solid server of New Mexico specialties is **Monroe's Restaurant,** with two locations: 6021 Osuna NE (881-4224) and 1520 Lomas NW (242-1111), near Old Town. The menus brag that Monroe's serves tons of green chile a year, and this certainly makes the growers in the Mesilla Valley very happy indeed. Monroe's has a beer and wine license. Open daily 9 a.m.–9 p.m. A downtown favorite is the **M&J Sanitary Tortilla Factory,** 403 Second Street SW (242-4890), so named because of its long history as a provider of quality tortillas for Albuquerque—obviously all of the ones served here are hot off the presses. The restaurant is justly famous for its extremely hot salsa and other Mexican and New Mexican specialty foods. Open 9:30 a.m.–4 p.m. daily for lunch and breakfast, may be open for dinner as hours vary.

Garcia's Kitchen, also downtown at 1113 Fourth Street NW (247-9149), should be renamed Garcia's Kitsch Kitchen because of its collection of the most ridiculous decorations you've ever seen, including a mechanical monkey on a tightrope. One of their specialties is *menudo* (tripe soup) with chiles, the so-called Mexican "breakfast of champions," renowned for its power to cure hangovers. Downtown location is open daily 6:30 a.m.–3:30 p.m. for breakfast and lunch only. Four other locations in town are open for dinner also, including a carry-out at 2525 Pennslyvania. Although not strictly New Mexican, **El Norteño,** 7306 Zuni SE

(256-1431) serves up great northern Mexican food, including soft tacos filled with *chorizo, carnitas*, or other meat specialties. Their "guaca-chile" dipping sauce is to die for. Don't be afraid to try their unusual *lengua* (tongue)—it's delicious. Open Thurs.–Sun. 10 a.m.–9 p.m. and Fri.–Sat. 9 a.m.–10 p.m.

The **Rio Grande Cantina,** 1100 Rio Grande NW (242-1777), has authentic Mexican decor and a classic outside patio. Their specialties include Mexican ceviche and *sopa de lima* (a tasty soup of chicken, chiles and lime), plus New Mexico fare and some nice seafood and burgers. The Little Ricky Burger, served on a homemade bun and spiced with green chile, is one of the best in the state—though other restaurants often claim that title. The Rio Grande Cantina is just off I-40 and has a full liquor license. Open 11:30 a.m.–1:30 a.m. daily. **Casa Chaco** in the Hilton at 1901 University NE (884-2500), serves nouveau-New Mexican dishes, and does and excellent job with innovative recipes such as Poblano Rellenos, which are Mexican chiles stuffed with lobster, sausage and brie cheese. Open 6 a.m.–2:30 p.m., and 5 p.m.–9 p.m. daily.

Undoubtedly, the award for best Mexican decor should go to **Garduños of Mexico** (three locations: 5400 Academy NE, 821-3030; 8806 Fourth Street NW, 898-2772; 10551 Montgomery NE, 298-5000). The restaurants are completely tiled in bright colors and feature Mexican antiques, piñatas, skylights, and plants—a very festive atmosphere. The selection of dishes is very wide, reflecting more of Mexico than just the corn and chile cuisine of the northern regions. Try the piñon-stuffed chile relleno. Open daily, 11 a.m.–9 p.m.

Other recommended New Mexican restaurants include: **Duran Central Pharmacy,** 1815 Central NW (247-4141); **Los Cuates,** 4901 Lomas NE (255-5079); and **Sadie's,** 6132 4th St. NW (345-5339).

BARBECUE

Henry Clopton, of **Henry's Old Time Barbecue,** is a BBQ philosopher: "Barbecue. That's the one you can be real with. You don't have to be too fancy about it. You don't have to be a phony to be a good barbecue man. Just do it the way you learned it back when you can remember." Henry's memories include nearly fifty years of smokin' and saucin', and quite simply, his barbecue is the best this writer—who was born in the South—has ever tasted. A sign on Henry's wall reads: "It's OK to eat these ribs with your fingers." Henry explains: "You see people come in and try to eat ribs and chicken with a fork. When they're through, they're more tired than they was when they came in." Henry's is located in the South

Valley at 4300 Coors SW (877-8383). Open 11 a.m.-9 p.m.
Tues.-Sat.
The Quarters, 905 Yale SE (843-7505), is an Albuquerque lunch
institution. I confess to having lunched there about once a week for
over eighteen years, about nine hundred times, so the excellence
of their sandwiches has been adequately tested. Their barbecue
is almost as tasty as that prepared by Henry Clopton, who was
the first cook at the Quarters before striking out on his own.
The adjacent liquor stores and wine shops offer perhaps the
best selection in the city. The Quarters, and its second location
at 4516 Wyoming Boulevard NE (299-9864), has a full liquor
license and the bartenders pour a stiff drink. Open 11 a.m.-3
p.m. and 5 p.m.-9 p.m. Mon.-Sat. Closed Sunday.
    With three locations in Albuquerque, Powdrell's Barbecue is cer-
tainly the largest barbecue operation in the state. The Powdrell
family members, close friends with Henry, prepare a smoky, tangy
product that compares favorably with Henry's. The most interesting location is in the historic Samuel Shalit House, 5209 Fourth
Street NW (345-8086). Open 11 a.m.-9 p.m. Tues.-Sun. Closed
Monday.
    Winner of Best Barbecue Sauce at the 1992 National Fiery
Foods Show, Robb's Ribbs, 2412 San Mateo Place NE (884-7422),
serves up delightfully spicy BBQ. Owner Robb Richmond's side
dishes, such as Corn Puddin' and Bread Puddin', are also great.
Open Tues.-Fri., 11 a.m.-2 p.m. and 4:30 p.m.-8 p.m., Sat.
11 a.m.-8 p.m.

NEW SOUTHWEST AND CONTINENTAL

Chef Rosa Rajkovic of the Monte Vista Fire Station, 3201 Central
NE (255-2424) was nominated for the 1991 James Beard Award of
Best Chef in the Southwest. Her creations almost defy description, ranging from New Southwest fare to imaginative combinations that change daily. The restaurant itself is striking; it's a
three-story former firehouse designed by famed architect John
Gaw Meem in the Pueblo Revival style. It was built in 1936 as a
WPA project, and the main dining area is the former bay for fire
trucks. The upstairs bar is a noted hangout for upscale locals.
Open Mon.-Fri. 11 a.m.-2:30 p.m., Mon.-Sat. 5 p.m.-10:30 p.m.,
bar open daily until 2 a.m.
    Scalo is a northern Italian grill located in the Nob Hill area at
3500 Central SE (255-8781) and it specializes in grilled meat and fish
as well as innovative pasta dishes. Open 11:30 a.m.-2:30 p.m. and

5 p.m.–11 p.m. Mon.–Fri., dinner only on Saturday 5 p.m.–
11 p.m. Closed Sunday. **Casa Vieja,** in nearby Corrales at Corrales
Rd. and Mockingbird Ln. (898-7489), serves classic French and
northern Italian cuisine in a restored adobe hacienda that has
authentic Southwestern ambience. Chef Jean-Pierre is a master of
veal dishes, crepes, and desserts, while wine expert Rob Kellner
maintains a wine list with selections that date back to before World
War II. Open daily for dinner only, 6 p.m.–10 p.m. Opens early
on Sunday at 5 p.m.

Lil's, at 2910 Yale Blvd. SE, in the Amfac Hotel near the airport
(843-7000), is a very intimate restaurant serving only 32 patrons
amidst chandeliers, silver, and cut glass. The service is superb, with
the staff working as a team in the small dining room. Rather than
just one waiter or waitress to a table, there are three or four. Specialties include tournedo's of Lil's, veal oscar, and broiled rack of
lamb. Dress up for this one (jacket and tie suggested) and call for
reservations first. Open 6 p.m.–11 p.m. Mon.–Sat.

One of Albuquerque's best restaurants is also one of its most innovative. **Restaurant André** in Fashion Square at Lomas and San
Mateo NE (268-5354) always astounds with its culinary creations.
Believe it or not, I splurged while researching this book and dined
on tournedos of elk with juniper berry sauce—for lunch! Open
11:30 a.m.–2:30 p.m. Mon.–Sat. 5:30–9 p.m. Mon.–Thurs. 5:30 p.m.–10
p.m. Fri. and Sat.

ASIAN

There are dozens and dozens of Chinese restaurants in Albuquerque, but most of them are not particularly outstanding. In keeping
with Albuquerque's love of fiery foods, it is the Szechwan and
Hunan places which are the best. Recommended are **Hunan's** (1218
San Pedro, 266-3300, and Coronado Center, 888-4848), open 11
a.m.–9:30 p.m. daily; and **Szechwan Chinese Restaurant,** 1605
Juan Tabo NE (299-9133), open 11:30 a.m.–9:30 p.m. Mon.–Sat.,
4:30 p.m.–9:30 p.m. for dinner only on Sunday. Also hot is food
served at the **Thai House,** 106 Buena Vista SE (247-9205), which
serves a great *gang gai,* a chicken chile curry. Open 11 a.m.–9 p.m.
Mon.–Sat. Closed Sunday. For sushi and other Japanese delicacies,
Minato, 10721 Montgomery NE (293-2929), is the place to go.
Open 11:30 a.m.–2 p.m., and 5:30 p.m.–9 p.m. Mon.–Fri., weekends dinner only 5:30 p.m.–9:30 p.m.

SEAFOOD

Even though the nearest ocean is a thousand miles away, Albuquerque seafood restaurants have fresh fish flown in daily from both coasts and the Gulf of Mexico, so there is no fear about eating seafood in the New Mexican desert. **Cafe Oceana**, 1414 Central SE (247-2233), was one of the first restaurants in the city to offer fresh fish and the citizens have repaid the favor by making the restaurant very popular. At least six fresh catches are offered daily—some cooked Cajun-style—and Cafe Oceana has a very popular Shrimp and Oyster Hour from 3 to 6:30 p.m. daily. Reservations are accepted only for parties of eight or more; full service bar. Open 11 a.m.–3 p.m., and 5 p.m.–11 p.m. Mon.–Fri. Dinner only on Saturday 5 p.m.–9 p.m., closed Sunday.

Seagull Street Fish Market and Restaurant, 5410 Academy NE (821-0020), doesn't have a beach, but it does sport a small outdoor lagoon with a fishing boat in it! Seagull Street often lists as many as twelve fresh catches a day, offers seafood sandwiches for lunch, and has a full-service bar and lounge. Open Sun.–Fri. 11 a.m.–2:30 p.m. and 5 p.m.–11 p.m., Saturday dinner only 5 p.m.–11 p.m.

STEAKS

Albuquerque has two restaurants that excel at serving beef. The **Old Timer's Cafe** (formerly Ogelvies), at 7100 Central SE (266-5564), offers extra-thick prime steaks that are aged and tender. The Steak Ogelvies, with a topping of crab in a bearnaise sauce, is highly recommended. Also excellent are the New Mexican entrées and grilled fresh fish. Open 11 a.m.–11 p.m. daily. The **Ranchers Club**, at 1901 University Ave. NE at the Hilton (884-2500) has been proclaimed one of the best restaurants in the state by two respected food critics, Russ Parsons and Robert Simon. Simon wrote that the Ranchers Club had "a distinct concept, fascinating decor, impeccable service, and wonderful food." Prime steaks, fish, and poultry are grilled over the diner's choice of four woods: mesquite, wild cherry, sassafras, or hickory. Accompanying the grilled entrées are twenty different sauces, butters, and condiments. Reservations and dressy clothes (jacket and tie) are suggested here. Open 11:30 a.m.–2 p.m. and 5:30 p.m.–10 p.m. Mon.–Fri, dinner only on Saturday 5:30 p.m.–11 p.m. Closed Sunday.

AMERICAN FOOD

Albuquerque has most popular franchised restaurants, so pick one, any one. A concession to New Mexico tastes in most such establishments is the addition of green chile as a side dish on the menus. Even McDonald's, that bastion of formatted, predictable food, allows its locations here to serve green chile on Big Macs. But of course, it's not nearly hot enough.

For pizza, consensus seems to be that **Nunzio's** tops the list in Albuquerque. They have seven locations and the original one is still in business near UNM at 107 Cornell SE (262-1555). Open 11 a.m.–10 p.m. daily, until 11 p.m. on weekends. Nearby is the **Frontier Restaurant**, 2400 Central SE, which specializes in inexpensive breakfasts and a chance to watch the widest — and wildest — possible cross-section of people in Albuquerque. Open 6:30 a.m.–midnight daily.

The 1950s have been re-created in at least two Albuquerque eateries. The **Route 66 Diner**, 1405 Central NE, has patio dining along old Route 66 (Central Avenue), and contrasts the present with historic photos on the wall. The food is classic diner fare, as is that of the **Owl Cafe**, 800 Eubank NE just off I-40, which features the chile cheeseburger made famous by the Cafe of the same name in San Antonio just south of Socorro.

Fred's Bread and Bagels, 3009 Central NE (266-7323), so named because Fred rhymes with bread, is a small bakery with a coffeehouse atmosphere that offers soup and sandwiches, including free-range turkey. The specialties here are green chile bagels (15 varieties) and green chile cheese bread. Open 7 a.m.–11 p.m. daily.

★ ★

SHOPPING

Albuquerque has it all — from huge shopping malls to very unusual specialty shops — and although there are stores in every section of the city, certain areas seem to specialize in specific types of establishments. For example, the Old Town area has most of the Native American art galleries and craft or curio shops while Uptown is the location for Winrock and Coronado Centers, the city's two malls. These malls are located just off I-40 east on Louisiana Boulevard and contain hundreds of shops that are mostly the usual national chains. There are, however, some shops that feature Indian jewelry and other regional specialty merchandise. For more unusual shopping, try Old Town or the Nob Hill/University area.

OLD TOWN

The Plaza, located at Central and Rio Grande, has been the focal point of community life in Old Town since the city's founding in 1706. The buildings that now house galleries and shops surrounding the Plaza were formerly residences, and even today a surprising number of people reside in Old Town, in apartments above the shops and in houses along the alleyways. The best place to start is the **Old Town Visitor Center** at 305 Romero NW (243-3215) where you can pick up a free copy of the "Old Town Map & Shopping Guide," which lists 25 galleries, eleven clothing stores, fifteen restaurants, 49 gift shops, 27 specialty shops, and 21 trading posts. (These figures seem to change weekly.)

"Doing" Old Town could easily take several days, especially if the Albuquerque Museum and the Museum of Natural History are included in the tour. Since it is unlikely that visitors would shop or dine in all 148 places, I'll describe a few of the most interesting. (Galleries have already been covered in the Arts and Crafts section and restaurants in the Dining section, above.) Most places are open seven days a week.

The **Covered Wagon**, 2034 South Plaza NW (242-4481), is one of the oldest shops in Old Town. It's owner, a real character named Manny Goodman, explains the history of his building: "This place was the number one house of prostitution in the whole state of New Mexico, and I'll tell you how I found out. About six months after we opened a man came in and looked around and said, 'You know, I met my wife right upstairs in the parlor there.' " The Covered Wagon now offers Native American arts and crafts rather than pleasures of the flesh, and it probably has the largest selection of souvenirs in Old Town. It's worth a visit just to meet Manny.

O'Grady's Old Town Trading Company, 400 San Felipe (247-4679), is tucked away in one of the many alcoves off the main streets. The shop offers authentic pre-Columbian and contemporary crafts as well as collector-quality Native American arts. **Nizhoni, Moses, Ltd.**, 326 San Felipe (842-1808), features an excellent selection of Hopi kachinas and also specializes in old and new Navajo weavings, Pueblo pottery, Taos furniture, and Navajo mud toys.

Two other trading posts close to Old Town both feature extremely large Native American jewelry collections and both advertise wholesale prices. **Gus' Trading Company**, 2026 Central SW (843-6381), has a huge room with aisle after aisle of cases filled with turquoise and silver. **Palms Trading Company,** 1504 Lomas NW (247-8504), has pottery from nineteen pueblos in addition to Hopi, Navajo, Zuni, and Santo Domingo jewelry. **Ortega's Chimayo Weavers,** 324-C San Felipe (842-5624), offers a wide range of handwoven woolen goods from the master weavers of northern New Mexico's Chimayo Valley. Open 10:30 a.m.– 5 p.m. Mon.–Sat. Another shop specializing in weaving is **Aceves Old Town Basket and Rug Shop,** 301 Romero (842-8022), which not only has a large selection of handwoven Chimayo rugs and blankets, but also baskets from around the world in which to carry them home. The Southwest-design pillows in both shops are outstanding.

Fine folk art from Latin America is the domain of **Pachamama,** 1909 Lomas NW (247-9669). In addition to antique and contemporary jewelry, the shop carries folk pottery, furniture, clothing, and textiles.

For enthusiasts of decorative ceramic tiles, there are two quite different shops in Old Town. **Territorial Tiles,** 400 San Felipe (243-3403), specializes in decorative tiles painted with Southwestern designs. These tiles are usually hung on walls or used as trivets, but they can also be utilized as accents when tiling walls or countertops. More functional tiles are sold by **Casa Talavera,** 621 Rio Grande (243-2413), which carries more than 150 patterns of the beautiful talavera style from Mexico as well as the Saltillo floor tiles which create the patterned floors so popular in New Mexico.

Gourmets interested in New Mexican cuisine should be sure to visit two Old Town shops that specialize in the necessary tools and ingredients. **Potpourri,** 121 Romero (243-4087), is a gourmet shop with a difference. Owner Abe Santillanes is an expert on Southwest cookery, and his shop reflects his interest with an excellent cookbook selection as well as many chile pepper specialty items. And speaking of chile peppers, the shop called **The Chile Pepper Emporium,** 328 San Felipe (242-7538), is one of several stores in the state worshipping what they call "the pungent pod." Peppers carries gourmet lines of chile food including an excellent selection of salsas from all over the Southwest. Non-food chile items include T-shirts, cookware, stationery, and decorations. Mail-order catalogue available also.

Since shopping wouldn't be true shopping without the quest for clothes, Old Town has several trendy shops to explore. Among the best are: **Sunbird,** 401-B San Felipe (behind the church), (242-0123); which features Mexican and South American apparel; **Leatherback Turtle,** 404 San Felipe (842-8496), carrying everything imaginable in beautiful leathers; and **The Harvest,** 328-A San Felipe (765-5763), which offers striking clothing from all over the world.

UNIVERSITY AND NOB HILL AREA

For shoppers who want something out of the ordinary, this area is the place to bring your cash and credit cards. The following three eclectic and downright odd shops feature toys for adults of all ages, mechanical creatures, gags, and hilarious (and often risqué) greeting cards: **Beeps** in Nob Hill Shopping Center at 3500 Central SE (262-1900) and **Martha's Body Bueno,** 3501 Central NE (255-1122). Equally unusual in its own right is **War Games West,** 3422 Central SE (265-6100), the only shop in the city devoted exclusively to what its name suggests.

The award for most unusual record shop in Albuquerque must certainly go to **Bow Wow Records,** 3103 Central NE (256-0928). Andy Horwitz has steadily increased his inventory of Third World music, compact disks featuring reggae, soca, zouk, and salsa — not to mention Tex-Mex. He also has a free full-color mail-order catalog.

Believe it or not, there are certain visitors to cities who, like me, spend much of their time haunting book shops as well as seeing the sights. The Nob Hill/University area is the best place for book lovers, as the most complete book stores in the city are located there. For used books, the best store is **The Bookstop,** 3412 Central SE (268-8898). Owner Jerry Lane has collected tens of thousands of great selections in all categories and will help locate books he doesn't carry. For new books, three bookstores particularly strong in Southwest nonfiction and contemporary fiction are **The Living Batch,** 106 Cornell SE (262-1619), which also carries a good selection of used books; **Salt of the Earth Books,** 2128 Central SE (842-1220), with its comprehensive collection of Latin American fiction; and the **University Bookstore,** Yale Boulevard on the UNM campus (277-5451), carrying the most complete selection of cookbooks and Southwest nonfiction. For visitors needing newspapers and magazines from all over the world, Albuquerque has two exceptional newsstands, **Newsland,** 2112 Central SE in the University area (242-0694), and **Page One,** located in the far northeast heights at 11200 Montgomery NE (294-2026).

THE FLEA MARKET

Ah, marvelous free enterprise! The Flea Market at the State Fairgrounds (Central and Louisiana) is an Albuquerque shopping tradition. It is open every Saturday and Sunday except during the State Fair in September. Starting as early as 7 a.m., several hundred vendors sell an incredible variety of merchandise to thousands of customers. And it's not just junk, either. Need a bargain on antiques, or clothing, or Native American jewelry? Looking for unusual gifts for friends and relatives? Want to take a forty-pound sack of fresh green chiles back home with you? Need some free entertainment for the kids? The Flea Market's the place. Admission and parking is free, and plenty of food is available. Bring cash because checks and credit cards are not usually accepted by the vendors.

★ ★

NIGHTLIFE

POPEJOY HALL
This rather intimate 2094-seat concert hall is the center for the performing arts in Albuquerque and has been described as "acoustically perfect." Located in the Fine Arts Center on the UNM campus, just north of Central at Cornell, Popejoy is the place to enjoy ballet, symphony orchestra performances, light opera, plays, and concerts. Popejoy's Performing Arts Series brings a wide variety of entertainment to Albuquerque, including concerts with singers such as Joan Baez, national dance companies from all over the world, road versions of Broadway plays, and serious drama. Popejoy's box office number is 277-3121.

The eighty-member **New Mexico Symphony Orchestra**, founded in 1932, is the state's official orchestra. It generally performs about twenty classical concerts a year and five "pops" concerts, at Popejoy Hall and different locations in Albuquerque and throughout the state. You can get more information by calling 842-8565. Season tickets are available for classical series.

For more than twenty years, the **Albuquerque Civic Light Opera** has been delighting lovers of musical comedy. The ACLOA generally stages five productions a year, eight performances each, from March through December at Popejoy Hall. Past shows have included "Camelot," "Hello Dolly," "South Pacific," "Kiss Me Kate," and "Kismet." ACLOA can be reached at 345-6577. Season tickets are available.

The **Southwest Ballet** has a troupe of about twenty professional dancers that performs fourteen shows in a twenty-week season November through April at Popejoy Hall and also at the KiMo Theatre. One popular ballet performed by the company is the Eugene Loring/Aaron Copland work "Billy the Kid," one of several different homages to the famous outlaw performed on stages around the state. For information on the current ballet schedule, call 294-1423. Season tickets are available.

KIMO THEATER

The pueblo-deco style KiMo theater building is a triumph because it's an historic building that was saved from destruction in the late '70s and was then restored by the city, which now subsidizes performances by many different artists, musicians, and dancers. Built in 1927, the KiMo was so named by Isleta Pueblo governor Pablo Abeita because the word meant "King of its Kind" in his language. The KiMo is the home of the New Mexico Repertory Theatre, which performs an eclectic mix of drama ranging from the works of Shakespeare to that of modern playwrights, particularly the works of lesser-known dramatists. The KiMo is located at 423 Central NW and Fifth downtown, ticket office (848-1370). Other performing arts centers in Albuquerque include the **Kiva Auditorium** at 401 Second Street NW in the Convention Center, a beautiful concert hall seating about 3500 (768-4575). **La Compania de Teatro de Albuquerque,** one of only ten Hispanic theatre companies in the country, gives bilingual performances of mostly modern works at 423 Central NW, 242-7929. The **Albuquerque Little Theatre,** which since 1930 has been presenting plays at its location, 224 San Pasquale SW, two blocks south of Central near Old Town, 242-4750. Season runs September through February.

TINGLEY COLISEUM

This rodeo arena on the State Fair grounds, located at Central Ave. between San Pedro and Louisiana, is the largest entertainment facility in the state, seating about 12,000. Rodeos, tractor pulls, mudbogs, professional boxing, and concerts featuring mega-groups like Starship or Alabama are all held here (not at the same time). Contact the State Fair grounds at 265-1791 for a schedule of events at Tingley. Tingley Coliseum was named, as was the "beach" of the same name, for former Albuquerque mayor and New Mexico governor Clyde Tingley, one of the state's most famous politicians and self-promoters.

★ ★

NIGHT CLUBS

Albuquerque is not the night club capital of the Southwest, but there are a few places to have some late-night fun: **Beyond Ordinary,** 211 Gold SW (764-8858); **Dingo Bar,** 313 Gold SW (243-0663); **Midnight Rodeo,** 4901 McLeod NE (888-0100); and **El Rey,** 624 Central SW (242-9300). A similar but smaller club is **Señor Buckets,** 4100 San Mateo NE (881-3110). Country music fans will enjoy the big-name recording acts on stage at **Caravan East,** 7605 Central NE (265-7877). Laughter is the best medicine at **Laffs Comedy Night Club,** 3100-A Juan Tabo NE (296-5653) where West Coast comedians appear quite often. Open Tues.–Sun. evenings.

★ ★
JUST FOR THE FUN OF IT

SANDIA PEAK SKI AREA
Atop Sandia Peak and accessible by Sandia Peak Aerial Tramway on Tramway Boulevard off either I-25 north or I-40 east, or by car twenty miles northeast via I-40 east, left on NM Hwy. 14 north, and left on NM Hwy. 165 west, the Sandia Peak Ski Area features 23 trails with 25 miles of skiing, four chair lifts and two Pomas. The runs are 35 per cent beginner, 55 per cent intermediate, and ten per cent advanced, with snowmaking on 35 per cent of the area. Cross-country trails are available and the snow here averages between 110 and 150 inches each year. Sandia Peak Ski Area is open during the season 8:30 to 4, and offers on-slope bars, restaurants, and a snack bar. The most easily accessible ski area in the state, Sandia Peak is located at No. 10 Tramway Loop NE, Albuquerque, NM 87122 (296-9585).

THE DOWNS AT ALBUQUERQUE
Quarter Horses and Thoroughbreds thunder down the State Fair Racetrack from late January through early June while horserace fans cheer from a glass-enclosed, climate-controlled grandstand. The Downs offers several different choices for seating, from the Jockey Club with its elegant buffet to trackside seating closer to the horses. Located at the New Mexico State Fair, Central Avenue between San Pedro and Louisiana (262-1188). General admission—free, Reserved $1, Turf Club $4, Jockey Club $6.

CLIFF'S
A medium-sized amusement park designed (obviously) for kids, Cliff's features a Galaxie roller coaster, a ferris wheel, log flume, bumper cars, ten kiddie rides, five snack bars, and other attractions designed to entertain and exhaust children. Open April–Oct., different hours every month; call for details. Located at 4800 Osuna NE at San Mateo (881-9373). $9.95 unlimited rides, live shows.

THE BEACH

Albuquerque is simply determined to have a beach. Since Tingley Beach is a joke and South Padre Island is a thousand miles away on Texas' Gulf coast, some enterprising business people have opened The Beach, New Mexico's only water park. The wet facilities here include a wave pool that builds breakers two to five feet high—perfect for body and tube surfing (no boards allowed). Four long, steep water slides provide thrills, or the desert beachgoer can float on the Lazy River, a quarter-mile-long, four-foot-deep moat that encircles the Beach.

All this water necessitates quite a staff of lifeguards—64, count 'em. The admission fee of $9.50 Wed. through Sunday for all persons over three years of age seems steep, but it lasts all day and includes all rides. Snack bars, an ice cream parlor, and picnic shelters are provided. Monday and Tuesday admission is $6.50. Every day after 4:30 p.m. admission is $5.00. Open every day 11 a.m.–9 p.m. from mid May through Labor Day. The Beach is located at 1600 Desert Surf Loop off I-25 north at the Montgomery/Montano exit west, then left over the freeway, left at second light at Alexander Street. For more information call 344-6111 or 345-6066.

THE PIT

Technically called University Arena, this 17,000-seat facility is known to basketball fans all over the United States as the home of the University of New Mexico Lobos. Roundball fans who are visiting the city during basketball season should attempt to find tickets to a Lobo game. The experience of sitting in a crowd screaming at the decibel level of a 747 taking off is simply electrifying. Since the Lobos win more than ninety per cent of their home games, almost all Lobo home games are sold out. The best bet for tickets is to check the classified ads a day or two before the game and expect to pay at least double what you would pay at the gate. Sometimes standing-room-only tickets are available. Call 277-2116 for ticket information. The Pit is located south of the University main campus at the corner of University Blvd. and Stadium Rd.

DUKE STADIUM

For baseball fans, Duke Stadium is the place to be in the summer. It is the home of the Albuquerque Dukes, the AAA farm club of the Los Angeles Dodgers and perennial powerhouse of the Pacific Coast League. The beautiful stadium seats 10,500 and half again as many fans squeeze in during big games. It's located diagonally

across the street from the Pit, at corner of University Blvd. and
Stadium Rd. (243-1791).

★ ★
GOLFING

Albuquerque has eleven public and private golf courses, including
the easily accessible University North and South Courses and
Puerto del Sol, all fairly close to the airport. The golf information
number for Albuquerque is 888-8115.

★ ★

HORSEBACK RIDING

A herd of 40 well-trained and equipped horses await equestrians
who wish to explore Tijeras Canyon, just east of the city. **Turkey
Track Stables** is located about thirteen miles from town just off
I-40 at exit 181. $15.00 for the first hour, $10.00 for additional
hours. Call 281-1772 for directions. **Sandia Trails** is located at
10601 4th Street NW. The rates are $15.00 per hour, and $20.00
for one and a half hours. Group rates are available. Three
hundred acres of wooded trails. Call 898-6970. Horseback riding
in the bosque along the Rio Grande is available from **Los Amigos
Round-Up,** 10555 4th Street NW, Alameda, on Sandia Pueblo.
Western banquet facilities are available for large groups or
conventions. Call for direction, 898-8173.

★ ★

BALLOONING

Visitors don't have to attend the International Balloon Fiesta in
order to float gracefully over the Duke City because several commercial enterprises offer safe balloon flights. **World Balloon Corporation,** with its blue balloons decorated as huge globes with the
major continents in yellow, notes that "ballooning is an
anachronism of today's high speed life style." Reach these balloon-
ists at 4800 Eubank NE (293-6800). Rates are $135 per person, and
group rates are available. Other popular ballooning outfits are
Duke City Balloonport, 4815 Hawkins (344-7334), rates $125 per
person, group rates available, and **Tours of Enchantment,** 5801
Jones NW (831-4285), $125 per person. **Rainbow Ryders Inc.** is

located at 430 Montclaire SE (1-800-725-2477, or 268-3401), rates
from $90 to $135, group rates available. **Braden's Balloons Aloft
Inc.** can be reached by writing to P.O. Box 174, Cedar Crest, NM
87008, or call 281-2714. Rates are $85 to $120.

PARKS AND PICNICKING

Virtually every one of the 130 parks in Albuquerque offers some
sort of picnicking facilities in addition to tennis, swimming and
golf. Probably the most interesting place to dine out, as it were, is
the **Elena Gallegos Picnic Area** in the foothills of the Sandias near
the Tramway. In addition to picnic tables, rest rooms, and a terrific
view of the Rio Grande Valley, this picnic area is the trailhead for
the **Piño Wilderness Trail,** which offers hiking and excellent nature-
watching. Another trail leading from this campground is **La Luz
Trail,** which takes the adventurous hiker to the top of Sandia Peak.
Elena Gallegos Picnic Area is reached by taking Tramway east off
I-25 north and following the signs. Albuquerque Parks and
Recreation has more information at 768-3550.

★ ★

OFFBEAT

ISLETA BINGO PARLOR
From I-25 south at night, the bright lights of this building give the
appearance of a UFO landing in the desert. But instead of little
green men, you'll find little greenbacks, if you're lucky. Isleta Bingo
Parlor is located on Isleta Pueblo at 11000 Broadway SE, 87105
(869-2614 or 1-800-843-5156).

SHOOTING RANGE STATE PARK
Weaponry aficionados can practice their sport here at the rifle,
pistol, skeet, and trap ranges. The fees are $3 for the rifle and pistol
ranges, and $3 a round for trap and skeet. The range is open
Wednesday through Sunday summer 7:30 a.m.–5:30 p.m., winter 9 a.m.–5 p.m. and is located off Paseo del Vulcan on the West
Mesa near the volcanoes. For directions, call (768-7824).

GALLES RACING TEAM
A tour of the workshop of the Indy car race team owned by Rick
Galles, whose principal driver is fellow Albuquerquean Al Unser
Jr, is available. The tour includes a visit to the team's wind tunnel,

an inspection of Galles' antique car collection, and stops at the on-site art gallery and gift shop. Reservations are by appointment only at 344-1556. Located at 2725 Broadbent Parkway. Admission is $2 per person for the two hour tour.

ANDERSON VALLEY VINEYARDS
They grow wine grapes in this desert? It may seem unlikely to visitors familiar with the wine-growing areas of California, France, and Italy, but the climate and soils of certain parts of New Mexico are excellent for grape cultivation and have been used for this purpose since Spanish Colonial times. The Anderson Valley Vineyards, started as a hobby by the late balloonist Maxie Anderson and his wife Patty in 1973, now produces more than 36,000 gallons of wine a year. The winery is open Tues.–Sat. noon–5:30 p.m., and Saturday 11 a.m.–5:30 p.m., Sunday 1 p.m.–4 p.m., with group tours by appointment—contact Anderson Valley Vineyards, 4920 Rio Grande NW (345-7744)

SPECIAL EVENTS

SPORT SHOW
Albuquerque just wouldn't be the same without this annual extravaganza, produced for more than 35 years by "Mr. Terrific," Frank Crosby, the World's Greatest Promoter of Thrill Spectacles—he claims this title himself. Held at the Albuquerque Convention Center, downtown at 2nd and Tijeras, his shows never fail to astound. Frank presents, on stage, the most fascinating personalities ever to appear in the state. Past attractions have included Johnny Weismuller, Mickey Rooney, Sally Rand, Tiny Tim, and Sandy Allen, the World's Tallest Woman. The New Mexico Sport Show is held in mid-February. Call 298-1002 for more information. Admission $3, children under twelve free.

THE GREAT RACE DOWN THE RIO GRANDE
Water-loving and water-desperate Albuquerqueans frolic along the runoff-swollen Rio Grande in mid-May during a bizarre raft race down the river. The race features fourteen different categories of everything afloat from bathtubs to rafts in the shape of castles. The fourteen-mile course provides perhaps the quickest tour of Albuquerque's bosque. Information is available from 768-3490. Best viewing is from the Central Avenue bridge area.

NEW MEXICO ARTS AND CRAFTS FAIR

The nation's second largest arts and crafts fair is held every year in late June along the tree-lined streets of the State Fairgrounds. More than two hundred artisans including ceramicists, leather workers, painters, sculptors, photographers, carvers, weavers, and woodworkers display their creations in an outdoor juried show. The fair also provides live entertainment and arts and crafts demonstrations. Information from 884-9043.

NEW MEXICO STATE FAIR

More than one million people attend this fair in early September. It's one of the biggest state fairs in the nation with a large midway, Native American and Spanish villages, quarter horse and thoroughbred racing, the PRCA rodeo with top country and western recording artists, and hundreds and hundreds of exhibits and food booths. The State Fair fairgrounds are bordered by Central, San Pedro, Lomas, and Louisiana, and more information is available by calling 265-1791.

ALBUQUERQUE INTERNATIONAL BALLOON FIESTA

Every year in early October, hundreds of thousands of people flock to the northern reaches of the city to watch the world's largest ballooning event. This nine-day fiesta, more than seventeen years old and still growing, is the most photographed event in the U.S. because of the colorful spectacle of as many as five hundred hot air balloons in mass ascension. In addition to the balloon spectacle, other events include a parade, daily air shows, and demonstrations by precision parachute teams. Visitors can participate in the excitement by wandering among the inflating balloons or by volunteering to become a member of a balloon chase crew. For exact dates and more information, contact the Albuquerque International Balloon Fiesta, 8309 Washington Place NE, Albuquerque, NM 87113 (821-1000). To reach the Balloon Fiesta site, take the Alameda west exit off I-25 north.

INTERNATIONAL ARABIAN CHAMPIONSHIP

This spectacular event occurs every other year in mid-October (1989, 1991, 1993, etc.) at the State Fairgrounds at Central and San Pedro NW, and is the showcase for some of the most expensive horses in the world — and their owners. The spectacle includes competition with costume events nightly, an extensive trade fair, decorated stalls, and very wealthy people. The Arabian show lasts a full week, with specialty shows at 8 a.m., 4:30 p.m. and 1:30 p.m. Admission is charged; call 243-3696 or 1-800-284-2282.

WEEMS ARTFEST

This winter art show occurs the first weekend of November at the Exhibit Halls, State Fairgrounds at Central and San Pedro NW. Second in size to the New Mexico Arts and Crafts Fair, the Weems Artfest includes 180 artisan exhibits plus a Children's Artmart where original arts and crafts can be purchased only by children under twelve. For details, call 293-6133 or contact the Weems Galleries.

★ ★
COMMERCIAL TOURS

Tours of nearby Indian Pueblos and national monuments are conducted by **Rocky Mountain Tours,** 1323 Paseo de Peralta (984-1684), **Tours of Enchantment,** 5801 Jones NW, 87120 (831-4285) and **Shuttlejack Olson/SW Grayline,** P.O. Box 25381, Albuquerque, NM 87125 (764-9464).

★ ★
RESOURCES

The main branch of the **Albuquerque Public Library** (768-5140) at 501 Copper NW at 5th Street, downtown, provides the easiest access to in-depth information about Albuquerque. **Zimmerman Library** (277-5761) at the University of New Mexico three blocks south of Lomas at Yale and Roma intersection, is the largest library in the state and is also open to researchers.

The **Albuquerque Convention and Visitor's Bureau** produces an informative annual publication, *Official Albuquerque Visitor's Guide.* To obtain a free copy, write P.O. Box 26866, Albuquerque, NM 87125 or call (1-800-284-2282). *Albuquerque Monthly,* P.O. Box 928, 87103 (255-4648) is published monthly ($12 year) and also produces *New Mexico Monthly,* and many guides to Albuquerque and the state. For additional information on galleries, *The Collector's Guide: Albuquerque,* ($4) is an annual publication which shows examples of the works of artists in Albuquerque's best galleries. It is published by Wingspread Communications, P.O. Box 13566, Albuquerque, NM 87192 (292-7537, 1-800-873-4278). Santa Fe and Taos edition ($5) and master edition ($9) also available. *Gallery News on the Radio,* a weekly radio program is also presented by *The Collector's Guide* on 96 Classical KHFM every Thursday and Friday at 8:55 a.m. and 4:55 p.m.

★ ★

NEARBY ATTRACTIONS

TURQUOISE TRAIL TOUR

The most direct route from Albuquerque to Santa Fe, I-25 north, is not the most interesting way to go. The Turquoise Trail Tour, as it's called, is a trip to Santa Fe by the "back way," or via I-40 east and then NM Hwy. 14 on the eastern side of the Sandias. It takes the visitor from desert to pine forests in a matter of minutes, and there are restaurants, galleries, and shops along the road in Cedar Crest and Sandia Park. Sandia Crest and Sandia Peak Ski area are also accessible off this route via NM Hwys. 165 and 536. Ten miles north of the Sandia Crest Highway intersection is the small town of **Golden,** the site of the Old Placers gold mine that created the first gold rush west of the Mississippi in 1828. It is one of many inhabited "ghost towns" in New Mexico and is famous because some of the largest gold nuggets ever found in North America including one that weighed an astonishing twelve pounds, were discovered in the appropriately named town. Legend holds that the prospector who found that nugget traded it for a case of whiskey. Strong drink on this tour will not be available until **Madrid** (pronounced Maa'-drid), a former coal mining "company town" that sits in the foothills of the Ortiz Mountains. Beginning in the 1920s and continuing through 1941, Madrid gained national fame for its spectacular display of Christmas lights — so spectacular that Transcontinental Airlines (TWA) flights were detoured over Madrid so the passengers could enjoy the view. The frame buildings scattered around the town were used until the last mine closed in 1954, but then they fell into disrepair and it seemed that Madrid would become a true ghost town. But enterprising young people began to buy and restore some of the buildings and Madrid has enjoyed a remarkable comeback; the town now boasts a museum, several shops, and an annual jazz festival.

The **Old Coal Mine Museum,** (473-0743), exhibits an extensive collection of mining tools and memorabilia and offers a tour inside a mine shaft. The **Mine Shaft Tavern,** open Memorial Day through Labor Day, purveys entertainment and strong drink and might even trade for a gold nugget. The former company store compound now houses four shops including the **Madrid Supply Company,** (471-9128), a source for paintings, jewelry, weavings, and glass, and **Madrid Earthenware Pottery** (471-3450), a studio featuring the work of four respected potters, plus rugs, and folk art.

The last stop on the Turquoise Trail is the reason for the name, since **Cerrillos** ("little hills" in Spanish) has been the source of some of the world's finest turquoise, mined mostly in the last two decades of the 1800s. The trail might well have been called the Gold or Silver Trail, since both of those precious metals were also discovered in Cerrillos. A gold strike in 1879 led to the building of the town by the Santa Fe Railroad and then silver was found as well, creating a boomtown with 21 saloons and four hotels. One of the largest silver mines in the area was Cash Entry, which was owned by a British company. During one period in the 1880s, the Cash Entry claimed wages paid to employees at an astounding $150,000 a month!

The Cerrillos boom ended abruptly after 1890 when all of the mines played out. The population, estimated at 2500 at its peak, wandered away and the town became a sparsely settled wayside stop and a picturesque reminder — as is Madrid — of the boomtown syndrome in New Mexico. Two interesting establishments in Cerrillos are the **What-Not Shop,** (471-2744), with a collection of everything under the New Mexico sun, including kachinas, antiques, and even snacks, and **Casa Grande,** a combination museum-gift shop in a sprawling twenty-room adobe hacienda that has exhibits describing the history of Cerrillos mining. For more information on the Turquoise Trail, write the Turquoise Trail Association, P.O. Box 303, Sandia Park, NM 87047 (281-5233 or 243-0605).

CORONADO STATE PARK AND MONUMENT

Often absurdly called "The Plymouth Rock of the West," Coronado State Park and Monument is the site where the Spanish conquistador Coronado spent the winter of 1540 — at the ancient pueblo of Kuaua, now a partially reconstructed ruin. It is located one mile northwest of Bernalillo via I-25 and NM Hwy. 44. There is an excellent museum and interpretive trail here, and camping with utility hookups and restrooms is available.

The discovery and plundering of New Mexico by the Spanish conquistadors was the result of one simple human characteristic: greed. Unbeknownst to the Indians of New Mexico, a European lust for treasure had, by 1533, destroyed two great Native American cultures, those of the Aztecs and the Incas. In both cases, Spaniards under the sign of the cross killed and plundered on an enormous scale. After they found vast amounts of gold and jewels in Mexico and Peru, the Spaniards were primed to believe any tale concerning treasure, and New Mexico was rumored to have at least three treasure hordes: the Seven Cities of Cibola; Quivira, with its streets paved with gold; and Sierra Azul, a mountain of solid silver. Francisco Vasquez de Coronado was given the task of finding these treasures, and the conquistador left Mexico City in 1540 with 250 cavalry and seventy infantrymen. He was forced to attack and defeat Cibola in order to learn it was really Zuni Pueblo, which had lots of corn but no gold. Frustrated and determined to salvage his expedition, Coronado pushed onward into New Mexico. He reached the Pueblo of Tiguex near what is now Bernalillo but was forced by winter weather to stay there. During his winter visit to what is now Coronado State Monument, Coronado made a reconnaissance of the Pueblo of Cicuye (modern Pecos), where he discovered a captive Plains Indian who told an amazing tale about a city to the east called Quivira, which had streets paved with gold. Even the common water jugs were made with gold instead of clay!

Coronado fell for the story completely and in the spring of 1541, he and his small army set out east along a path approximating that of old Route 66. Finally, in July, after 77 days of travel on his quixotic quest, he and his small band finally arrived at Quivira near what is now Manhattan, Kansas. The streets were not golden in Quivira — they were made of mud and buffalo chips. In fact, metal did not exist among these impoverished Plains Indians, who hovered on the edge of existence in grass huts. As historian Charles Lummis noted, "Every eyewitness who then or thereafter saw the Quiviras, describes them as utter barbarians, clothed only in skins, eating raw meat, and having no bread, no metal, no towns, no arts whatsoever." So much for the golden water jars.

After wasting months following two nonexistent treasures, Coronado was furious. He ordered his guide strangled and then returned to Tiguex Pueblo. An injury and subsequent illness forced him to abandon the expedition and return to Mexico City without treasure to face the consequences of complete and utter failure: He was fired and fined for his misdeeds by the Viceroy and New Mexico was ignored by the Spanish for nearly forty years.

Even though there is a monument named after him, it should be pointed out that far from being the hero legend has made him today, Coronado was a paid adventurer in search of gold no matter what the cost, including Indian lives. Incidentally, Isleta Pueblo governor Pablo Abeita gained further fame on May 29, 1940, during the dedication of Coronado State monument. He embarrassed New Mexico Governor John Miles by stating in a speech during the dedication ceremonies: "Ninety per cent of the white man's history is wrong. I don't agree with all this talk about Coronado, and I don't know what you mean by Spanish culture. The Spaniards got lost on the ocean and accidentally ran across this continent. They thanked God for giving it to them and stuck a flag in it. They never asked the Indians how they felt about it." For more information on Coronado State Park and Monument, call (867-5351). Take US Hwy. 85 seventeen miles north to Bernalillo, then one mile west on NM Hwy. 44. Museum, campgrounds (867-5589) and hiking trails are adjacent to Kuana Pueblo. The park is open daily; admission is $2 for adults.

SANDIA PUEBLO
Located just eight miles north of Albuquerque off I-25 (take Tramway exit west off I-25 north, then north on NM Hwy. 313 for four miles). Sandia is today a fairly modern pueblo even though it dates to about 1300. In the early seventeenth century, the Franciscans constructed the mission of San Francisco here, but it was destroyed during the pueblo revolt of 1680 and wasn't rebuilt until the early 1890s. Fear of Spanish reprisals drove the Sandia people out of the area to take refuge with the Hopi. The Sandias celebrate their annual feast day on June 13. Visitors should remember that alcohol, sketching, recording, and photography are forbidden on tribal land.

The Sandias have a diversified income base that includes a large gravel operation and **Sandia Pueblo Bingo Parlor** (898-0852), which can be reached by exiting west on Tramway Rd. off I-25 north. Sandia also has a fine trading post, **Bien Mur,** located at the Tramway Road exit east off I-25. Here the visitor can find turquoise and silver jewelry, baskets, rugs, sandpaintings, and other Indian crafts. Bien Mur is open seven days a week and can be reached at 821-5400. For more information on Sandia Pueblo, call 867-3317.

SAN FELIPE PUEBLO
Famous for its beautiful ceremonial dances, San Felipe is located along the Rio Grande at the foot of Black Mesa, about ten miles north of Bernalillo one-half mile off I-25 on NM Hwy. 313. During the Green Corn Dance on the Feast Day of San Felipe (May 1), hundreds of men, women, and children dance in a bowl-like depression in the plaza.

San Felipe is essentially a farming community and no crafts are produced at the village. Photography, sketching, and tape recording are forbidden on tribal lands. For more information, contact the tribe at 867-3381.

SANTO DOMINGO PUEBLO
Located just off I-25 forty miles north of Albuquerque on NM Hwy. 22, Santo Domingo Pueblo has a small museum and gas sta-

tion to serve visitors. Most of the Indians here make their living through farming, developing commercial property, and employment in Albuquerque or Santa Fe.

The pueblo has always had a reputation for secrecy, which dates back to their resistance against Spanish control—they even destroyed their own pueblo in 1692 rather than submit to reconquest. In the past they carefully hid their native ceremonies from the Spanish, but today they perform an annual Corn Dance on August 4th, which is open to the public. The Corn Dance is one of the most exciting of all pueblo ceremonies, featuring dancers, singers, drummers, and clowns called *koshares*. Santo Domingo jewelry is similar to the shell and turquoise ancestral decorations uncovered in excavations, essentially, and the traditional pottery is generally black and red on a cream base.

No visitor's permit is required here, but a small parking fee is charged on ceremonial days. No alcohol, tape recording, photography or sketching is allowed. The tribal phone number is 465-2214.

ISLETA PUEBLO
Named "little island" because it originally was surrounded by the Rio Grande, Isleta is a progressive farming community fifteen miles south of Albuquerque just off exit 209 of I-25. Many of the people here are employed in Albuquerque, and much tribal revenue comes from leasing lands, since the pueblo is the second-largest in terms of area. The tribe maintains Isleta Lakes, where fishing for bass and catfish is allowed with a permit available at the lakes. In the center of the pueblo is a tribal marketplace, which, along with other stores scattered around the pueblo, offers bargains on cigarettes and other merchandise.

The annual feast day, in honor of St. Augustine, is September 4th. Photography is not allowed at Isleta. For more information call 869-3111.

BELEN AND LOS LUNAS
Although these two communities, located south of Albuquerque via I-25 or NM Hwy. 314, are separate towns, they tend to merge together. Ranching and farming are still important in the area, although many of the residents here commute to jobs in Albuquerque.

The name Los Lunas tends to confuse people who always expect Spanish adjectives to agree with nouns. Yes, it is true that "las lunas" would mean "the moons," but the word "los" in front of a surname means that the translation of Los Lunas is "place where the Luna family lives." In this case, the name refers to the family of Solomon Luna, who was a famous politician in territorial times. The **Luna Mansion,** just one and one-half miles east of the Los Lunas exit off I-25, with an southern mansion architectural style more suited for Virginia than New Mexico, has been completely restored and is now an excellent restaurant. To make reservations for dinner at this National Historic Landmark, call 865-7333. Open for dinner only Mon.–Thurs. 5 p.m.–10 p.m., Fri.–Sat. 5 p.m.–10:30 p.m., and Sunday Brunch 11 a.m.–2 p.m., 4:30 p.m.–9:30 p.m.

The name "Belen" is Spanish for Bethlehem, and this small city of 12,000 just off I-25 was named such by religious settlers in 1741. In 1880 the Santa Fe Railroad opened a system through Belen and in 1897 followed with an east-west line, making the "Hub City" a major railroad center. Unlike Albuquerque, Belen managed to save its railroad hotel, the **Harvey House,** at 104 N. 1st Street (864-5903), which has been completely restored and now serves as home for the **Valencia County Museum,** which is open Sundays and Tuesdays 2 p.m.–4 p.m. Also in the building is the Greater Belen Chamber of Commerce, 864-8091. For more information, contact the Belen Chamber of Commerce, 221 S. Main Street, Belen, NM 87002.

Senator Willie Chavez State Park is located along the Rio Grande off NM Hwy. 47 and offers hiking trails, a picnic area, a playground, and rest rooms. **Rio Grande Veterans Memorial Park** is located east of the Valencia Campus of the University of New Mexico just off Rio del Oro. As you stroll along beautifully land-scaped trails, you'll see plaques and monuments commemorating New Mexicans who died in defense of their country, from the Mexican-American War of 1848 to the Vietnam Conflict.

LAGUNA PUEBLO
It's called the "newest" New Mexico pueblo because Laguna was founded in the late 1690s by Cochiti and Santo Domingo rebels who were still fighting the Spanish after de Vargas subdued the pueblos in 1692-4. The name is odd today because even though "laguna" is Spanish for "lake," there is no lake at this pueblo (popu-lation about 5200), 45 miles due west of Albuquerque on I-40. However, the name was probably derived from the presence of a lake that was in the area when the pueblo was founded, but which has since has dried up and is now a meadow that helps feed Laguna's cattle and sheep. Since the uranium boom in Grants ended because of the end of nuclear power plant construction, the pueblo now depends heavily on livestock. Many Lagunans work for vari-

ous tribal industries, some of which have U.S. government defense contracts.

The village, visible from I-40, is one of several communities including Paguate, Mesita, Encinal, Casa Blanca, and Seama that make up the pueblo. The pueblo celebrates St. Joseph's feast day every September 19 with a large fair that attracts both pueblo and Navajo people. Fishing is allowed at Paguate Reservoir, with permits available in Paguate, eight miles north of Laguna on NM Hwy. 279. Permission must be obtained from the staff officer of each village before photos can be taken within the pueblo boundaries. Visitors should check with the tribal office or call 552-6654; a guide service is available.

San Jose Mission Church at Laguna is the most interesting building at the pueblo. The massive structure dates from 1706 and is listed on the National Register of Historic Places. The interior features elaborate red, yellow, and green religious decorations, and a beautifully carved altar. All the work in the church was completed by Indian craftsmen. Laguna Pueblo can be reached at P.O. Box 194, Laguna, NM 87026 (522-6001).

ACOMA PUEBLO

Without question the most spectacular Indian pueblo in the state, Acoma (population about 4000) rests high atop a mesa rising 365 feet from the surrounding valley. The pueblo, which vies with the Hopi Pueblo of Oraibi in Arizona as the "oldest continually inhabited community in the U.S.," is about 65 miles west of Albuquerque and about twenty miles from Laguna. Take exit 102 off I-40 and follow the signs along NM Hwy. 23.

Coronado's men were the first Europeans to visit Acoma, in 1540. They reported that the pueblo was "one of the strongest ever seen, because the city was built on a high rock." They also remarked that "the ascent was so difficult that we repented climbing to the top." Fifty years later, the Spaniards feared Acoma's military might and the fact that the pueblo was situated upon a natural fortress, so Juan de Oñate sent a detachment of soldiers to Acoma demanding—as was the Spanish way—tribute and supplies. The Acomas pretended to acquiesce and lured the soldiers up the mesa with the promise of cornmeal, then attacked the force and killed thirteen Spaniards, including Juan de Zaldivar, the leader of the expedition.

A punitive expedition under the direction of Zaldivar's brother attacked Acoma the following year with a force of seventy armed and armored conquistadors. After a three day battle that may have cost as many as eight hundred Indian lives, Sky City was captured

and mostly destroyed. The Spaniards took revenge on the pueblo
by punishing the Acoma survivors severely. The men had one foot
cut off and were made slaves for 25 years; women and children
were divided between the Church and the Crown as slaves for
twelve years.

In 1680, the Acomas had their chance for revenge against the
Spanish during the Pueblo revolt. They murdered the Church priest
and joined the rest of the pueblos in routing the Spanish soldiers
and settlers, who retreated to El Paso. Acoma's residents resisted
the Spanish until 1699, when they were the last pueblo to again
yield to the invaders.

The "Sky City," as it's called, is opposite from another impressive
formation, four-hundred-foot-high **Enchanted Mesa** to the east,
which figures prominently in Acoma legend as the original home of
the pueblo until a storm closed the trail to the top during prehistoric times. Visitors to Acoma must stop at the Visitors' Center
and register to take the Acoma tour — it is against tribal regulations
for visitors to drive or walk up to the top of the mesa on their own.
There are admission fees ranging from $4 for adults to $2 for children, plus additional fees for photography ranging from $4 (if you
want to use your Instamatic) to $300 for professional photograph-
ers. A shuttle bus accommodating thirteen visitors at a time transports the tours from the visitor center to Sky City atop the mesa.
The tour lasts one hour and gives a comprehensive overview of the
history and culture of Acoma.

On the contemporary tour the first stop is at the **Church of San
Esteban Rey,** one of the finest examples of Spanish colonial mission
churches. This often-photographed church was built about 1629
with forced labor from the surviving Acoma slaves and was restored by the Museum of New Mexico in 1923. Every single piece
of building material, including the forty-foot roof beams, was
laborious carried up steep, narrow trails by burros or men. The
painting of Saint Joseph displayed inside the church was the gift of
Phillip II of Spain and was the subject of a lengthy dispute between
Acoma and Laguna during the mid-1850s. Believing the painting to
have miraculous powers, the Lagunas borrowed it from the Acomas and refused to return it, relented, and then stole it back after
they returned it to Acoma. War between the two neighboring
pueblos was averted through a decision by the U.S. District Court
in Santa Fe awarding possession of the painting to Acoma. On their
way to Laguna to fetch the painting, a committee of Acomas found
the painting under a tree about halfway to Laguna.

On the tour, you will encounter both crumbling and restored
structures perched on the edge of the cliff where only about fifty

inhabitants live year-round. There is also a natural cistern that captures and stores rainwater; it was the subject of a famous photograph, "At the Old Well of Acoma," by Edward S. Curtis. The pottery sold by Acoma women along the tour, and at the visitor center, is a result of a centuries-long ceramic tradition and includes bowls, jars, and figurines of animals, birds, and humans, decorated in the traditional black and white style. A flyer issued by the pueblo describes the pottery poetically: "Never in the form of a perfect sphere, or in design a perfect pattern, but more a transference of feeling in design and artistry transmitted through the delicate hands of the creator. The form and designs all revert back to nature, birds, mountains, and clouds. It is considered to have a life and spirit of its own. Therefore the break in design pattern is not to imprison this life, but to let it breathe freely as we do."

Back at the visitors' center, a permanent museum exhibit entitled "One Thousand Years of Clay: Pottery, Environment, and History," explains in detail Acoma's ceramic tradition. The Visitors Center also houses the Native Food Shop and the Craft Shop, which offer jewelry and native foods. Fishing for both rainbow and German brown trout is available at nearby **Acomita Lake** for a fee of $2.75 a day plus a valid NM fishing license. There are snack bar and restroom facilities at the lake, but boating and fishing are prohibited.

Acoma Pueblo is open from 8 a.m.–7 p.m. during the summer and spring, and 8 a.m.–4 p.m. during the fall and winter. The pueblo is closed to all visitors July 10–13, the weekend of October 2, and Easter weekend. Fiesta day is September 2nd, when the Harvest Dance and the Annual Feast of San Estevan is held. The festival was the subject of another famous photograph by Edward S. Curtis, "Feast Day at Acoma."

For further information on Sky City, contact the Pueblo of Acoma, P.O. Box 309, Pueblo of Acoma, NM 87034 (552-6604).

GRANTS

Grants, about sixty miles west of Albuquerque via I-40, is a small town (9000 inhabitants) with a lot of pride. It has somehow managed to survive the Uranium mining industry collapse that left most of the town's labor force unemployed. The former "Uranium Capital of the World" was founded in 1881 by three brothers and was known as "Grant's Camp." The Santa Fe Railroad used the town as a stop to load coal, and for many decades it was a lumber-milling town where the trees from nearby **Mt. Taylor** were processed.

Mt. Taylor, one of the sacred mountains of the Navajo, is impossible to miss since Grants literally sits in its shadow. The 11,300-foot peak is named after Zachary Taylor, 12th President of the U.S., but a more interesting name for it is *dzil dotlizi*, or "turquoise mountain" in the Navajo language. The mountain marked the southern boundary of the Navajo Nation, and Navajo mythology holds that it was built by First Man and First Woman with earth brought up from the underworld—not too far off, considering the Mt. Taylor's volcanic origins. According to Navajo legend, First Man and First Woman fastened the mountain to the ground with a knife and adorned it with rain, game, and turquoise.

During the late Pliocene, about two million years ago, the east peak of Mt. Taylor detonated in precisely the same manner as did Mount St. Helens in recent years. A huge explosion, combined with ash and lava flows, ripped an eight-square-mile gash in the mountain. Called the amphitheater, this center dwarfs the 2100-foot-deep crater left by the Mount St. Helens eruption. The mountain is part of Cibola National Forest, and two campgrounds, **Coal Mine** and **Lobo Canyon,** can be reached by taking NM Hwy. 547 from exit 85 of I-40.

NEW MEXICO MUSEUM OF MINING

"Go Underground!" is the motto of this interesting museum that recreates a uranium mine known as "Section 26." Former miners act as tour guides and lead visitors below ground by way of an elevator. The first stop is the Station, a work area where miners gather when blasting is in progress. The next stop is the mine proper, where ventilation shafts, mining equipment, chutes, and huge drilling machines are described by the guide.

Some readers might not think such a museum would be very interesting. After all, uranium, because of its nuclear connection, is not the most popular mineral in the world these days. However, years ago I took a tour deep into a working uranium mine as our small group of journalists was lowered one mile into the earth in a huge metal bucket. It was a thrilling and fascinating experience, and although this museum tour is tame by comparison, it is no less interesting. Claustrophobes should remain on the surface and gaze at Mount Taylor.

The New Mexico Museum of Mining is located at 100 Iron Street at Santa Fe Avenue, 287-4802. Hours are Mon.–Fri. 10 a.m.–noon and 1 p.m.–4 p.m., Saturday 10 a.m.–4 p.m., and Sundays 1 p.m.– 4 p.m. Admission is $2, children eight and under free.

★ ★
LODGING AND DINING

Don't expect big-city luxury accommodations here — the motels are decidedly normal. However, they do make a good base of operations for explorations of nearby attractions. The largest motel is the **Econo Lodge** (287-4426), on Santa Fe Ave. (take exit 85 off I-40 east), with 212 rooms and a large outdoor pool. At the intersection of E. Spur Hwy. and I-40 is **The Inn Best Western** (287-7901), with 125 rooms and an indoor pool.

Recommended restaurants include **La Ventana Steak House,** 110½ Geis Street (287-9393), where you can order extremely good New Mexico style steak with chiles while sitting in comfortable leather booths. It is open 11 a.m.–11 p.m. Mon.–Sat. but is closed Sunday. (Bar stays until 2 a.m.) Also good are **Jaramillo's Mexi-Catessen,** 213 N. 3rd (287-9308), open 10:30 a.m.–7:30 p.m. Mon.–Fri., closed weekends; the **Monte Carlo Cafe,** 721 W. Santa Fe (287-9250), open 7 a.m.–10 p.m. daily.

BLUEWATER LAKE STATE PARK

One of the prettiest lakes in the state is Bluewater, located about 28 miles west of Grants off I-40, via NM Hwy. 412 south (exit 63). Situated 7400 feet above sea level on the northeast flank of the Zuni Mountains and surrounded by piñon and juniper trees, the lake is a mile wide by seven miles long and has about 25 miles of shoreline.

The deep blue water here is stocked with rainbow trout and channel catfish, and boat rentals are available. Picnicking and camping sites are available for a nominal charge, and stores nearby furnish food, recreational supplies, and fishing licenses. For information, call 876-2391.

EL MALPAIS NATIONAL MONUMENT

New Mexico's newest National Monument is probably the most difficult to explore because its brutally rugged terrain consists of 84,000 acres of abrasive basaltic lava. In order to tour El Malpais, which means badlands in Spanish, take NM Hwy. 117 south from I-40 until it intersects County Rd. 109, which loops back to NM Hwy. 53 and then to I-40. There is no visitor center yet, but one is planned. Along the way, stop at the overlooks, and the picnic areas and be sure not to miss La Ventana, New Mexico's largest natural arch, not quite eighteen miles south of I-40. Be extremely careful; the sharp lava can easily shred shoes and car tires. Southwestern author J. Frank Dobie has vividly described the malpais: "In it are pits of glazed walls so steep that only a creature of four padded feet would attempt descent to their barren floors. Horrific chasms, made by the lava's contracting when cooled, cut and crisscross the beds so that a person trying to progress in a certain direction will be twisted in labyrinthian isolation."

At least four separate lava flows—some moving as fast as 25 miles an hour—covered the McCarty's Valley south of Grants perhaps as recently as 1500 years ago, which means there must have been human witnesses to the river of fire. Navajo mythology holds that the lava is the blood of Big Snake, a monster killed by Monster Slayer to make *Dinetah*, the land of the Navajos, safe for humans. The first Europeans to cross the malpais were a party of cavalrymen sent ahead from Zuni by the Spanish èxplorer Coronado in August, 1540. Captain Hernando de Alvarado, who led the party, was hardly in a partying mood when the trip ended. He wrote that the trail was barely passable and was exceedingly rough on the feet of horses and men alike.

Badlands they might be to the untrained eye, but as with other desert areas, there is a surprising amount of life in the malpais. In fact, the area includes three distinct plant zones. Yuccas, cholla cactus, grasses, and even junipers eventually take root amidst the lava in blown-in dirt and sand. Larger trees such as ponderosa pine, Douglas fir, and aspen grow in the *kipukas*, oasis-like depressions or clearings in the lava. Rodents such as mice, jackrabbits, and kangaroo rats move in next, and they attract the predators— coyotes, hawks, owls, and snakes. Incredibly, there are 156 species of wildlife which survive the harsh conditions of the McCarty's malpais: nine reptiles and amphibians, 39 mammals, and 108 birds. Even trout are reputedly found in the lava, surviving in deep pools either spring-fed or filled with rainwater runoff.

The malpais has assumed a prominent position in recent legend with stories of outlaw escapes across the lava and treasure tales claiming that the Lost Adams Diggings were hidden somewhere in the 119 square miles of convoluted basalt. The malpais is so formidable, so hostile, that it seems like a natural place to hide a treasure. A few minor treasures have been retrieved from the lava: an occasional gold nugget, an iron chest filled with $10,000 in Confederate bills and several Indian water jars filled with bones and Spanish coins. Every small find fuels the hope that a big bonanza is hidden somewhere in the lava. But any major treasure find remains elusive, though not for lack of legends.

The Pueblo Revolt against the Spanish in 1680 produced many tales of hidden silver, and the lava beds feature prominently in the general legend. The mission churches of Zuni and Acoma reputedly contained 52 *atajos* (burro-loads) of gold and silver coins, bars, and statues. During the revolt, the Indians of those pueblos sacked the churches, killed or routed the priests, and captured the holy treasures. Determined to destroy or hide all things valuable to the Spaniards, the Indians reputedly transported the treasure deep into the malpais directly south of Grants. But no one has ever found it.

In October, 1897, a train robbery near Grants revived tales of booty concealed somewhere in the McCarty's flow. The eastbound Santa Fe passenger train made its usual stop at Grants to pick up coal and was hijacked by a gang of bandits who forced the engineer to uncouple the passenger cars and pull the mail, express, and baggage cars to a predetermined spot east of town. There the gang dynamited the door of the express car and escaped with about $100,000 in gold, silver, and currency. They were followed by a posse but disappeared into the malpais. Legend holds that the bandits fought among themselves over the division of the loot and some members of the gang were killed. One of the survivors of the gun battle buried the booty somewhere in the lava, hoping to return later and claim it. But he could never find it, and neither can anyone else. Another legend tells that the train robbery loot was hidden in the "Hole in the Wall," a 14,000 acre "island" of grass and trees in the center of the flow which was too high for the lava to cover.

A final treasure story illustrates the fact that J. Frank Dobie was not exaggerating the roughness of the malpais. In 1936, a Lockheed Vega was flying a $100,000 cash contribution from California oil men to presidential candidate Alf Landon in New York. During the flight, the pilot of the Vega radioed ahead to Albuquerque to request that the airport remain open until he arrived. He never made it. Somewhere over the lava fields, the Vega was spotted by another pilot. It was flying very low and apparently that was the last time the courier plane was ever seen. Although many air and ground searches were made to find the plane and the missing cash, not one has been successful. Treasure expert Thomas Penfield concluded that the remains of the plane were at the bottom of a large crevasse in the lava. Visitors wishing to continue the search for such missing treasures should be forewarned that getting lost in the malpais is equivalent to a death sentence. Compass readings are not accurate because of the iron content of the lava, so take the advice of the federal government: "Never travel alone; carry plenty of food and water; travel only during spring or fall; and leave word with a reliable person as to where you are and when you're expected to return."

ICE CAVE AND BANDERA CRATER

One of the more unusual attractions in the malpais is the Perpetual Ice Cave, located 26 miles southwest of Grants on County Rd. 109 just off NM Hwy. 53. The miniature glacier inside this cave hasn't melted since it was first seen by Europeans when Coronado was given a tour of the cave by Zuni guides in 1540. Although one of the most popular visitor sites near Grants, the Ice Cave is privately owned by the Candelaria family and receives no state funding, so a $2 admission fee is charged.

Summer temperatures in the malpais reach well over 100 degrees F., yet 75 feet below the surface the temperature hovers just below freezing at an even thirty degrees — enough to keep the fifteen-foot-thick block of ice solid. Such a wonder has kept people guessing for centuries; How was the cave formed? How did the ice get there in the first place? and What keeps it frozen?

The origin of the cave is easily explained. Molten lava solidifies at different rates as it cools, depending upon the thickness of the flow, the temperature of the ground and air, and the precise chemical composition of the lava. Lava that solidifies first next to the ground tends to cause the flow to pile up, causing "blisters" and "blowholes." If the surface of the lava cools first, forming a crust, sometimes the flow beneath the crust flows through completely, creating lava "tubes" that may be more than a mile long. Occasionally a portion of one of these tubes will collapse, creating a small cavern. Fanciful early theories held that the lava had flowed over a glacier and melted it, or that there was some chemical process involving ammonia at work in the cave.

Fortunately for the reputation of science in this high-tech state, E.R. Harrington published the solution to the puzzle in the July 1940 issue of *New Mexico* magazine. The cave faces south, which means that the winter sun can enter the cave, but the hot summer sun cannot. Harrington conducted studies of air circulation and temperature during all seasons and concluded that the ice is formed during the winter as water seeps into the cave through cracks in the lava and meets dense, cold air that is sinking into the cave entrance. As the weather warms, the air circulation diminishes as the warmer air rises and leaves the cave. The lack of circulation keeps the lower cave temperature constant, enabling the mass of ice to resist melting. Besides, any small amount of melt would take heat from the air surrounding the ice mass, thus lowering the temperature of the air even more. The malpais above the cave also acts as an excellent insulating material.

The source of at least one of the McCarty's flows is **Bandera Crater**, located at the end of a one and one-half mile walk from the Ice Cave. The name means flag in Spanish, because the U.S. Cavalry from Fort Wingate near Gallup raised the American flag on the top of the cone. A trail through the malpais leads to the crater, which has trees on its slopes and a deep deposit of ash inside.

Bandera is what is known in volcanologist circles as a breached cinder cone, and it is one of many in the state. Cinder cones are formed when blobs of molten lava solidify as they are shot out of the central vent of a volcano and pile up in the shape of a cone. Often the cinder cone is too weak to contain the lava which soon begins to fill it up, and the bottom of the cone collapses. The basaltic lava flows from the rupture rather than from the cone and the building of the cone ceases as rivers of molten lava fill up nearby valleys, as with the McCarty's flow.

The Bandera cone rises 450 feet above the lava, but the trail ends at the breached part of the crater, about half-way up. A core of hardened lava also remains amidst the ash inside the crater. Millions of years from now, erosion will make this lava a towering volcanic neck similar to Shiprock or Cabezon farther north in New Mexico.

The Ice Cave and Bandera Crater are open 8 a.m. to one hour before sunset daily, all year round. There is a trading post and snack bar here, but no lodging or gasoline. Reach the attraction at 12000 Ice Cave Rd., Grants, NM 87020 (783-4303).

EL MORRO NATIONAL MONUMENT

Located 43 miles west of Grants on NM Hwy. 53 is one of the earliest examples of what some would now call grafitti. At the base of a two-hundred-foot-high sandstone bluff are inscriptions dating from Anasazi times (c. 1200 A.D.) through colonial days in New Mexico. Inscription Rock, as its often called, is a sort of Who's Who of Southwestern history, a register of carved Indian, Spanish, Mexican, and American names and messages.

Because there is a water hole at the base of El Morro ("the bluff"), the site became a favorite camping place for many travelers and even became a home for some. There are unexcavated pueblos atop the bluff and thousands of petroglyphs within the 1278-acre site. Although history tells us that it is likely that many Spanish explorers, such as Coronado and Chamuscado, passed El Morro, the first European message inscribed on the rock was that of Juan de Oñate, who stopped at El Morrow in 1605 after exploring the

Colorado River basin and the Gulf of California (the "sea of the south"). He wrote, in Spanish, "Passed by here the Adelantado Don Juan de Oñate from the discovery of the Sea of the South, the 16th of April, 1605." Oñate is also credited as the founder of the first Spanish settlement in New Mexico, that of San Juan near present-day Santa Fe, in 1598.

After the Pueblo Revolt of 1680, Don Diego de Vargas undertook the task of reconquest, which he accomplished with little violence. In 1692, he inscribed the following message on the rock: "Here was General Don Diego de Vargas who conquered for our holy faith, and for the Royal Crown, all of New Mexico at his own expense, year of 1692."

The first American inscription was made by Lt. J.H. Simpson, who wrote, "Lt. J.H. Simpson & R.H. Kern, Artist, visited and copies these inscriptions September 17, 18th, 1849." One of the more unusual visits to Inscription rock was made eight years later when Lt. Edward F. Beale passed by with a caravan of camels—yes, camels— which had been imported for use in the desert Southwest. Incidentally, the camel experiment failed and for years afterward there were feral camels wandering about New Mexico, Arizona, and Texas.

Visitors to El Morro can view these inscriptions, but it is against federal law to add any more. There is a visitor center, a self-guiding trail, a small campground, and a picnic area. The monument is open 8 to 8 daily during the summer and 8 a.m.–5 p.m. during the winter. Space in the campground is available on a first come, first served basis. Contact El Morro National Monument, Ramah, NM 87321 (783-4226).

ZUNI PUEBLO
The initial goal of Coronado's 1540 expedition into New Mexico was to search for the legendary Seven Cities of Cibola and to appropriate gold and emeralds. Imagine his surprise when Cibola turned out to be Zuni Pueblo (sometimes spelled Zuñi), complete with adobe mud buildings and ferocious inhabitants who proceeded to attack his expedition. Ever the conquistador, he launched a frontal assault against the pueblo—a few hundred Spaniards versus thousands of Indians. Because the Spaniards had superior weaponry, they managed to subdue the Zunis, but not without injury; Coronado suffered an arrow wound in the foot that would plague him throughout his futile search for gold in New Mexico. The fabled city of Cibola yielded but one treasure: food for the starving expedition.

Zuni is much more hospitable today. Located on NM Hwy. 53 about thirty miles south of Gallup via NM Hwy. 602, it has the largest population of any of the pueblos, about eight thousand people who till the fields, tend to their herds of sheep and cattle, and create the world-famous Zuni silver-and-turquoise jewelry. The town itself resembles many New Mexico rural communities. But before visitors start visiting, they should check in at the tribal government office (782-4481) and obtain permits for photography, buying jewelry, camping, or visiting sights such as the **Village of the Great Kivas.** The ruins of three ancient pueblos in the village provide evidence that there may have been seven cities here after all.

In many pueblos, the most important and spectacular building is the mission church. Zuni is no exception, and **Our Lady of Guadalupe Church** has undergone many transformations. First built sometime between 1630 and 1666, the church was completely destroyed during the Pueblo Revolt of 1680 and then rebuilt after the return of the Spanish. It remained basically intact until 1849, when it was destroyed again during local unrest. It was restored to its present excellent condition in 1968.

The interior of Our Lady of Guadalupe reveals the merging of two religions — Zuni gods in harmony with Catholic saints. The interior walls are decorated with murals of Zuni figures representing each season. A live recreation of the figures on these murals occurs each year in late November or early December in the Shalako Ceremony, called by Albuquerque author Tony Hillerman "the most dramatic and colorful ceremonial in the Western Hemisphere." This re-creation of the return of the Zuni Council of Gods to the pueblo features six Shalakos, messenger birds portrayed by Zuni men wearing elaborate, ten-foot-high costumes who perform graceful, swooping dances that last all night long. The Shalako dances are usually witnessed by thousands of spectators from all over the state. Visitors should remember that photography, tape recording, or sketching of the ceremonies is expressly forbidden by tribal law. While at Zuni, shop at the village cooperative for the silver jewelry for which these people are so famous. Especially notable are the inlay work with turquoise and coral, and the exquisite petit point work. The Zunis also fashion a limited amount of traditional pottery which resembles that of Acoma.

Zuni has an excellent school system (the only school district in the state created exclusively for a pueblo), and a Zuni Tribal Band which is often called the Million Dollar Band because of the amount of silver and turquoise jewelry worn by the band members. For more information on Zuni, write Zuni Pueblo, P.O. Box 339, Zuni, NM 87327.

GALLUP

Gallup is a town with an image problem. Since it is the center of trade for the enormous Navajo Reservation, its regular population of 18,000 swells enormously when thousands of Navajos descend upon it to shop. Unfortunately, it is also the only place some of those people can purchase alcoholic beverages, since sale of alcohol is prohibited on Navajo lands. As a result, the visitor often sees inebriated Navajos along the downtown streets — certainly not the image the city fathers — or Navajo tribal leaders — want tourists to have of Gallup. There appears to be no solution to this problem; visitors should simply ignore the situation and mind their own business.

Of course, Gallup has its good image too. It's a community that loves spectacular shows, parades, and fiestas (see the entry for Red Rock State Park, below), and it's the Indian jewelry capital of the world. More than seventy shops specialize in Indian jewelry and other crafts, and nearly every restaurant and motel has designated areas for the sale of Indian arts and crafts.

The town was founded in 1881 after the Atlantic and Pacific Railroad laid down tracks here. The railroad was so important to the small village that it was named Gallup in honor of David L. Gallup, one of the first paymasters who settled here. After rich coal deposits were found north of town, miners came to Gallup from all over the United States and from foreign countries. But the coal boom ended when railroads switched to diesel fuel. Similarly, the uranium boom and bust cycle has affected Gallup much like it has Grants. But somehow, these New Mexico towns always seem to bounce back.

★ ★
TOURIST INFORMATION

GALLUP CHAMBER OF COMMERCE
103 W. 66th Ave., Gallup, NM 87301 (722-2228)

★ ★
LODGING

Gallup has more than seven thousand motel rooms, so finding a room here shouldn't be a problem. Perhaps the most interesting place to stay is **El Rancho Hotel,** built when Gallup was experiencing another kind of boom — a boom in motion picture production. Westerns were big business for Hollywood during the 1930s and

'40s, and Gallup was chosen as a location for several reasons: the scenery — particularly the towering red rocks — was spectacular; it was reasonably close to Hollywood and situated along a major railroad; food and lodging were very inexpensive; and there were thousands of cowboy and Indian extras in the area.

In 1937, D. W. Griffith's brother "Griff" opened El Rancho Hotel in Gallup to serve the needs of the movie industry. It was the on-location home of such movie greats as Errol Flynn, Betty Hutton, Alan Ladd, Burt Lancaster, Lee Remick, and Gregory Peck. Between 1937 and 1945, more than 24 movies and many episodes of television shows were shot in Gallup, including "Paint Your Wagon" and "Have Gun, Will Travel." El Rancho has celebrated that fact by naming each of its rooms after an actor or actress who stayed there. Appropriately enough, the Presidential Suite is named for ranch-loving Ronald Reagan, who stayed at El Rancho while filming parts of "Death Valley Days."

Such was the public side of the "showplace of the desert," as it was called in those days. The secret side of El Rancho was that the hotel was a notorious illegal casino, complete with escape tunnels in case of raids. Such a raid occurred in the early '40s, when federal agents closed down El Rancho and smashed the gambling machines.

As often happens with such colorful establishments, the El Rancho gradually faded from the scene, unable to compete with the newer chain hotels. For a while, it appeared that El Rancho would be headed for oblivion like Albuquerque's Alvarado. As recently as July, 1987, the hotel was in bankruptcy court and citizens feared it would be torn down to make room for a car wash or a discount store.

But Gallup Indian jewelry entrepreneur Armand Ortega saved El Rancho by purchasing it from the court and completely restoring it to its former glory. Its amenities include a huge stone fireplace in the lobby, a split-log staircase, and a balcony decorated with autographed photographs of the film stars who lived — and gambled — there.

El Rancho Hotel still beckons along old Route 66 at 1000 E. Hwy. 66 (863-9311).

Two modern chain hotels, the **Holiday Inn** and **The Inn Best Western**, round out the choice accommodations for Gallup. The new Holiday Inn, 2915 W. Hwy. 66 (722-2201), is quite nice, with 212 units and amenities including the "Holidome" indoor recreation center, sauna, and whirlpool. The restaurant there, **Nicole's**, serves continental cuisine and is reputedly the most expensive in Gallup. The Inn Best Western, 3009 W. Hwy. 66 (722-2221), has half the number of units as the Holiday Inn, but it does have tennis courts.

Bed and breakfast buffs will delight in **Stauder's Navajo Lodge,** located twenty miles east of Gallup just off I-40 at Coolidge (862-7553). Here, while experiencing the great scenery of the Hollywood westerns, visitors can stay in charming apartments in white stucco buildings with red tile roofs.

★ ★
DINING

Imagine opening the menu at the simply named **Pedro's Mexican Restaurant** (107 Burke Drive, 863-9755) and finding a dining selection called "The Nightmare." It's not as bad as it sounds: In fact, The Nightmare is a dream of a steak smothered — New Mexico style — in green chile and cheese. And it costs less than $10. Pedro's is a favorite with locals and visitors alike because huge portions, like the traditional Mexican combination plate, are very reasonably priced. A full liquor license helps too. Open for dinner only Tues.-Sat. 5 p.m.-10 p.m.

Another recommended restaurant is **The Butcher Shop** 2003 W. Hwy. 66 (722-4711).

★ ★
SHOPPING

In Gallup visitors have the chance to go blind from the brilliance of what is undoubtedly the largest collection of turquoise and silver anywhere on the planet. Under New Mexico law, Indian-type jewelry that is machine made must be labeled as such. The best Indian jewelry is handcrafted, so concentrate on the non-tourist merchandise.

A visit to **Richardson's Trading Company and Cash Pawn,** 222 W. Hwy. 66 (722-4762), is like a trip back in time. The building's vaulted ceilings, combined with the stuffed game animals on the wall, give the store a true trading post atmosphere. Long-time traders in Gallup, the Richardsons have a fine collection of "old pawn," which means collectible Navajo bracelets, rings, and squash blossom necklaces that were exchanged for cash long ago. Other excellent jewelry stores are **Tobe Turpen's Indian Trading Company,** 1710 S. 2nd Street (722-3806), and **O. B. Indian America,** 3330 E. Hwy. 66 (722-4431), which has a "double category" policy regarding the sale of Indian jewelry. This policy means that the company sells both the very finest (and most expensive) jewelry, as well as inexpensive, tourist-oriented merchandise. **Rio West Mall,** located just off I-40 at exit 20 (722-7281), has about sixty shops and restaurants. Here, large department stores are interspersed with Indian arts and craft galleries.

RED ROCK STATE PARK
Set amidst dramatic red sandstone cliffs just six miles east of downtown Gallup, Red Rock State Park is a remarkable facility. It combines a spectacular natural setting with a rodeo arena seating eight thousand, a museum, a convention center, an auditorium seating eight hundred, an outdoor amphitheater, a balloon launch site, two campgrounds with picnic areas, rest rooms, and showers, boarding stables, a restaurant, the **Historic Outlaw Trading Post** (built in 1888) and a Post Office. For detailed information, Red Rock State Park can be reached at P.O. Box 328, Church Rock, NM 87311 (722-3839).

The **Arena** at Red Rock is the location for all kinds of events: rodeos, mudbogs, circuses, balloon fiestas, concerts, and demolition derbies. The biggest show of all at this state park is the Inter-Tribal Indian Ceremonial, held for four days starting the second Thursday every August. During this event, the Indoor and Outdoor Marketplaces present the country's most complete and varied displays of authentic Native American arts and crafts, including jewelry, baskets, pottery, rugs, kachinas, paintings, sculpture, leather, and beadwork. There are four afternoons of all-Indian rodeo during the Ceremonial plus three evenings and one afternoon of Indian dances. For tickets, contact the Inter-Tribal Indian Ceremonial Association, P.O. Box 1, Church Rock, NM 87311 (863-3896 or 1-800-233-4528).

For more information on Gallup, contact the Gallup Convention and Visitor's Bureau, P.O. Drawer "Q," 103 W. 66 Avenue, Gallup, NM 87305 (722-2227 or 1-800-242-4282).

HUBBELL'S TRADING POST
Although this attraction is located in Ganado, Arizona, it's worth including in this guidebook because it is the best example of a relic of the past, the reservation trading post. It's about an hour from Gallup; take US Hwy. 666 north from Gallup and turn left on NM/Ariz. Hwy. 264 to Ganado and turn left at the Exxon station. The trading post here was established in 1878 by Don Lorenzo Hubbell, also known as "Lorenzo the Magnificent" by President Teddy Roosevelt, who gave him the title because of his reputation for legendary hospitality.

From the beginning, the Navajos trusted Hubbell and depended upon him as their link with the world of the white man. He was their guide, their teacher, and a trusted friend who took part in the Navajo Nation's negotiations with the federal government. As one source described it, "The trading post was like Christmas or a World's Fair to the Navajos. Across the long miles with horses and wagons they came to this world of wonder and excitement. It was more than a place to meet old friends and relatives. The store was a center for news, quiet gossip, and endless talk about sheep and cattle."

It still is. Despite the fact that most other trading posts have disappeared, Hubbell's carries on business much in the same way it has for more than a century. It is also a National Historic Site administered by the National Park Service, complete with Visitor Center and museum. The Visitor Center has interpretive displays of the history of the site, while the former Hubbell home has been converted into a museum with interpretive tours conducted every thirty minutes. Summer hours are 8 to 6, winter hours 8 to 5, and a campground, gasoline, and food are available. Contact Hubbell's Trading Post, P.O. Box 388, Ganado, AZ 86505 (602-755-3254).

FARMINGTON

The name of this community of 40,000 derives from the fact that the town was originally a market for vegetables and grain in the 1870s, when it was called, simply, Farming Town. Farmington's location at the confluence of the Animas, San Juan, and La Plata rivers insured that the town had plenty of irrigation water and it soon became the agricultural and commercial center of the Four Corners area — the only place in the U.S. where the corners of four states meet. A monument 61 miles northwest of Farmington on US Hwy. 160 commemorates this geographical fact.

Farmington is another boom-bust community that has experienced the roller coaster ride of the oil and gas industries. Like Grants, the city has now learned that diversification of its income base is the key to survival. So, in addition to energy, Farmington depends on agriculture, tourism, light manufacturing, food processing, and retail trade for its livelihood. Two nearby towns, Aztec and Bloomfield, are considered to be part of the Farmington trade area.

★ ★
TOURIST INFORMATION

FARMINGTON CHAMBER OF COMMERCE
203 W. Main, Suite 401, 87401 (326-7602 or 1-800-448-1240)

FARMINGTON HISTORICAL MUSEUM

A small but diverse museum with displays covering both the natural and cultural history of the Four Corners region, the Farmington Museum specializes in local history between the years of 1876–1912. One of the most popular permanent attractions of the museum is a replica of a frontier business street from this frontier era. There is an interesting children's experience gallery with educational exhibits for hands-on participation. The museum houses a specialty gift shop in the museum, which is located at 302 N. Orchard (599-1174). Admission is free and hours are Tues.–Fri. noon–5 p.m. and Saturday 10 a.m.–5 p.m.

★ ★

LODGING

Farmington has more than 1200 motel rooms, and more lodging is available in nearby Aztec and Bloomfield. The following Farmington motels are recommended: **The Inn at Farmington** is a Best Western operation located at 700 Scott Ave. (327-5221 or 1-800-528-1234) which features an indoor heated pool and saunas surrounded by tropical plants and a refrigerator in every room; also good are the **Holiday Inn** (600 E. Broadway, 327-9811), with an outdoor pool and fitness center, and **La Quinta** (675 Scott Avenue, 327-4706 and 1-800-531-5900), which also has an outdoor pool as well as three restaurants within walking distance.
The Vogt Ranch B&B is on the historic register and is located in Ramah (783-4363). **The Inn at the Post** offers lodging at the Nageezi Trading Post, complete with a general store, in Nageezi (632-3646); and the **Silver River Inn** is an adobe hacienda overlooking the San Juan River (325-8219).

★ ★

DINING

Surprisingly enough, one of Farmington's best restaurants is located at the airport. The **Señor Peppers** in the Municipal Airport at Navajo and Municipal Rd (327-0436), specializes in New Mexican cuisine but also offers steaks and seafood. It is open 6:00 a.m.–10 p.m. daily. Another good New Mexican restaurant is **The Paddock** at 315 N. Auburn Ave. (327-3566). **The Trough,** located two miles east of Farmington on US Hwy. 550 (334-6176) in Flora Vista, has rather rustic decor but just might serve the best food in the area.

It is open Mon.–Thurs. 5:30 p.m.–10:30 p.m., Fri. and Sat. 5:30
p.m.–11:00 p.m., closed Sunday. Other recommended restaurants
include **K.B. Dillon's,** 101 W. Broadway (325-0222) and **The Brass
Apple** in the Holiday Inn (327-9811).

★ ★
SHOPPING

There is a 65-store mall here, the **Animas Valley Mall,** 4601 E.
Main (326-5465), which claims in its ads that it is "the only
shopping center in the entire U.S. that combines authentic
Southwestern Indian art with modern shopping convenience."
Numerous trading posts in and around Farmington include
Foutz' Indian Room, with one store at 301 W. Main (325-9413), and
another location in Kirtland—**The 550 Store,** with an extensive
collection of Indian rugs, sandpaintings, and sculptures. Another
is the **Hogback Trading Company** (598-5154), a large (10,000
square foot) shop owned by the Wheeler family, traders in the
Farmington area since 1871. Hogback offers Navajo baskets and
rugs, pottery, jewelry, and sculpture, and the store is located six
miles east of Shiprock, 3221 Hwy. 64 at the tiny town of
Waterflow. Also in Waterflow is **Bob French Navajo Rugs,** 3495
Hwy. 64 (598-5621), not only one of the state's largest dealers in
Navajo rugs, but also a dealer in baskets and kachinas.

★ ★
JUST FOR THE FUN OF IT

Farmington has a well-organized parks and recreation department
that promotes the **Connie Mack World Series Baseball Tournament,** a seven-day, seventeen-game competition involving the best
high school teams from the mainland United States and Puerto
Rico. Scouts from colleges and various pro baseball teams scout for
talent at this tournament, which attracts 55,000 spectators to four-
thousand-seat Ricketts Park, at 1101 Fairgrounds Rd. at Main
Street, recently voted to be one of the best amateur baseball parks
in the country. The Connie Mack World Series takes place in early
August; for more information, call 599-1184.
San Juan Downs, located halfway (about six miles) between
Farmington and Bloomfield on US Hwy. 64, offers parimutuel betting on a mix of twelve Quarter Horse and Thoroughbred races a
day on weekends and holidays during the season, early May

through Labor Day. Gambling fans can also bet on races at other tracks, including the Preakness and the Kentucky Derby. Clubhouse, reserved, and general admission ($1.50) is available—the Clubhouse is quite comfortable. Complete food and beverage service is available on all three levels. Post time is 1:30 p.m.; for more information, call 326-4551.

Budding agronomists will enjoy a tour of the **B-Square Ranch,** home of former New Mexico governor Tom Bolack. About five hundred acres of riverside farmland where the Bolacks grow trophy-winning unusual vegetables is on public display. Tours of the fields, greenhouses and the Electromechanical Museum are available for no fee, but advance reservations are required—call 325-7873. Call 325-4275 for reservations to tour Bolack's African trophy room. The farm is located at 3901 Bloomfield Highway (US Hwy. 64).

A new outdoor musical drama, the **Anasazi Pageant,** is held June through September at Lion's Wilderness Park, Wed.–Sat., a $300,000 outdoor amphitheater located north of the San Juan College campus and follow College Blvd. until it turns into a dirt road, then proceed two miles farther to park. Ads for the show romantically describe it as "a musical pageant about a white man and an Indian woman whose love and courage shaped our history." For more information on the Anasazi Pageant, or the Four Corners region in general, contact the Farmington Convention and Visitors Bureau, 203 W. Main, Suite 401, Farmington, NM 87401 (326-7602).

SHIPROCK

The Navajos call it *tse bida hi,* "the rock with wings," and they have a legend which holds that Shiprock was the location of the nest of the Winged Monster, which was killed by Monster Slayer, who was then rescued from the top of this huge rock by Spider Woman.

Shiprock, west of Farmington via US Hwy. 550 and US Hwy. 666, looks like a perfect spot for a monster's nest; its impressive bulk towers 1700 feet above the Mancos Plain—about twenty stories higher than the Empire State Building. It is so striking that the Navajos have several creation-type myths that explain its origin: that Shiprock was a great bird—or a ship—which carried the tribe to the area and then turned to stone, or that the Navajos were cast up from the earth at this point, and Shiprock is a symbol of that voyage.

Indeed, Shiprock was cast up from the earth, but geologists tell us the upheaval took place millions of years before the Navajos arrived. Shiprock is the core of an ancient volcano and it is alternately called a volcanic neck or a volcanic plug. Whatever it's called, the formation is simply lava that has solidified in the central conduit of a cinder cone of a volcano. Rain and wind erosion over millions of years have removed the cone and surrounding pumice and ash, leaving only the harder, solidified basalt to face the ravages of time and nature.

And ravaged Shiprock has been. Because this formation is an intrusive volcanic neck, the rising magma in the volcano never broke the surface of the ground. So the erosion not only had to remove the earth and rock around the solidified basalt plug, it had to peel away an additional half mile of material above it!

SALMON RUINS

In 1969, San Juan County voters approved a $275,000 bond issue to preserve ruins and a burial mound on the land of homesteader P.M. Salmon, who had protected the site from the ravages of vandals and pot hunters. These ruins have been excavated under the direction of the San Juan County Museum Association, which maintains the Archaeological Research Center and Library on the site.

Built in the shape of the letter "C," part of the pueblo was four stories high and contained more than seven hundred rooms. The roof beams of the pueblo were timbers cut thirty miles away in Colorado and floated down the Animas River. The pueblo at Salmon was abandoned about the year 1200 and was then occupied by the Mesa Verdeans, who also left the area about seventy years later (more about this mystery below, in the section on Chaco Culture National Historical Park).

Salmon Ruins are located on US Hwy. 64, two miles west of Bloomfield. The visitor center has displays of excavated artifacts which reveal the influence of Chaco Canyon on this pueblo, and the Salmon homestead cabin has been restored. Admission is $1 for adults and $.50 for children six to sixteen. Seniors, group tours, and children under six free. Museum and gift shop hours are 9 a.m.–5 p.m. daily and weekends. Call 632-2013 for additional information.

AZTEC RUINS NATIONAL MONUMENT

Don't look for Aztec Indians here; these ruins have no connection with that early civilization. The name "Aztec" was mistakenly applied to this ruin more than a century ago when settlers believed that such magnificent structures could only have been built by a more advanced culture than the supposedly primitive "locals," the pueblo people.

The true inhabitants of the pueblo were, of course, the Anasazi, ancestors of the puebloan people who built the U-shaped, three-story structure that covered three acres in the 12th century. The Anasazi abandoned the pueblo, which was eventually resettled by the Mesa Verde people.

Before venturing into the ruins, study the displays at the visitor center and museum to learn explanations of the ancient pottery, baskets, implements, and stone tools uncovered at this site. Nowadays, everyone realizes that the Anasazi were well-advanced in their own right.

Aztec was a large pueblo, featuring one complex of stone blocks three stories high and containing more than 500 rooms—enough space for a thousand inhabitants, though in all probability only a few hundred lived here at any one time. One spectacular sight is the Great Kiva, or underworld ceremonial chamber, the largest one ever excavated. It is 48 feet in diameter and was restored in 1934 by Earl H. Morris of the American Museum of Natural History. Massive columns support a roof estimated to have weighed more than ninety tons.

Aztec Ruins National Monument is located about a mile north of Aztec off US Hwy. 550, right on Ruins Rd. (334-6174). Admission fees are $1 for adults or $3 a carload. There are picnic tables and rest rooms on site, and camping is available at a nearby campground.

In the nearby town of Aztec, the **Aztec Museum,** 125 N. Main (334-9829), has pioneer history exhibits and Anasazi artifacts. It is open Mon.–Sat. 10 a.m.–4 p.m., winter hours. Summer hours May–Sept. Mon.–Thurs. 10 a.m.–5 p.m., Sat. 10 a.m.–4 p.m. Another fascinating ancient Indian ruin site is located in nearby Colorado. **Mesa Verde National Park,** between Durango and Cortez just off US Hwy. 160, features the spectacular Cliff Palace and other pueblos built into the cliffs, as well as ruins of earlier dwellings. Call (303-529-4461) for information.

NAVAJO LAKE STATE PARK

Navajo Lake, formed behind Navajo Dam about forty miles east of Farmington, is the third largest lake in New Mexico with 200 miles of shoreline and 15,000 surface acres. The **San Juan River Recreation Area,** below the dam seventeen miles east of Aztec via NM Hwy. 173 (632-1770) offers some of the best trout fishing in the U.S. This riparian environment stretches to the **Cottonwood Campground** and makes bankside trout fishing comparatively luxurious with its paved trails and elevated fishing platforms. But park rules are strict here: only fly fishing is allowed for the first three miles below the dam, and fish shorter than twenty inches must be released.

The lake itself is widely utilized for sailing, motor boating, water skiing, and fishing for Kokanee salmon, black bass, catfish, crappie, brown trout, and other finned species. Access to the lake is from two separate sites, both of which offer camping. **Pine River Site,** 632-2278, 25 miles east of Bloomfield on NM Hwy. 511 (off US Hwy. 64), has a marina, a visitor center, and a 5000-foot paved airstrip. **Sims Mesa Site,** 27 miles east of Bloomfield on NM Hwy. 527 off US 64 (320-0885), also has a marina, boat ramps, and rest rooms. A good contact for fishing information is **Abe's Fly Shop,** 339 Hwy. 173 right before it intersects with NM Hwy. 511 (632-2194).

ANGEL PEAK RECREATION SITE
Angel Peak, thirteen miles southeast of Bloomfield via NM Hwy. 44, is so-named because the 7000-foot eroded mountain appears to have sandstone "wings." Early Spanish explorers created a legend that Angel Peak represented an angel that presided over the nearby badlands, called *bisti* in the Navajo language. There are sixteen campsites at the site.

BISTI BADLANDS
Located forty miles south of Farmington on NM Hwy. 371, this 4000-acre area is administered by the Bureau of Land Management and is one of the weirdest above-ground places in the state. Bisti and nearby De-Na-Zin are both wilderness areas established by the San Juan Basin Wilderness Preservation Act of 1984, which protects them from coal strip-mining operations.

The landscape here consists of eroded shale and sandstone rocks that have formed fantastic mushroom-shaped formations called "hoodoos," a legacy of the end of the Cretaceous Period, 65–70 million years ago, when dinosaurs roamed the region. Fossils of dinosaurs, crocodilians, turtles, and primitive mammals have been collected here since the 1880s. Visitors may roam amidst the hoodoos, but disturbing any part of the wilderness area is forbidden by federal law.

CHACO CULTURE NATIONAL HISTORICAL PARK
The most extensive archaeological attraction in New Mexico, Chaco Canyon (as it's usually called), was the center of the Anasazi civilization, the most advanced ancient North American culture and one that pre-dates the Aztecs of Mexico. A vast network of prehistoric roads connected Chaco with about seventy pueblo sites of the same era, design, and masonry. These sites, called outliers,

include Salmon and Aztec ruins, described earlier.

More than a dozen large ruins and hundreds of smaller sites are found in the this remote national park. The largest ancient pueblo ever built, **Pueblo Bonito**, is a four- and five-story, D-shaped structure that rests at the foot of a sandstone cliff. Pueblo Bonito contained more than six hundred rooms, thirty kivas, and the excellent stone masonry work in the walls of the pueblo resembles a tile mosaic.

Visitors wandering through Chaco Canyon should be aware that these ruins raise quite a few mysteries about the Anasazi culture here. Among the questions are: Why did the Chaco culture evolve to such a complex state in one of the harshest environments of the Southwest? How did Chaco support its large population? Where did the Anasazi find the hundreds of thousands of huge logs they used in constructing the complex apartment-like pueblos? Considering the fact that the Anasazi lacked wheel technology, why did they construct hundreds of miles of roads? How sophisticated was their "archaeoastronomy"? And finally, the most famous riddle of the ancient people the superstitious Navajos called "enemy ancestors": Why did the Anasazi culture collapse?

Archaeologists have suggested many theories to solve these mysteries. The most likely explanation for questions raised about the harsh environment and the support of the large population is that the Anasazi made the most out of their environment through elaborate irrigation systems which trapped, conserved, and distributed rain water to crops. Also, the population of the larger pueblos has been exaggerated because of the large number of rooms. Many of these rooms probably were not residences but storage rooms for trade goods, which brings up the possibility that pueblos like Bonito might have been primarily used for trade and ceremonial purposes. This theory is supported by the fact that very few Anasazi burial sites have been found in Chaco Canyon.

It is true that more than 200,000 log beams were hand-carried by the Indians from forests thirty to fifty miles away. But the building of Pueblo Bonito took place over nearly a hundred years, so not only was transporting these logs feasible, such logging certainly did not decimate the forests of Mount Taylor or the Chuska range in Arizona. As for the roads, some scientists speculate they were used for seasonal migrations from the outliers to Chaco, the center of the Anasazi world. The much-publicized "Sun Dagger," a supposed solar calendar to track the passage of the sun, is probably a religious sun shrine and not an actual calendar.

The greatest mystery of all is the so-called "disappearance" of the Anasazi. Popular stories imply that the Anasazi mysteriously vanished, as if a mass kidnapping by aliens in UFOs snatched them away overnight. In reality, there are many possible explanations for why the Anasazi left Chaco, including drought, warfare, disease, or disruption of trade. A better term than disappearance is "abandonment," for that is precisely what happened at Chaco Canyon over dozens of decades. The ancestors of the modern pueblo Indians were highly mobile and they regularly built pueblos and then abandoned them to move on and build others.

Visiting Chaco Culture National Historical Park is not easy, but it's well worth the effort. It's best to plan a day trip and bring along food and beverages. The park is located 56 miles south of Bloomfield. Take NM Hwy. 44 south of Bloomfield—that's the easy part. Then turn right at Blanco Trading Post on NM Road 57 for the hard part—twenty miles of gravel and dirt road. Facilities are limited here; campsites with fireplaces and water are available, but no hook-ups. There is a visitor center with a museum and restrooms. Check road conditions by calling the park at 988-6716. Check road conditions by calling the park at 988-6716.

CHAMA

The Chama Valley in northern New Mexico is the land of outdoor activities which range from hunting to snowmobile racing to riding a narrow gauge railroad. Since the snow depth in the valley occasionally exceeds ten feet, winter sports are particulary enjoyable.

Chama was first settled in 1744 and was essentially a ranching and logging community until the coming of the Denver and Rio Grande railroad and a gold strike in the late 1800s. Chama Peak, which is actually located across the state line in nearby Colorado, towers 13,200 feet above the town and prompted the creation of an interesting legend. In the spring, when warm chinook winds melt the snow, the form of a gigantic letter "J" appears near the peak. Early explorers assumed the letter was a sign from St. John and promptly named all the mountains between Albuquerque and Colorado "Las Sierras de San Juan," now called the southern Rockies. The "J" phenomenon is caused by unmelted snow which is packed into a deep, J-shaped ravine and is thus the last snow to melt on the peak.

One of the main attractions in Chama is the Rio Chama, which offers excellent fishing for rainbow and German brown trout for about four miles below this town of 2000 people. Many of the best places to stay in Chama are located along the river, and they cater to trout fishermen (and fisherwomen).

★ ★
TOURIST INFORMATION

CHAMA CHAMBER OF COMMERCE
P.O. Box 306A, Chama, NM 87520 (756-2306)

CUMBRES AND TOLTEC SCENIC RAILROAD
Built in 1880 to serve the mining towns between Denver and
Durango, the Cumbres and Toltec is the finest remaining example
of a vast network of narrow-gauge steam railroads that served the
Rocky Mountains, and today it is a National Historic Site as well
as a popular motion picture set. The dramatic 64-mile journey from
Chama to Antonito, Colorado takes six and one-half hours, making this train "the slowest railroad in the west." The trip,
available from late May to mid Oct., is fascinating, passing
through Toltec Gorge and the 10,000 foot-high Cumbres Pass.
Passengers ride in coaches with comfortable seating as they
observe spectacular rock formations, rushing creeks, tall forests,
and lots of wildlife.

An open sightseeing car is available for the adventurous, and a
refreshment car and simple rest room facilities are also available.
Passengers may choose to return to Chama by train or van, or send
someone ahead to Antonito with the family car. Round trip fares
vary between $27 and $41 for adults, depending upon travel
options selected, and overnight packages that include hotel accommodations are available. For details, write Cumbres and Toltec
Scenic Railroad, P.O. Box 789, Chama, NM 87520 (756-2151).

★ ★
LODGING, DINING, AND SHOPPING

Along the banks of the Rio Chama are four recommended lodges,
including **Spruce Lodge** on US Hwy. 84 south of Chama (756-2593
or 756-9989); it has fourteen cabin units with kitchenettes; **River
Bend Lodge** (756-2264), with large rooms and large beds; **Little
Creel Lodge** (756-2382), offering cabins with kitchens and fireplaces; and the largest lodge in Chama, **Elk Horn Motor Lodge**
(756-2105 or 1-800-532-8874), with 35 units (22 are cabins)
equipped with color television. Other nice accommodations
include: **Oso Ranch Lodge** located two miles south of town on
US Hwy. 84 (756-2954), with its large log lodge and custom hunts
for elk and mule deer; and the completely renovated **Chama
Trails Inn** located at junction of US Hwy. 84 and NM Hwy. 17
(756-2156).

★ ★ ★ ★ ★ ★ ★ ★ ★ ★ ★ ★ ★ ★ ★ ★ ★ ★ ★ ★
ECLECTIC LODGING NEAR CHAMA

Corkin's Lodge is a fisherman's dream on a lake near Chama
(588-7261), while **Unser's Oso Ranch and Lodge,** an 800-acre
ranch owned by the racing Unser brothers (756-2954), is for
hunters. **The Jones House** is a town B&B with craft and nature
seminars (800-288-7851) and the **Gandy Dancer** is a Victorian B&B
in Chama (756-2191). **DeMaster's Lodge** has large guest rooms
and a greenhouse garden hot tub (756-2942).

DULCE
Located thirty miles west of Chama via US Hwy. 64-84, Dulce is
the headquarters of the **Jicarilla Apache Reservation,** a
750,000-acre reserve that extends about 65 miles south from the
Colorado border. On the reservation, Dulce, Stone, Mondo, and
Enbom lakes have excellent trout fishing available with a permit
from the tribe, and camp sites can be reserved at the lakes. Hunting
for deer, elk, and turkey is available from September through
December, and the waterfowl shooting season extends from October to January. For more information on the Jacarilla reservation,
    An excellent restaurant is **Brazos Beef 'n' Bottle** (588-7304), which
is usually open only during the summer and fall season in nearby
Brazos, nine miles south of Chama via US Hwy. 84 to County Rd.
512, then seven miles to the lodge.
    For shopping, check out the **Cumbres Mall,** (756-2472) across the
street from the railway depot, which has shops and the **Unicorn
Gallery,** which features the art of northern New Mexico's artists. In
nearby Los Ojos is **Tierra Wools** (588-7231), a weaving cooperative
with workshop and showroom featuring clothing, rugs, blankets,
and pillows. Also in Los Ojos is **Casa de Martinez,** PO Box 96, Los
Ojos, 87551 (588-7858), a bed and breakfast inn set in the old
Martinez hacienda. The house dates back to 1868 and is listed on
the State Register of Historic Places, and is located thirteen miles
south of US Hwy. 84. Open Feb. 1–Oct. 31.
    The Chama Chamber of Commerce is the place to contact for
brochures and other information. Write Box 306A, Chama, NM
87520 or call 756-2306.
contact Jicarilla Game and Fish Department at 759-3255.
    For lodging in Dulce, the **Jicarilla Inn Best Western** on US Hwy.
64 (759-3663) is recommended.

HERON AND EL VADO LAKE STATE PARKS
Several dams have been constructed along the Rio Chama for irrigation and recreation purposes. **Heron Reservoir,** (588-7470), a

medium-sized lake with about six thousand acres of water, is located twenty miles south of Chama and fourteen miles west of Tierra Amarilla on NM Hwy. 95. It has been designated a "quiet lake," which means that motorboats are limited to trolling speed. Thus it is a favorite place for sailboaters, especially that breed of boat known as a Hobie Cat. Races and regattas are popular on this lake during the summer because of the dependable breezes that spring up on the lake every morning.

There is a visitor center with interpretive displays here, plus camping and picnicing sites, a marina, utility hookups, boat ramps, and rest rooms. The primary fishing on both Heron and El Vado lakes is trout-oriented, featuring Kokanee salmon, plus rainbow, lake, and German brown trout. A good place to stay nearby is **Stone House Lodge** (588-7274) on NM Hwy. 95, about one mile west of Heron Dam. The lodge offers rustic cabins that overlook El Vado Lake, as well as RV sites and a general store.

The lovely five-and-one-half mile Rio Chama Trail allows hiking or cross-country skiing from Heron Lake to **El Vado Lake,** which boasts of a 5000-foot landing strip for fly-in fly fisherman who want to fish amidst the timbered mesas surrounding this lake. El Vado, which is located 27 miles southwest of Chama via US Hwy. 64-84 and NM Hwy. 112, is celebrated for its ice fishing. A marina and boat rentals are available at El Vado Lake.

Between El Vado Dam and Abiquiu Dam, the Rio Chama is a wild and beautiful river and a favorite with river rafters and kayakers. For information, contact the Bureau of Land Management in Taos, 224 Cruz Alta Road, 87571 (758-8851), or get in touch with one of several private companies that specialize in raft tours. Among these companies are: Far Flung Adventures, P.O. Box 707, El Prado, NM 87529 (758-2628 in summer, 915-371-2489 in winter or 1-800-359-2627); Wolf Whitewater River Company, P.O. Box 666, Sandia Park, NM 87047 (281-5042).

Echo Canyon Amphitheater, just north of Abiquiu Dam on US Hwy. 84, is a U.S. Forest Service area with a campground and picnic tables. Echo Canyon is a near-perfect natural amphitheater created by millions of years of wind and water erosion. As its name implies, Echo Canyon reverberates with perfect echoes of sounds made in front of the formation.

ABIQUIU

This tiny town about 55 miles south of Chama on US Hwy. 84 was once a stop on the Spanish Trail from Santa Fe to Los Angeles. In the late 1700s it was the final outfitting point for trappers and traders heading to the Chama area. It is close to two popular attractions, **Abiquiu Lake** and **Ghost Ranch Living Museum.** Abiquiu Lake is fairly small, about four thousand acres, but it offers good fishing for catfish, crappie, largemouth bass, and rainbow trout. Except for camping sites, the only lodging available in the area is the **Abiquiu Inn** (685-4378) on US Hwy. 84, about one-half mile south of Abiquiu, a twelve-room motel with a laundromat, RV camping space, gallery, restaurant, and gift shop.

The Ghost Ranch Living Museum, located about fourteen miles northwest of Abiquiu on US Hwy. 84, is actually the visitor center of the Carson National Forest (685-4312) and it is operated in cooperation with the Ghost Ranch Living Museum Foundation. Ghost Ranch is so-named because of legends of *brujas*, or witches, said to inhabit nearby canyons. Here the Forest Service maintains a visitor center, a small but excellent zoo featuring native New Mexico wildlife, and the world's smallest national forest, the one-and-one-quarter-acre Beaver National Forest.

In 1947, an archaeological team from the American Museum of Natural History, under the direction of George Whitaker, uncovered a jumble of dinosaur bones at Ghost Ranch. Hundreds of dinosaurs were piled on top of each other and crisscrossed in every direction. These dinosaurs were identified as Coelophysis (pronounced see-low-FY-sis), an agile carnivorous creature about five feet tall that ran on its back legs. The reconstructed, fleshed-out form of Coelophysis has been immortalized as the New Mexico State Fossil and is the official logo for the New Mexico Museum of Natural History in Albuquerque. There is a display describing Coelophysis at the visitor center.

Ghost Ranch hours are 9 a.m.–5:30 p.m. daily from May through September and 8 a.m.–4:30 p.m. Tues.–Sun. during October to May.

JEMEZ MOUNTAIN AREA

About a million years ago, the largest volcano in the western hemisphere, about 25,000 feet, towered above the rest of what is now called the Jemez Mountains, a range located between Chama and Bernalillo. Molten rhyolitic rock had been building up and accumulating in a magma chamber beneath that volcano for eons. This magma contained a high concentration of volcanic gasses — mostly steam — that built up enormous pressure in the chamber.

Finally, the pressure had to be relieved and when the magma finally broke through the rock, it exploded with a force that made Mount St. Helens seem like a firecracker by comparison. The Valles Explosion, as it's called, was probably on a scale with Krakatoa and it sent gases and ash from the site at speeds of more than one hundred miles an hour, covering everything in its path. Significant ash deposits from this explosion have been found as far east as Nebraska.

After the magma chamber was emptied of its lava and ash, the entire mountain collapsed into itself and formed a caldera, or vast crater, similar to Crater Lake in Oregon. The collapse, according to some estimates, trimmed nearly 16,000 feet off the mountain and transformed it into the huge meadow now called Valle Grande ("great valley"), located between Jemez Springs and Los Alamos on NM Hwy. 4.

Many books and articles state flatly that the Valles caldera is the largest volcanic crater in the world. It is not, but the confusion is the result of matters of measurement and definition. Valle Grande has been variously described as measuring nineteen by fourteen miles, twelve to fifteen miles in diameter, or 160 square miles in area. In other words, measuring calderas is imprecise at best. Also, there are two types of calderas: the central ones, like Valles, and fissural calderas, which develop in an oblong shape.

Actually, Valle Grande is the third-largest crater in the world. The largest is the fissural crater which contains Lake Toba in Indonesia and the second-largest is the Buldir Depression, a totally submerged central caldera in the Bering Sea. Both of those are considerably larger than this meadow, but it is safe to assert that Valle Grande is the largest non-submerged, non-fissural crater on the planet.

Today the Jemez Mountains are part of the **Santa Fe National Forest,** and are a popular recreation site for residents of Albuquerque and Santa Fe. **Fenton Lake State Park,** 24 miles northwest of Jemez Springs via NM Hwys. 4 and 126, is a small (thirty-acre) but very popular lake offering fishing for German brown and rainbow trout plus hunting for deer, turkey, and elk. Park facilities include camping and picnicking sites, a five-mile hiking or cross-country skiing trail, a boat ramp, and toilets. No motor or sail boats are allowed on Fenton Lake.

Other camping sites in Jemez Mountains include **Battleship Rock,** six miles north of Jemez Springs on NM Hwy. 4, **Redondo,** eleven miles northeast of Jemez Springs on NM Hwy. 4, and **San Antonio,** nine miles northeast of Jemez Springs via NM Hwy. 4 and 126. For more information, contact Santa Fe National Forest, P.O. Box 1689, Santa Fe, NM 87501 (988-6940) or the ranger station in Jemez Springs, P.O. Box 98, 87025 (829-3535).

JEMEZ SPRINGS

Here is a picturesque and thoroughly charming town nestled in the spectacular Jemez Valley, located 41 miles northwest of Bernalillo via NM Hwys. 44 and 4. There are hot springs and bath houses to visit here, evidence of geothermal activity which has persisted eons after the explosions which created the Valle Grande. The **Soda Dam,** one mile north of town, is a calcium carbonate deposit caused by hot springs, which partially blocks the Jemez River, a good stream for rainbow trout. There is a geological irony here, for the newest rocks in the state, formed by the Soda Dam, are in the same location as the oldest ones. The pink granite cliffs next to the Soda Dam are from Precambrian times, more than 570 million years ago, about half the age of the earth.

Via Coeli Monastery, headquarters for the Catholic order of the Servants of the Holy Paraclete and the Handmaidens of the Sacred Blood, is a retreat for priests and nuns. Founded in 1947 by Fr. Gerald Fitzgerald at the site of Clay's Resort (established in the 1920s), the monastery here has acquired a number of other properties in the Jemez Valley, including Rancho Chico above the Soda Dam (829-3586). At **Jemez State Monument,** in Jemez Springs, are the remains of a pueblo and Spanish mission called Guisewa, which was abandoned in the early 1630s. One of the most impressive ruins in the state, the site was declared a state monument in 1935. There is a small visitor center here that provides information about the history of the area from the viewpoint of the Jemez Indians, and an interpretive trail runs through the ruins of the San Jose de los Jemez mission church, $2.00 fee, 16 years and older. Picnicking is permitted. For more information, call 829-3530.

JEMEZ PUEBLO
Set amidst red and yellow sandstone cliffs is this thriving pueblo community of about two thousand people. Jemez was first established about 1625 when area pueblo Indians occupying a number of smaller sites were consolidated in the Jemez Valley by the Spanish. A tribe always hostile to the Spanish, the Jemez joined the Pueblo Revolt of 1680 and resisted reconquering for more than twenty years. In 1703, most of the tribe came out of hiding and rebuilt their present village at the site of an earlier settlement. They were joined in 1836 by the last survivors of Pecos Pueblo east of Jemez, who also spoke the Towa language.

A community that existed previously by farming and crafts such as their black, tan, and red pottery, the Jemez have diversified. In addition to tending their fields of corn and melons, many of the Jemez people work at the pueblo's light industry or for nearby lumber mills. Pueblo men and women are also employed by the U.S. Forest Service.

The Jemez are well known for their dancing, and the major ceremonies are performed on August 2nd, the Feast of Our Lady of the Angels, when the Old Pecos Bull Dance celebrates the ancestors of the Jemez, now-extinct Pecos Pueblo, and November 12th, the Feast Day of San Diego.

Fishing is available with the proper permit at **Sheep Spring Fish Pond,** on NM Hwy. 4 just south of the pueblo, and at **Holy Ghost Spring** just off NM Hwy. 44 west of San Ysidro. There is no admission fee, but no photography is permitted in Jemez. For detailed information contact tribal officials at Jemez Pueblo, P.O. Box 78, Jemez Pueblo, NM 87024, 834-7359. To get there, take NM Hwy. 44 west from Bernalillo, then NM Hwy. 4 north (San Ysidiro exit) about 10 miles.

ZIA PUEBLO
Located off NM Hwy. 44 about eighteen miles northwest of Bernalillo, Zia is essentially a ranching pueblo where sheep, cattle, and goats are raised. Those inhabitants of Zia who are not ranchers have jobs in Albuquerque. Zia potters are known for their polychrome pottery, and their sun symbol has been adopted as the New Mexico State Insignia. Fishing is allowed with a permit at **Zia Lake,** two miles west of the pueblo.

No visitor's fee or permit is required, but photography, recording, and sketching are prohibited. All visitors should check in at the governor's office. The feast day is August 15th, when a Corn Dance is celebrated. Reach pueblo offices at 867-3304.

SANTA ANA PUEBLO
Here is another small pueblo also on NM Hwy. 44 about ten miles west of Bernalillo, which often appears deserted because most of the Santa Anas live outside the village proper. The pueblo is open to the public only on the following days: January 1 and 6, Easter, June 24 and 29, July 26 (annual feast day), and December 23–28. Other times of the year it is completely closed. No visitors fee.

As usual, photography, sketching, and tape recording are prohibited. Call tribal offices at 867-3301 for additional information.

PART II

Santa Fe and the Northeast Quadrant

SANTA FE

In just a few short decades, Santa Fe has become the magical city of the Southwest, a destination for artists, writers, tourists, and of course, entrepreneurs. The city's reputation for tolerance of individuality has had much to do with its attraction as a place to live; its reputation as the latest trendy place to visit is the result of hundreds of magazine and newspaper articles and coffee table books about the scenery, the art scene, the cuisine, the architecture, and the Santa Fe look in clothing and jewelry—all are part of the so-called "Santa Fe style."

Such slavish worship of a single city astounds long-time residents of New Mexico, who remember that just a few years ago most people in this country did not realize that New Mexico was a state of the Union. Except when making money off it, residents of Santa Fe think all this hoopla is beneath them; in fact, they adopt an attitude known as "Santa Fe blasé," which means if something or someone is nationally known, it will be completely ignored in Santa Fe. A perfect example of Santa Fe blasé is the Coyote Cafe, owned by anthropologist-chef Mark Miller, which is certainly one of the finest restaurants in Santa Fe, if not the entire country. The Coyote is now the largest-grossing, single-establishment restaurant in the city, but it must depend upon tourism for ninety percent of its business. The locals think the restaurant is just too trendy.

Thus Santa Fe residents view the huge influx of hundreds of thousands of tourists each year as just another invasion and occupation of the capital city. After all, during approximately four hundred years of history, Santa Fe has been controlled by Indians, Spaniards, Indians again, Mexicans, Americans, Confederates, Americans again, and now, primarily Texans and Californians. Such a lengthy history has led to many claims of antiquity for buildings, such as the "oldest house in the United States" and the "oldest mission church in the United States." Santa Fe itself is often referred to as the "oldest continually occupied city in the United States," "the oldest seat of government in the United States," and sometimes simply, "the oldest city."

Sorry folks, it's just not that old. Four hundred years is simply the tick of a clock when compared to, say, the six thousand years which have elapsed since the city of Sumer was established on the site of Babylon. Santa Fe was established by Juan de Oñate in 1610, 45 years after St. Augustine, Florida was settled, but that fact does not qualify either city for the title of the oldest. Since the Seminoles predated the Spaniards, and Santa Fe rests upon the ruins of an ancient pueblo, the "Oldest City in the U.S." title must go to an Indian settlement rather than a Spanish town. In reality, Santa Fe is the second-oldest city founded by Europeans in this country. No one knows for certain which Indian ruin is the most ancient, but the consensus seems to be that Acoma Pueblo is the oldest continually occupied settlement in the Southwest, dating to about the year 1000, or six hundred years before Santa Fe.

As devoted to peaceful enterprises as it is today, it is surprising that the history of Santa Fe turns upon violence. Its great distance from Mexico City led to strife between the military and the clergy and an inability of inhabitants to fight off raids by hostile Indians. In 1680, Santa Fe was evacuated because of the Pueblo Revolt and remained under Indian control for twelve years until it was reoccupied by the Spanish, led by Don Diego de Vargas, in 1692.

During the centuries that followed, the Spanish crown was, by law, the only supplier of trade goods to its colonies, and particularly New Mexico. Any European merchandise that arrived in Santa Fe was transported by mule train all the way up the Chihuahua Trail from Mexico City. But the French who had settled Louisiana discovered a route to Santa Fe by way of the Lower Arkansas River, a route that paralleled, but pre-dated the Santa Fe Trail. Thus was born the great Southwestern tradition of smuggling, as the Frenchmen used every trick in the contraband book to avoid the Spanish soldiers.

In 1821, Mexico declared its independence from Spain and Santa Fe came under Mexican control, thus opening the famous Santa Fe Trail to trade — and more smuggling. Since the Mexican custom houses just outside Santa Fe charged 750 pesos per wagon for imports, goods would often be cached just outside town and smuggled onto store shelves during the night.

Texas forces tried to conquer Santa Fe and all the land east of the Rio Grande in 1841, but failed in the attempt. Five years later, the war between Mexico and the United States brought Santa Fe permanently under the control of the American Army and General Stephen W. Kearny.

During the Civil War, Confederate forces captured Santa Fe and much of the Rio Grande Valley all the way down to Las Cruces, but the Rebels' victory was short-lived as Union troops triumphed at the battles of Apache Canyon and Glorieta Pass.

Although military conflict in New Mexico ended with the Civil War, peace did not come to the Santa Fe and the rest of the territory. As historian Warren Beck described the situation: "During the period following the Civil War and lasting approximately until the turn of the century, New Mexico experienced a wave of rampant lawlessness unparalleled in the history of the United States. It was an era when stealing, killing, and lynching were so common as to be hardly worthy of mention in the press. . . . Other parts of the nation had experienced a breakdown in law and order, but in few areas had it lasted or been as complete as it was in the territory of New Mexico."

Reasons for the wave of lawlessness include New Mexico's reputation for being a land of great treasures, it's remoteness, which tended to attract criminals on the run, and the fact that the federal government back in Washington regarded the territory as an outpost in a wilderness and virtually ignored the needs of the citizens there. During the years immediately following the Civil War, Santa Fe and the northeast quadrant of New Mexico witnessed a dazzling diversity of crime including the death of a judge in a gunfight, the theft of a government fortune, the mass murder of nine innocent travelers, and a colossal diamond hoax. We'll get into all of these stories as we tour Santa Fe, the Central Highlands, and the northeast section of the state.

During the years following World War I, Santa Fe began to emerge from obscurity as the city — and the rest of the state — was discovered by artists such as Peter Hurd and Georgia O'Keefe,

authors such as Willa Cather and D.H. Lawrence, as well as other
prominent sculptors, poets, photographers, and musicians. The
high concentration of artists in the city, combined with Santa Fe's
tradition as an Indian trading center, produced one of the top art
sales markets in the world. More than 150 art galleries, concentrated principally around the Plaza and along Canyon Road, now
feature local as well as international artists, and special events such
as Indian Market in mid-August ensure that the ancient artistic
traditions are kept alive.

Santa Fe is one of the few cities in the Southwest that is designed
for pedestrians: The best sightseeing, lodging, dining, and shopping
is located in the central downtown area. Santa Fe Plaza, bordered
by Palace Avenue, Lincoln Street, Old Santa Fe Trail, and East San
Francisco Street, was once the end of the Santa Fe Trail and now
is considered to be the center of the city. This National Historic
Landmark is the location for the annual Indian and Spanish art
markets, as well as for religious processions, concerts, fiestas, and
year-round people-watching. Most of the downtown attractions
are within ten blocks of the Plaza.

The best way to visit Santa Fe if one is not driving is to fly in
to Albuquerque, take a shuttle (see "Tours," below) from the airport to your place of lodging in the City Different. After walking
to see the downtown sights for a few days, rent a car and visit the
surrounding area.

* *
TOURIST INFORMATION

SANTA FE CHAMBER OF COMMERCE
P.O. Box 1928, Santa Fe, NM 87501 (983-7317)

SANTA FE CONVENTION & VISITORS BUREAU
P.O. Box 909, Santa Fe, NM 87504 (984-6760 or 800-777-2489)

* *
HISTORIC SIGHTSEEING

LORETTO CHAPEL
Why not start off the tour of Santa Fe by getting married beneath
a miraculous staircase? The Loretto Chapel, located at 211 Old
Santa Fe Trail, was built in the 1873 on the grounds of the Loretto
Academy, a school established by the Sisters of Our Lady of Light.

It was the first gothic structure built west of the Mississippi.
P. Mouly, the architect for the chapel (which is modeled after the
Sainte-Chapelle in Paris), was shot and killed by John Lamy,
nephew of the famous archbishop Jean Baptiste Lamy, before he
could complete the plans.

During construction of the chapel, there appeared to be no possible way for singers to climb to the choir loft in the back except
with a ladder. Legend holds that after the sisters prayed to San Jose,
the patron saint of carpentry, an itinerant woodworker appeared
at the chapel and offered to build a staircase which would solve
their problems.

The result was a winding spiral staircase that makes two complete turns yet has no center support. It has been in use for more
than a century and has spawned a legend that it has some miraculous powers. According to one article, "To this day, engineers and
architects remain baffled by the staircase's mysterious strength."
Skeptics have noted that finely crafted wood can be as strong as
steel under certain circumstances, while the original sisters believed
that the carpenter, who refused payment, was actually San Jose
himself.

The Loretto Chapel also features stained glass windows and
nineteenth century gems on display for a voluntary donation.
Romantic couples wishing to exchange vows beneath this strong,
but twisted structure should call the Inn at Loretto, 988-5531. As
a result of controversery within the Catholic Church over the
miracle of the stairway, Catholic wedding ceremonies are no longer
performed here.

ST. FRANCIS CATHEDRAL

Santa Fe's most famous church is St. Francis Cathedral, at San
Francisco St. and Cathedral Place. It was begun by Santa Fe's first
archbishop, Frenchman Jean-Baptiste Lamy in 1869, who is buried
beneath the altar. The Romanesque architecture of the church is in
sharp contrast to the rest of the buildings in the Plaza area, and is
a reminder that not all of Santa Fe's buildings have been pueblo
style. The cathedral features the "oldest representation of the
Madonna in the U.S.," a statue of La Conquistadora which was
brought to the city by Don Diego de Vargas during his reconquest
twelve years after the Pueblo Revolt of 1680.

The cathedral, which was partly the inspiration for Willa
Cather's novel, *Death Comes for the Archbishop*, is open to the
public on a daily basis, and the Feast of Corpus Christi is celebrated
in late May or early June with a noon mass and a procession
around the Plaza. For information, call 982-5619.

SANTUARIO DE GUADALUPE
Located at 100 Guadalupe and Agua Fria streets, the Santuario
features displays of Spanish colonial art and religious artifacts,
including a large painting of Our Lady of Guadalupe, patron saint
of Mexico, completed by Jose de Alzibar in 1783. This mission,
which has three-foot-thick adobe walls, was built in the 1780s
by Franciscan missionaries. The Santuario is maintained by the
Guadalupe Historic Foundation (988-2027), which believes in the
"living preservation" concept and in keeping with this philosophy,
presents events such as music, art, and drama in the sanctuary.

BARRIO DE ANALCO HISTORIC DISTRICT
Now known as East De Vargas Street, this neighborhood was first
settled by Mexican-Indian mercenaries in the early 1600s, making
this area "one of the oldest continually inhabited streets in the U.S."
The narrow street is the site of the historic Crespin, Bandelier,
Alarid, and Boyle houses, which are marked by commemorative
plaques.

SAN MIGUEL CHAPEL AND THE "OLDEST HOUSE"
One of the oldest mission churches in the U.S., San Miguel Chapel
at 401 Old Santa Fe Trail and De Vargas Street was totally rebuilt
(including new foundations and walls) after it was burned to the
ground during the Pueblo Revolt, so to say that this building is the
oldest church is a fallacy akin to claiming one has Abe Lincoln's
original axe, except for three new handles and four new heads.

Inside the chapel is a nice collection of religious artifacts including painted deer and buffalo hides, and what is supposedly the "oldest bell in the United States," cast in 1356 in Spain. The chapel is
maintained by the Christian Brothers (983-3974).

Behind the San Miguel Chapel is a privately owned gift shop
which proclaims to be the "oldest house in the United States." This
claim is totally unsubstantiated because the structure was built in
1610 on the site of an Indian pueblo dating back to 1250, and enlarged in 1740. Hours for May through October 9 a.m.–4:30 p.m.
Mon.–Sat., November through April 10:30 a.m.–3:30 p.m. Open
Sundays all year 1 p.m.–4:30 p.m. with Sunday mass at 5 p.m.
Visitors are always welcome.

STATE CAPITOL BUILDING
Called the "Roundhouse" by locals, the State Capitol (Paseo de
Peralta and Old Santa Fe Trail) was built in 1966 in the shape
of the Zia symbol, which is representative of the circle of life, the
four winds, four directions, four seasons, and the four sacred

obligations — which we hope the legislators uphold. The six-and-a-half acre grounds are planted with more than one hundred varieties of trees and shrubs.

Visitors to the State Capitol may take guided tours of cultural and historic displays, or attend the legislature in session during the winter. For details call 827-4011.

★ ★
MUSEUMS AND LIBRARIES

PALACE OF THE GOVERNORS
Built in 1610, this palace on the Plaza was originally part of the royal presidio of Don Pedro de Peralta, the first colonial governor of New Mexico, and served as the residence and offices of succeeding Spanish, Mexican, and American governors. It has undergone many transformations over the centuries, including a major renovation in 1909 that used original plans found in the British Museum as a reference. The building is famous for its long *portal*, or porch, where many prisoners of war have been hanged. These days, however, the portal serves a much more peaceful purpose: to shade Indian craftsmen who sell their wares to visitors.

The Palace of the Governors, often called the "oldest continually used public building in the United States," is part of the Museum of New Mexico system and offers exhibits on the four hundred years of New Mexico history and the frontier experience, as well as a photo gallery and a stagecoach area. Admission to each of the Museum of New Mexico facilities is $3 for adults and $1.25 for children, with group rates available or you can purchase a pass to all the museums for $5. The Palace of the Governors is open 10 to 5 daily; call 827-6483 for more information.

Museum of New Mexico facilities is $3.50 for adults and children under 16, free, with group rates available or you can purchase a pass to all the museums for $6.00 for two days. The Palace of the Governors is open 10 a.m.–5 p.m. daily; call 827-6483 for more information.

MUSEUM OF FINE ARTS
Located just off the Plaza at 107 W. Palace Ave. and Lincoln Street, the Museum of Fine Arts houses a permanent collection of more than eight thousand works of regional art by such luminaries as Georgia O'Keefe, the Taos masters, and Native American sculptors.

Completed in 1917, this museum was the first structure of the Pueblo Revival architectural style built in Santa Fe and is a melding of six of the Spanish churches founded by Franciscan missionaries—Acoma, San Felipe, Cochiti, Laguna, Santa Ana, and Pecos. The museum was built because the artists of Santa Fe and Taos had no place to display their works, since art galleries were unknown in those days. Because pressure from the art community led to the construction of the museum, the early policy of the museum was to allow any local artist to use its exhibition space. This unrestricted policy led to the comprehensive collection of regional art.

The Museum of Fine Arts is open 10 a.m.–5 p.m. daily, but is closed Mondays in January and February, and can be reached at 827-4468. Admission is $3.50; children under 16, free.

LABORATORY OF ANTHROPOLOGY AND
THE MUSEUM OF INDIAN ARTS AND CULTURE
Located in the Camino Lejo museum complex (south of town, turn left off Old Santa Fe Trail on Armente, turn left at stop sign, right at next four-way stop, then go one hundred yards to Camino Lejo, and turn right to museum), which also includes the Museum of International Folk Art, and the Wheelwright Museum, the Laboratory of Anthropology is a combination museum, library, and research facility. Built in 1931, the laboratory features one of the world's finest collections of Indian pottery, basketry, textiles, jewelry, and clothing—more than 50,000 pieces.

The laboratory is the official repository for all archaeological artifacts found in the state, and regular exhibits feature both prehistoric and historic Indian cultures.

Adjacent to the laboratory is the Museum of Indian Arts and Culture, which displays the most interesting artifacts in the state's vast collection. Anyone writing about Southwest archaeology or anthropology should consult the 15,000 volume library here. The laboratory, like the museum, is open 10 a.m. to 5 p.m. daily (827-8941).

MUSUEM OF INTERNATIONAL FOLK ART
The Camino Lejo complex is also the home of the largest folk art museum in the world. The Museum of International Folk Art has collected more than 120,000 objects from one hundred countries, including the amazing lifetime collection of architect Alexander Girard and his wife, Susan. This museum specializes in ethnic costumes, textiles, and toys, with particular emphasis on Hispanic folk art. Many of the objects are humorous or whimsical.

The museum also offers folk art performances, traveling shows, demonstrations, and lectures. Hours are 10 a.m. to 5 p.m. daily, admission is $3.50 for adults, children 16 or under, free, and the museum phone number is 827-6350.

WHEELWRIGHT MUSEUM

The final museum at the Camino Lejo complex is devoted to preserving the spirit of Navajo ceremonialism, which is the reason the building is shaped like a Navajo *hogan*. Founded in 1937 by Mary Cabot Wheelwright, the museum has the largest sandpainting collection in the world as well as extensive holdings of Navajo jewelry and textiles.

The focus of the museum has broadened within the last few years to include works of all American Indian cultures. This private museum produces single-subject exhibits (basketry, pottery, weaving, jewelry and other crafts) in the main hall and requests a $2 donation. Hours are 10 a.m. to 5 p.m. Monday through Saturday and 1 p.m. to 5 p.m. Sundays. For more information, call 982-4636.

SCHOOL OF AMERICAN INDIAN ARTS RESEARCH CENTER

This school, which has an endowment of $13 million, conducts archaeological digs in New Mexico and around the world, has an active press which publishes many books, and houses what is undoubtedly the most complete collection of pueblo Indian pottery in existence. More than seven thousand pieces of pottery, including 78 pieces by famous San Idelfonzo Pueblo potters Maria and Julian Martinez, reside in climate-controlled vaults at the school.

Although the research center is accessible to scholars and Native Americans daily, it is open to the public only by appointment and during tours every Friday at 2 p.m. $15.00 per person for a 2 hour tour. The School of American Research is housed in the eccentric Amelia White estate called El Delirio ("the madness" or "foolishness") at 660 Garcia Street (982-3584).

INSTITUTE OF AMERICAN INDIAN ARTS MUSEUM

Located at the Institute of American Indian Arts at Cathedral Place, the museum puts its permanent collection on display every June through August. It also produces four or five major exhibitions, featuring the works of the faculty and students at the institute, throughout the year. The museum is open Monday through Friday 8 a.m. to 5 p.m., closed weekends. Admission is free and more information is available by calling 988-6281.

OLD CIENEGA VILLAGE MUSEUM

Imagine a small colonial village that has been restored to the way it was during the seventeenth and eighteenth centuries – with chapel, shepherd's kitchen, *torreon* (defensive tower), weaving rooms, and village store. Then imagine this village as a living museum, complete with volunteers dressed in authentic costume who demonstrate weaving, spinning, threshing, and blacksmithing. The Old Cienega Village Museum, located fifteen miles south of Santa Fe off I-25 at exit 271, is part of Rancho de las Golondrinas ("Ranch of the Swallows"), the last stopping place along the thousand-mile El Camino Real ("Royal Road") between Mexico City and Santa Fe.

The museum features special Spring and Harvest Festivals during the first weekends of June and October, where Spanish folk dances with traditional music are performed. Open houses are held the first Sunday in July, August, and September, when visitors may take self-guided tours. Every Wednesday and Saturday during the summer, guided tours are offered at 10 a.m. The museum is closed from November through March; tours may be arranged during other times by calling 471-2261 for reservations.

NEW MEXICO STATE LIBRARY

This library, which is open to the public, is the repository of tens of thousands of books and documents relating to New Mexico and the Southwest and is quite a resource for the researcher. It is located at 325 Don Gaspar Ave. near S. Capitol Street (827-3800), open 8 a.m.–5 p.m. Mon–Fri., closed weekends. The History Library is located at 110 Washington Street and Palace Ave. in the Palace of the Governors building (827-6474).

★ ★
GALLERIES

Santa Fe is the third-largest retail art center in the country, behind New York and Chicago, and with something like 150 art galleries to see, I'd advise you to pick up a copy of one of the three full-color guides to the galleries and artists (see Resources, below), decide which styles of art are interesting, then plan your visits accordingly. Obviously every one of these galleries cannot be described in this guide, so the recommendations which follow are by no means complete, but rather give an overview of the extraordinary selection of artistic expression available in the City Different.

Andrew Smith Gallery, 76 E. San Francisco on the Plaza (984-1234), is one of the finest photographic art galleries in the

U.S., offering photography by Edward S. Curtis, Ansel Adams, Annie Liebovitz, Josef Karsh, and many others.

Channing-Dale-Throckmorton, 53 Old Santa Fe Trail (984-2133), has an interesting collection of art from indigenous peoples—Native American, Eskimo, African, Oceanic, and Pre-Columbian.

Elaine Horwitch Gallery, 129 W. Palace Ave. (988-8997), is one of the major contemporary art galleries in the Southwest and always has a collection of startling works.

Fenn Gallery, 1075 Paseo de Peralta (982-4631), is perhaps the most famous gallery in Santa Fe and carries an impressive collection of the most famous artists of the region.

The **Gerald Peters Gallery,** 439 Camino del Monte Sol (off Canyon Rd., 988-8961), occupies the original 1920s home of writer Mary Austin and features American, classic Western, and Taos School works. Famous artists represented include Albert Bierstadt, Georgia O'Keefe, and Diego Rivera. The owners also have a gallery in Dallas, TX at The Crescent Court, 2200 Cedar Springs, Suite 320 (871-3535).

Presden Gallery, 125 E. Water Street (983-1014), offers a wonderful collection of contemporary Southwestern art which is striking, colorful, and often humorous.

The **Rainbow Man,** 107 E. Palace Ave. (982-8706), has been in business since 1945 and offers Southwestern folk art, handcrafted Southwestern furniture, and a large collection of the Indian photography of Edward S. Curtis.

Santa Fe East, 200 Old Santa Fe Trail (988-3103), offers late nineteenth and early twentieth century American art by such luminaries as Karl Bodmer, George Catlin, Thomas Hart Benton, and Leon Gaspard. Additionally, it features the work of contemporary painters and sculptors and a fine collection of designer Southwestern jewelry. A gallery magazine is available by calling or writing.

Santa Fe Print Gallery, 439 Camino Del Monte Sol (983-5987), specializes in decorative and historic antique prints and rare maps from such talent as Audubon, Bodmer, Catlin, Currier and Ives, and Mercator-Hondius.

Shidoni Gallery and Sculpture Garden, five miles north of Santa Fe on Bishop's Lodge Rd. (988-8001), is the largest and one of the finest sculpture galleries in the country. There are several beautiful sculpture gardens with large works cast in steel and bronze. There is also a foundry where visitors may watch the pouring of molten metal into elaborate molds every Saturday.

Zaplin-Lambert Gallery, 651 Canyon Rd. (982-6100), specializes in nineteenth and twentieth century paintings, watercolors, drawings and prints of the American West, plus select works of the Taos and Hudson River Schools and early American impressionists

Other recommended galleries are: **C. G. Rein Gallery,** 203 W. Water St. (982-6226); **Dewey Galleries,** 74 E. San Francisco on the Plaza (982-8632); **Dalton-Cordova Gallery** (984-7972) and **Ventana Gallery** (983-8815) at the Inn of Loretto; **Sena Galleries,** 112 W. San Francisco St. (982-8808); **Christine's at La Fonda** (989-9664) in La Fonda Hotel; and **Waxlander Gallery,** 622 Canyon Rd. (984-2202).

★ ★
LODGING

Without a doubt, **La Fonda,** 100 E. San Francisco (982-5511) is the most famous and historic hotel in New Mexico. A brochure entitled "The History of La Fonda," published by the hotel, claims that the hotel has been in existence since 1610, the founding date of Santa Fe. That date is a bit misleading because although there might have been a *fonda* ("inn") near the plaza then, it certainly was not the same building which sits there now. The present structure was built in 1920 and has been enlarged and remodeled several times since then.

Known as "The Inn at the End of the Trail," La Fonda has certainly played an important role in the history of Santa Fe. Before the present structure was built, an earlier version of the inn was a stopping place for mountain men, trappers, merchants, and gamblers who traveled the Santa Fe Trail in search of wealth. The discovery of gold in the Ortiz Mountains south of Santa Fe in 1828 contributed to a flood of prospectors—and hotel patrons.

After New Mexico became as U.S. Territory in 1851, La Fonda was purchased by Anglo-American owners, who changed its name to the U.S. Hotel and expanded its gambling operations. In 1857, the Honorable John P. Slough, Chief Justice of the Territorial Supreme Court, was shot to death in the hotel's lobby by attorney W.L. Rynerson, who was later acquitted of murder because the judge supposedly drew his derringer first. Soon afterward, the hotel again changed names, this time to The Exchange Hotel.

During the Civil War, the Confederate Army controlled Santa Fe briefly and Brigadier General H.H. Sibley quartered his staff in the hotel, and was there drinking in the hotel's saloon when he received word of the defeat of his troops at Glorieta. After the war, the Exchange gained a reputation in the West for great food, but those glory days faded near the end of the nineteenth century. By 1907 the great hotel had begun to deteriorate and soon became an ordinary boarding house; in 1919 the hotel was demolished.

The site at the corner of Old Santa Fe Trail and East San Francisco Street was purchased by private investors and a new hotel was built in 1920. The venture was unsuccessful and La Fonda did not begin to flourish until it was purchased by Fred Harvey in 1926. As part of the renowned Harvey House chain of hotels for forty years, La Fonda became the premier hotel in the state and was the starting point for the Harvey Company's famed Indian Detours, which allowed train passengers to explore the wonders of the state by automobile for the first time. Since that time, La Fonda has retained its reputation as a first-class destination.

Early hotel registers from La Fonda reveal hundreds of celebrity guests: Kit Carson, Gen. William T. Sherman, Ulysses S. Grant, Pres. Rutherford B. Hayes, Billy the Kid, and Sheriff Pat Garrret (not at the same time). More recent celebrities include: Jimmy Stewart, John Travolta, Diane Keaton—the list seems to be endless.

Because of its popularity, reservations for La Fonda far in advance are suggested. La Fonda has 150 rooms, twenty suites, a lounge, restaurants, galleries, and an excellent newsstand.

The Bishop's Lodge, located three miles from the Plaza on Bishop's Lodge Rd. (take Washington Street from downtown, which turns into Bishop's Lodge Rd.) (983-6377), is small (35 rooms) but it's a Mobil Four-Star resort hotel with an outdoor heated pool and plenty of other amenities. The name derives from the fact that this lodge was formerly the home and chapel of Archbishop Lamy. The setting is superb: it sits on one thousand acres in the foothills of the Sangre de Cristo Mountains. The Bishop's Lodge is open only during the months of April through October.

The largest hotel in Santa Fe, **Eldorado,** 309 W. San Francisco (988-4455), is one of the most beautiful. Its lobby floors are tiled with the lovely Saltillo tiles from Mexico upon which sit pots full of huge cacti. The walls of the lobbies are painted with Indian designs and hung with striking art from the Elaine Horwitch Gallery. In fact, the hotel offers a free brochure describing an art and interior design tour of the hotel, which was designed by the architectural firm of McHugh, Lloyd, the same firm that created the facility for the Santa Fe Opera. Eldorado features 213 rooms, five suites, three restaurants, a rooftop pool, whirlpool and sauna, galleries, and a shopping arcade.

Hilton de Santa Fe, 100 Sandoval Street (988-2811), is built around the historic Casa de Ortiz and is just a block and a half from the Plaza. The hotel, part of the giant Hilton chain, is built in Territorial rather than Pueblo style, and offers 155 rooms, four suites, and two restaurants. The Piñon Grill, located in the older part of the hotel, is particularly recommended.

One of the newer hotels in the City Different, **Hotel Santa Fe,** Paseo de Peralta at Cerrillos Rd. (982-1200 or 800-825-9876), is nicely designed with 131 rooms and suites that have mini-bars and microwaves.

The **Hotel St. Francis,** 210 Don Gaspar Ave. (983-5700) was known for forty years as the De Vargas Hotel, which was built in the 1880s and was destroyed in a spectacular fire. The hotel was rebuilt in 1924 and underwent a $6-million renovation and name change in 1987–88. The 85 rooms here have high ceilings, brass and iron beds, antiques, and porcelain pedestal sinks in the baths. Its restaurant, Francisco's, is good, and the hotel—unbelievable as it may seem—serves high tea in its lobby every afternoon.

The Inn at Loretto, 211 Old Santa Fe Trail (988-5531), is a long-time favorite of visitors and is adjacent to Loretto Chapel (see entry under HISTORIC SIGHTSEEING above). The Inn, now a Best Western, features its own shopping mall with fifteen shops and galleries, including a liquor store. There are 136 rooms, three suites, a heated outdoor pool at the Inn, plus a beauty salon, restaurant, and lounge.

Small but impeccably designed, the **Inn of the Anasazi,** 113 Washington St. (988-3030 or 800-688-8100) has 59 luxurious, unique rooms and suites featuring gaslight kiva fireplaces, hand-crafted furnishings, mini-bars, VCRs, and coffee makers. The restaurant of the same name is superb.

At **Inn of the Governors,** 234 Don Gaspar Ave. (982-4333), visitors will find 99 rooms and twenty suites in a Territorial-style building with a walled outdoor patio. The amenities here include a heated outdoor pool, fireplaces in the rooms, Spanish Colonial furniture, hand-painted valances and headboards, and balconies with views of the mountains.

The intimate (36 rooms, one suite) **Inn on the Alameda,** 303 E. Alameda (984-2121) includes breakfast as part of the room rate, although it does not offer a restaurant *per se*. It is a European-style inn with *concierge* and a spa.

La Posada de Santa Fe, 330 E. Palace Ave. (986-0000 or 1-800-727-5276), is one of the most inviting places to stay in the

state. Situated on six landscaped acres a short walk from the Plaza,
La Posada has 120 suites, traditional rooms, and *casitas* ("little
homes"), each of which is unique. The main lodge, once part of a
nineteenth-century mansion, has Victorian decor, a popular
lounge, and an excellent restaurant.

Located in nearby Tesuque, **Rancho Encantado** (982-3537) is an
"enchanted ranch" featuring a main lodge, casitas, cottages, and
condominiums — 54 in all. Among the amenities here are tennis
courts, swimming pools, a horse stable, and hot tub, as well as the
Cantina Bar and a fine dining room and restaurant which are open
to the general public as well as to guests. Rancho Encantado is
designed for visitors seeking seclusion and is open year-round.
Mailing address is Rt. 4, Box 57C, Tesuque, NM 87501.

Additional recommended Santa Fe hotels include: **Inn on the
Alameda,** 303 E. Alameda (984-2121 or 800-289-2122); **Pecos Trail
Inn,** 2239 Old Pecos Trail (982-1943); **Hotel Plaza Real,** 125 Wash-
ington Ave. (988-4900 or 800-279-7325); and **Vista Clara Spa and
Health Retreat,** Galisteo 111 in Lamy (983-8109 or 800-247-0301).

Recommended **Bed and Breakfast Inns** of Santa Fe include
Preston House, 106 Faithway (982-3465), a restored 1886 Victorian
home; **Grant Corner Inn,** 122 Grant Ave. (983-6678), a collector's
heaven filled with antiques and artifacts; **Pueblo Bonito,** 138 W.
Manhattan (984-8001), with its seclusion and corner fireplaces;
and **El Paradero,** 220 W. Manhattan (988-1177), a restored 150-
year-old adobe Spanish farm house.

★ ★

ECLECTIC LODGING NEAR SANTA FE

Choose between the **Fort Marcy Compound,** downtown condos,
320 Artist Road (800-745-9910), and **Los Pinos Guest Ranch,** on the
Pecos River (757-6213). Also contrasting are the **Galisteo Inn,** a 250-
year-old hacienda in Galisteo (982-1506) and **Santa Fe Suites,** an all-
suite hotel on Galisteo St. (800-331-3131). **Pueblo Bonito** offers a
secluded adobe compound at Manhattan and Galisteo Sts. (505-984-
8001), while the **Inn on the Paseo** is a quaint B&B right off the Plaza.
Also recommended are: **Casa del Rio,** a B&B in Española (753-2035);
The Abiquiu Inn on Highway 84 in Abiquiu (800-447-5621); **Rancho Jacona,** adobe casitas with fireplaces, twenty minutes from
Santa Fe (455-7948); **Casitas de Santa Fe,** adobe casitas in the historic district (983-2832); **Dancing Ground of the Sun,** 4 intimate
casitas just off the Plaza (800-645-5673); **Inn of the Animal Tracks,**

a whimsical B&B with handcrafted furniture; **Territorial Inn,** an elegantly remodeled 100-year old home one block from the Plaza (898-7737); **La Posada de Chimayo,** traditional hacienda in the historic valley (351-4605); and **Pueblo Hermosa,** a downtown resort atop Rosario Hill (984-2590).

★ ★
DINING

There are probably more fine restaurants per capita in Santa Fe than anywhere else in the country. As is true of New Mexico in general, people living in and visiting the City Different love their food spicy hot. In fact, a recent study by the *Whole Chile Pepper* magazine determined that Santa Fe is the fiery food capital of the country, on the basis of the number of "Mexican" restaurants compared to population. Despite that fact, visitors should note that there is a wide variety of cuisines available to sample because Santa Fe attracts great culinary artists as well as great visual artists. Recommended restaurants are described below, grouped by type of cuisine offered. Since Santa Fe restaurants usually are crowded, especially during the summer, calling in advance for hours and reservations is suggested.

NEW MEXICAN

The Shed, 113½ E. Palace Ave. (982-9030), is located in historic Sena Plaza, which dates back to 1692. Chef-owned and operated for more than 32 years, The Shed offers the classic corn and chile cuisine of New Mexico. Highly recommended are their blue corn enchiladas with red chile sauce and the outstanding mocha cake and other desserts. The Shed is open only for lunch Mon.–Sat., closed Sunday. **Tomasitas,** 500 S. Guadalupe Street (983-5721), features a similar New Mexican menu with particularly good green chile. Open 11 a.m.–10 p.m. Mon.-Sat., closed Sunday. **The Guadalupe Cafe,** 313 S. Guadalupe St (982-9762) also specializes in New Mexican corn and chile cuisine, but with a difference—the menu offers crabmeat-seafood enchiladas and other delicious experiments. Open Tue.–Thurs. 7:00 a.m.–2 p.m., 5:30 p.m.–9:00 p.m. Friday until 10 p.m., Sat.–Sun. brunch served 8 a.m.–2 p.m. Funky surroundings and great spicy food characterize two other New Mexican restaurants, **Tiny's Lounge,** 1015 Pen Road Shopping Center, at St. Francis and Cerrillos Rd. (983-9817). Open 10 a.m.–2:00 a.m. Mon.–Sat., closed Sunday; and **Maria's New**

Mexican Kitchen, 555 W. Cordova Rd. (983-7929). It is open 11
a.m.–10 p.m. daily.
Other recommended New Mexican restaurants include: **Peppers
Restaurant and Cantina,** 2239 Old Pecos Trail (984-2272), open
11 a.m.–9:30 p.m. daily; **La Tertulia,** 416 Agua Fria (988-2769),
open 11:30 a.m.–2 p.m. and 5 p.m.–5:30 p.m. daily; and the **Blue
Corn Cafe,** 133 Water Street (984-1800), open 11 a.m.–11 p.m.
daily.

MEXICAN AND NEW SOUTHWESTERN

The **Old Mexico Grill,** 2434 Cerrillos Rd. at College Plaza (473-
0338), specializes in dishes from Old Mexico rather than New, such
as mole poblano, paella Mexicana, and carne asada a la Tampi-
quena. Many specialties are grilled over mesquite wood, or prepared on a French rotisserie. **The New York Times** noted: "The
dishes are filled with flavor, light and vibrant." Open 11:30 a.m.–
3 p.m. and 5 p.m.–9 p.m. Mon.–Sat., for Sunday dinner 5
p.m.–9:30 p.m. **The Coyote Cafe,** 132 W. Water Street (983-1615),
offers a truly unique dining experience because anthropologist-
turned-chef Mark Miller prepares a different menu each day as
he re-creates Southwestern and Latin American dishes that
pre-date the arrival of Europeans. It is difficult to suggest any
one particular menu item because they change so much, but here
are some samples from past menus: barbecued duck crepas, corn
crepes layered with roast duck, barbecue sauce, and corn chile
relish; red chile quail, fresh Texas bobwhite quail marinated in
dried chiles and wild mushrooms; and grilled prime ribeye, a
pecan-grilled ribeye steak with roasted garlic and orange-chipotle
butter. Incidentally, Mark is now a celebrity chef of the highest
order, with more than one hundred articles written about him
and his culinary artistry. Miller has not only taken Santa Fe by
storm, but also has made a national name for himself. He was
the chef at the farewell dinner for George Schultz at the State
Department in 1988. Dinner is served 6 p.m.–9:30 p.m., Sat. and
Sun. brunch, 11:30 a.m.–2 p.m. Lunch in Rooftop Cantina open
May–Oct. 11:30 a.m.–9:30 p.m., 7 days. Reservations are recommended.

SEAFOOD AND STEAKS

The Bull Ring, 414 Old Santa Fe Trail (983-3328), is one of Santa
Fe's oldest dining establishments and is a center of political activity

during winter legislative sessions because of its proximity to the Roundhouse. The restaurant is housed in a rambling, 150-year-old adobe hacienda and the enclosed outdoor patio is a comfortable spot to indulge in the Bull Ring's excellent steaks. Open 11:30 a.m.– 9:30 p.m. Mon–Sat., closed Sunday. The **Ore House,** 50 Lincoln Ave. (983-8687), features a balcony that overlooks the Plaza and 64 different types of margaritas. Recommended dishes are the Steak Ore House, a center-cut filet wrapped in bacon and served with a mushroom Bearnaise sauce; the New Zealand rack of lamb; and the steamed mussels. Open 11:30 a.m.–10:30 p.m. Mon.–Sat. The restaurant serves only dinner on Sunday, but the bar opens on Sunday at noon, and also stays open until 2 a.m. every night.

INTERNATIONAL

The Pink Adobe, 406 Old Santa Fe Trail (983-7712), is the oldest (founded in 1944) and probably the most famous restaurant in Santa Fe. Owner Rosalea Murphy still oversees the kitchen and attends to the myriad of details necessary to the proper operation of a great restaurant. "The Pink," as it's affectionately called, has a menu that might be described as a collision of cuisines — Creole and New Mexican, with a touch of French. The most popular dish is Steak Dunigan, a New York cut smothered in mushrooms and green chile sauce. The Dragon Room bar at the restaurant was once voted one of the nineteen best bars in the world by *Newsweek International.* For celebrity-watching, The Pink is *the* place in Santa Fe. Open 11:30 a.m.–2 p.m., and 5 p.m.–9 p.m. Mon– Friday, dinner only 5 p.m.–9 p.m. Sat.–Sun. *Always* call for reservations at the Pink.

CONTINENTAL

The Compound, 653 Canyon Rd. (982-4353), is another famous and written-about restaurant in Santa Fe. It is located in an old adobe hacienda renovated by noted architect Alexander Girard on Canyon Road, among artists' studios and galleries. Salmon, veal, lamb, and duckling are commonly on the menu at The Compound, which is often called Santa Fe's most romantic restaurant. Open 6:30 p.m.–9 p.m. for dinner only Tue.–Sat. Closed Sun.–Mon. Reservations required.
La Casa Sena, 125 E. Palace, in Sena Plaza (988-9232) is part of a complex built in the late 1860s by Major José Sena. The building is on the National Historic Register, and in its heyday hosted ter-

ritorial governors and even Col. Kit Carson of Taos. Its historic architecture, combined with extensive collections of Southwestern,
Indian, and Taos art, gives the restaurant an elegant, yet warm
ambience. Interesting dishes from a recent menu included Filete Bis-
tec, a mesquite-grilled filet of beef with a Hatch green chile and tree
oyster mushroom sauce; and Corona del Cordero, a rack of fresh,
prime Rocky Mountain lamb marinated in red chile pesto, served
with jalapeño jelly and red chile-piñon cream sauce. Open daily 6
p.m.–9:30 p.m.; Sat. and Sun. 11:30 a.m.–9:30 p.m.

The elegant **Inn of the Anasazi,** 113 Washington Ave. (988-
3030) offers tempting dishes like Venison Chile with Aged
Cheddar Quesadilla, Navajo Flatbread with Fire-Roasted Sweet
Peppers, and Vegetable Empanadas with Yellow Mole. Guests
may dine in the Library, the Wine Cellar (700 bottles on display),
or in one of the private dining rooms. Open daily 7 a.m.–10:30
a.m., 11:30 a.m.–2:30 p.m., and 5:30 p.m.–10 p.m.

The Southwest meets Asia at **Santacafe,** one of Santa Fe's
toniest spots at 231 Washington Ave. (984-1788). The menu
changes seasonally, but some recent menu choices included
Smoked Pheasant Spring rolls with Four-Chile Dipping Sauce,
Grilled Filet Mignon with Mole Verde Sauce, and Oriental Duck
Breast with Sweet and Sour Sauce. Don't miss the Santacafe
Brownie All-the-Way for dessert. Open Mon.–Sat. 11:30 a.m.–2
p.m. and 6 p.m.–10 p.m., closed Sun.

Owned by the same folks who run Albuquerque's excellent
Scalo, **Pranzo,** 540 Montezuma in Sanbusco Center (984-2645),
also offers fine Northern Italian fare, such as Lombata di Vitello,
a large char-grilled veal chop with fried onions and red pepper
aioli, and Ravioli d'Anatra Pomodoro, ravioli with duck, wild
mushrooms, sundried tomatoes, and a spicy fresh tomato sauce.
Open for lunch, Mon.–Sat. 11:30 a.m.–3 p.m., and dinner
Mon.–Sun., 5 p.m.–10 p.m.

★ ★

SHOPPING

In addition to its art galleries, Santa Fe has quite a collection of
unusual shops. Many of these shops fall into that gray area between the formal art gallery and the boutique or design studio,
offering such items as "wearable art," "craftworks," and "designer
jewelry." Since there are so many of these stores to choose from,
only a few can be briefly described here. Many of the shops listed
sell more than one category of merchandise — clothing, jewelry,
and craft items, for example.

CRAFTS AND IMPORTS

For a great selection of Mexican pots, folk art, handwoven rugs, and pottery, **Jackalope Pottery,** 2820 Cerrillos Rd. (471-8539) is the place. Mexican tiles, metal work, pots and other imports are also featured at **Artesanos Imports,** 222 Galisteo Street (983-5563). **Handcrafters Gallery,** 227 Galisteo Street (982-4880) has museum-quality crafts including ceramics, fiber, cast paper, wood, and metal objects. **The Givingness Gallery,** 309 San Francisco Street at the Eldorado Hotel (988-4721) features the hand-painted gourds of Robert Rivera. Indian pottery, country antiques and folk art highlight **Robert F. Nichols Americana,** 419 Canyon Rd. (982-2145). **Chris O'Connell Spider Woman Designs,** 225 Canyon Rd. (984-0136), is a striking weaving studio offering handwoven textiles and clothing. Masterpieces of American Indian art are featured at **Morning Star Gallery,** 513 Canyon Rd. (982-8187). The **Davis Mather Folk Art Gallery,** 141 Lincoln (983-1660) specializes in New Mexican animal woodcarvings and Mexican folk art. Perhaps the largest collection of local folk art, Indian jewelry and folk art from around the world is found at the **Santa Fe Store,** 211 Old Santa Fe Trail at the Inn of Loretto (982-2425).

INTERIOR DESIGN

Two fine shops featuring Oriental rugs, kilims, and dhurries are **Seret and Sons,** 149 E. Alameda (988-9151), and **Santa Fe Oriental Rugs,** 212 Galisteo Street (982-5152). **Santa Fe Pottery,** 323 S. Guadalupe (988-7687), specializes in handcrafted stoneware, lamps, tableware, and accessories. For New Mexican and South-western-style furniture, try **Southwest Spanish Craftsmen,** 328 S. Guadalupe (982-1767), **Doolings of Santa Fe,** 525 Airport Rd. (471-5956), and **The Sombraje Collection,** 403 Canyon Rd. (988-5567). There are several shops in Santa Fe which feature accessories for the home from all over the world: **Foreign Traders,** 202 Galisteo Street (983-6441), **Nomads of Santa Fe,** 207 Shelby Street (986-0855), and **World Arts,** 219 Shelby (986-1446). Collectors of minerals, seashells, and fossils should visit the **Mineral and Fossil Gallery,** 127 W. San Francisco St. (984-1682). For Indian items such as Navajo blankets and rugs or Pueblo pottery, visit: **Joshua Baer and Company,** 116½ Palace Ave. (988-8944) and **Indian Trader West,** 204 W. San Francisco (988-5776).

KITCHEN ITEMS

Visitors eager to bring New Mexican cuisine back home with them should stop by **The Chile Shop,** 109 E. Water Street (983-6080), and see the incredible collection of chile pepper–related items, including *ristras,* prepared foods, books, kitchen items, and even dinner ware. **Nambe,** 112 W. San Francisco (988-3574) and 924 Paseo de Peralta (988-5528), is famous for its handcrafted silver bowls and trays. **Hand Maiden,** 102 E. Water (982-8368), specializes in handcrafted stoneware by New Mexico artisans. Imported ceramics and gourmet specialties are among the offerings at **Casafina,** 125 Lincoln Avenue (988-4800).

CLOTHING

Visitors in search of the "Santa Fe look" in clothing should visit the following shops. **Suzette International** at La Fonda, Old Santa Fe Trail and W. San Francisco (982-8228), specializes in wearable art. **Origins,** 135 W. San Francisco (988-2323), describes itself as "folk art to fantasy" and sells such unusual clothing as a Yakima Indian velvet cape with cowrie shells. Fine leather clothing is found at **Salamander Leathers,** 78 E. San Francisco (982-9782) and at the **Blue Rose,** 131 W. San Francisco (983-8807). **Spirit,** 109 W. San Francisco (982-2677), has a unique collection of garments made of natural fiber. For elegant boots and such specialties as lizard pumps, **Santa Fe Footwear,** 112 W. San Francisco (983-1340), is the place to set foot, as is **Tom Taylor Custom Belts, Buckles, and Boots,** at La Fonda (984-2231).

Other recommended clothing stores are **Yarrow Collection,** 223 W. San Francisco (982-2030), **Nancy Block Design,** 338 Camino Del Monte Sol (983-3177), **Handwoven Originals** (982-4118) and **Spirit of the Earth** (988-9558) at the Inn of Loretto, **Char,** 104 Old Santa Fe Trail (988-5969) **Nancy Lewis,** 209 Galisteo Street (988-4400), **Styles of Santa Fe,** 112 W. San Francisco (982-5675), **Sundance Originals** (988-4668) and **Zephyr Clothing** (988-5635), both in Sena Plaza at 125 E. Palace Ave., **Santa Fe Weaving Gallery,** 124¹/2 Galisteo Street (982-1737) and **Laise Adzer,** 125 Lincoln Ave. (989-9322).

JEWELRY

In addition to the galleries and shops already listed, many of which carry jewelry, the following shops are recommended. **Ross LewAllen Jewelry,** 105 E. Palace Avenue (983-2657), owned by Ross LewAllen, the creator of the earcuff, offers exotic jungle jewelry. **Nancy Brown,** 111 Old Santa Fe Trail at La Fonda (982-2993), features handcrafted work in silver and gold by local artists as well as her own jewelry designs. Two shops specializing in gold originals are **Antony Williams/The Golden Bough,** 211 Old Santa Fe Trail at the Inn at Loretto (982-3443) and **Golden Web,** 102 E. Water Street in El Centro Mall. **Ornament,** 209 W. San Francisco (983-9399) carries contemporary and traditional adornment and specializes in turquoise. That traditional blue stone is also the specialty of **Douglas Magnus/Heartline,** 905 Early St. (983-6777), which presents jewelry made from turquoise mined in the legendary Tiffany Cerrillos mines. Silver is the specialty at **The Passionate Eye Gallery,** 235 Don Gaspar Street (984-1606), and at **Contemporary Craftsmen Gallery,** 100 W. San Francisco. Recommended shops for traditional Indian turquoise and silver jewelry include **Storyteller Indian Arts Gallery,** 228 Old Santa Fe Trail (982-6819), **Ortega's Turquoise Mesa** (988-1866) and **Kiva Trading Post** (982-4906), both on the Plaza, **Koshare Trading Company,** 312 Sandoval Street (988-3042), and **Indian Trader West,** 204 W. San Francisco (988-5776).

BOOKS

Footsteps Across New Mexico, 211 Old Santa Fe Trail at the Inn at Loretto (982-9297) , is a bookstore with a large collection of titles about New Mexico, plus a theatre with a multi-media historical show about the state. The largest collection of art books in the state can be found at the **Santa Fe Bookseller,** 203 W. San Francisco (983-5278). **Los Llanos,** 500 Montezuma, is one of the most complete bookstores in the city, with an excellent selection of titles on travel, the Southwest, and art. Perhaps the best used and rare bookstore is **Nicholas Potter Bookseller,** 203 E. Palace Ave. **Horizons,** 328 Guadalupe, is a fascinating shop specializing in books about nature, science, and astronomy. For Western and Native Americana titles, visit **Parker Books of the West,** 142 W. Palace (988-1076) and **Great Southwest Books,** 960 Camino Santander (983-1680).

PERFORMING ARTS

SANTA FE OPERA
It might seem odd that one of America's finest opera houses is located seven miles from the Plaza in the foothills of the Sangre de Cristo Mountains, but opera fans have supported this open-air facility for more than 35 years. Founded in 1957 by John Crosby, the Santa Fe Opera has been successful because of its unique location and because its productions are every bit as good as, say, those in New York City.

The 1773-seat amphitheater has a nearly 360-degree panoramic view of mountains, mesas, and sky, as well as the lights of Los Alamos. Its productions utilize the talents of as many as five hundred singers, musicians, directors, designers, and painters. Featured operas include every noted composer, including Strauss, Mozart, Wagner, Puccini, and Stravinski.

The opera season runs from late June through August, and tickets are generally very difficult to obtain, especially at the last minute. By tourist standards, the tickets are also expensive, ranging from $15–$83. Mon.–Thurs., $20–$88 Fri. and Sat. Occasionally, standing room only tickets are available for $6 on sale at 8 p.m. The best chance for obtaining seats is to request an annual brochure and reservation from the Santa Fe Opera, P.O. Box 2408, Santa Fe, NM 87504 (982-3855). The opera is located seven miles north of town on U.S. Hwy 84/285 near Tesuque.

SANTA FE CHAMBER MUSIC FESTIVAL
Another high point in the cultural scene of Santa Fe, the Chamber Music Festival, is held for six weeks beginning the second week of July through the third week of August and features a musical tour of the world. In addition to classical concerts performed at St. Francis Auditorium in the Museum of Fine Arts and the Santuario de Guadalupe, the festival offers composers' forums, National Public Radio broadcasts, conversations with musicians, and a composer-in-residence program. For ticket information, contact the Santa Fe Chamber Music Festival Box Office, P.O. Box 853, Santa Fe, NM 87504 (983-2075).

CENTER FOR CONTEMPORARY ARTS
Offering more than one hundred film and video presentations yearly in its 143 seat theatre, the center also offers seven annual shows

of painting, sculpture, and photography. The Center is located at
291 E. Barcelona (982-1338). For a calendar of events, write P.O.
Box 148, Santa Fe, NM 87504.

ORCHESTRA OF SANTA FE and
THE SANTA FE SYMPHONY

For more than sixteen years the Orchestra of Santa Fe, under the
direction of William Kirsche, has presented baroque, classical, and
contemporary programs at the Lensic Theatre, one block from the
Plaza on W. San Francisco Street. The season for the orchestra
runs from the third week in September to the first week in May.
For tickets and information, call 988-4640 or write P.O. Box 2091,
Santa Fe, NM 87504-2091.

The larger orchestra, the Santa Fe Symphony, also performs
September through May, but at Sweeny Center. Five concerts a
year under the direction of Stewart Robertson feature classical and
contemporary works. For ticket information, call 983-3530.

Other performing arts groups and facilities include **Greer Garson
Theatre** at College of Santa Fe, on St. Michael's Dr. (473-6511),
Santa Fe Community Theatre, 142 E. De Vargas Street (988-4262),
Santa Fe Desert Chorale, 219 Shelby Street, which performs at
Santuario de Guadalupe in Santa Fe, and Keller Hall at UNM cam-
pus in Albuquerque (988-7505), and the **Santa Fe Concert Associa-
tion** (984-8759 or 243-5646).

★ ★
NIGHTLIFE

Except for lounges in the various hotels and restaurants, the nightclub scene in the City Different is virtually nonexistent. One exception is **Chez What,** 213 W. Alameda (982-0099), which always
seems to attract interesting musical acts. On any given night, one
might find a reggae group from Jamaica, a standup comic from
Los Angeles, or performances by legendary rock, blues, and folk
singers. Likewise, **Paolo Soleri Amphitheater,** an outdoor concert facility located on the campus of the Santa Fe Indian School,
1501 Cerrillos Rd., is the location for summer concerts featuring
rock, blues, and third-world music. For information, contact
Allegro Music at 471-9112 or Ticketmaster in Albuquerque (884-
0999). Events info. (842-5387).

The **Maria Benitez Spanish Dance Company** features internationally renowned Maria Benitez and her Estampa Flamenca dance

troupe and musicians, who perform from July through September at the Picacho Plaza Hotel, 750 N. St. Francis Dr. For more information, call 982-5591.

★ ★
JUST FOR THE FUN OF IT

The Downs at Santa Fe, located nine miles south of town just off I-25, offers Quarter Horse and Thoroughbred racing June through Labor Day in one of the most picturesque racetracks in the country. Racing days are Wednesday, Friday, Saturday, and Sunday; exotic wagering includes a daily double, quinella, twin trifecta, two regular trifectas, Santa Fe Six, and exacta. Senior citizens receive free admission and a seat in the Turf Club on Wednesdays; ladies receive the same privileges on Fridays. Call 471-3311 for racing details.

Ten Thousand Waves, a Japanese health spa three and one half miles from town on Hyde Park Road on the way to the Ski Basin (988-1047), is a great place for people who love hot tubs, saunas, cold plunges, and massages. Also available at Ten Thousand Waves are facials, herbal wraps, salt glows, and aromatherapy, which utilizes the essential oils of flowers and plants to, according to the management, "rid the body's lymphatic system of toxins." Open 10 a.m.–9:30 p.m. daily except on Tuesdays open only in the evening from 4:30 p.m.–9:30 p.m. Call 982-9304 for reservations and summer hours.

Santa Fe Ski Basin, located thirteen miles northeast of Santa Fe on NM Hwy. 475, has forty trails of which eighty per cent are for intermediate or advanced skiers. There is an on-slope bar here, plus a restaurant and cafe. The annual snowfall at the upper altitude of 12,000 feet averages 190–250 inches, so there is not too much need for snowmaking equipment, which is only used on about 25 per cent of the trails. Cross-country skiing is available on a 4.6–kilometer groomed track. The ski season usually runs Thanksgiving through Easter depending on snowfall. For details call 982-4429 or 983-9155.

Hyde Memorial State Park is located near the Ski Basin on NM Hwy. 475 (983-7175) and is used as a base camp for backpackers and skiers who venture into Santa Fe National Forest and the Pecos Wilderness Area. The park has a skating pond, a sledding area, camping and picnicking sites, utility hookups, and rest rooms. There is a restaurant and general store at the park.

★ ★
SPECIAL EVENTS

There is never a lack of activities in Santa Fe. **Fiesta de Santa Fe,** established in 1712 by Don Diego de Vargas to commemorate the reoccupation of New Mexico by the Spanish is, really and truly, the oldest continuous community festival in the United States. It begins the Friday after Labor Day with the spectacular burning of Zozobra, a forty-foot-tall effigy representing Old Man Gloom. Crowds of up to 50,000 spectators assemble to witness this burning, which symbolically removes all the sadness of the previous year. After Zozobra burns out, the party moves to the Plaza for two more days of parades, dancing, singing, religious processions, and booths filled with arts, crafts, and traditional food. For more information, call 988-7575.

Indian Market, held around the Plaza during a weekend in mid-August for nearly seventy years, is probably the finest single show of Indian arts and crafts in the nation, although the folks around Gallup might dispute that claim. All objects for sale in the booths must be Indian-made, and the finest pieces are judged in a juried competition. Collectors travel from all over the world for this event, and hotel rooms are difficult to find. For more information, call 983-5220.

Spanish Markets, held during the last weekend in July for nearly forty years, showcase the arts and crafts of New Mexico's Hispanic artisans. Exhibitors must be a least one-quarter Hispanic to sell their crafts, which include *santos, retablos,* embroidery, weavings, tinwork, jewelry, and handmade furniture. The markets include a Traditional Spanish Market, held on the Plaza, and a Contemporary Spanish Market held in the courtyard of the Palace of Governors. For more information, write to the Spanish Colonial Arts Society, P.O. Box 1611, Santa Fe, NM 87501 or call 983-4038.

Rodeo de Santa Fe started in the late 1940s and has steadily grown into a popular regional competition. In early July, between three and five hundred entrants compete for nearly $30,000 in cash prizes at the Rodeo Ground (seats 5500) on Rodeo Road, just off Cerrillos Road. For details, call the Convention & Visitors Bureau (984-6760 or 1-800-777-2489).

Other special events include the **Santa Fe Festival of the Arts** (988-3924), occurring the last two weeks of May, and the **Fall Festival of the Arts** held the second and third weekends in October (For a complete schedule, write 1050 Old Pecos Trail, Santa Fe, NM

87501); the **Mountain Man Rendezvous and Buffalo Roast** (827-6473), held in mid-August at the Palace of the Governors in conjunction with trade fair; and the **Winterfestival** (1-800-982-SNOW), a skiing extravaganza and competition that runs in the second week in February. Events are held in various locations including the Eldorado Hotel.

★ ★
TOURS AND TOUR GUIDES

For transportation between Santa Fe and Albuquerque International Airport, as well as for group tours, a dependable operator is **Shuttlejack** (982-4311 or 1-800-452-2665).

Guided tours of Santa Fe and northern New Mexico are readily available—here is just a sampling. The **Santa Fe Chile Line** (989-8595) is a trolley service that runs between major chain hotels and historic sites. **Chamisa Touring Service**, Rt 7, Box 125SC, Santa Fe, NM 87505 (988-1343), run by Sandy Clarke, Ph.D., provides anthropologist and educator guides for in-depth tours for both individuals and groups. Two comprehensive services featuring every conceivable type of tour are **Rocky Mountain Tours,** 1323 Paseo de Peralta, Santa Fe, NM 87501 (984-1684) and **Rojotours,** 228-A Old Santa Fe Trail, Santa Fe, NM 87501 (983-8333). Air and land expeditions of Monument Valley (Utah) and the Grand Canyon leave from Santa Fe via **Southwest Safaris,** P.O. Box 945, Santa Fe, NM 87504 (988-4246). Rafting expeditions are provided by **Rio Bravo River Tours,** 1412 Cerrillos Rd. (988-1153 or 1-800-451-0708).

★ ★
RESOURCES

For detailed information about the City Different, consult *Santa Fe Visitor's Guide,* Santa Fe Convention and Visitors Bureau, Sweeny Center, P.O. Box 909, Santa Fe, NM 87504 (984-6760 and 1-800-528-5369); *The Collector's Guide to Santa Fe and Taos,* a guide to art galleries ($5) from Wingspread Communications, P.O. Box 13566, Albuquerque, NM 87192 (292-7537); *The Santa Fe Catalogue,* P.O. Box 1007, Aspen, CO 81612 (303-925-5109).

NEARBY ATTRACTIONS

Pecos National Monument, 25 miles west of Santa Fe via I-25 to Pecos exit, in Pecos go right two miles on NM Hwy. 63 to monument. One of the largest ancient pueblos in New Mexico, Pecos was visited in 1540 by Coronado when it was called Cicuye. The village featured a four- and five-story structure with 660 rooms. It was later conquered by Gaspar Castaño in 1591 and the Franciscans founded the Mission de Nuestra Senora in the early 1620s. The Pueblo Revolt of 1680, an epidemic in 1788, and raids from the Comanches led to the abandonment of Pecos in 1838, and the remaining inhabitants moved to Jemez Pueblo.

Now a small, quiet National Monument, Pecos offers a self-guided tour of the pueblo and mission ruins, which were excavated between 1915 and 1929 by famed archaeologist Alfred V. Kidder. Picnicking, rest rooms, and drinking water are available here, but no camping or other facilities. For further information on Pecos National Monument, call 757-6414.

SANTA FE NATIONAL FOREST
The mountains that loom behind the City Different are part of Santa Fe National Forest, a vast 1.5 million acre forest in three sections. Picnicking and camping are available at more than 45 recreation sites, including: **Black Rock Canyon,** eight miles north of Santa Fe on NM Hwy. 475; **Aspen Vista,** thirteen miles north of Santa Fe on NM Hwy. 475; **Holy Ghost,** fifteen miles north of Pecos via NM Hwy. 63; and **Ev Long,** sixteen miles northwest of Las Vegas via NM Hwy. 65.

For further details about camping, picnicking, hunting, or fishing in Santa Fe National Forest, call the Santa Fe office, 988-6940. For information about hiking and camping trips conducted by outdoor organizations, contact Santa Fe Group of the Sierra Club (983-2703 or 983-8870).

COCHITI PUEBLO
This small pueblo is located about thirty miles south of Santa Fe via I-25, then right on NM Hwy. 22 about ten miles. The Cochiti people are known for the drums they make out of hollow cottonwood logs and for their ceramic story-teller dolls. The ancestral home of the pueblo is located in Bandelier National Monument while the current farming community is along the banks of the Rio Grande. The pueblo leases land to the town of Cochiti Lake and

operates services, including a commercial center and an eighteen-hole golf course, for the town. There is no admission fee to the pueblo but cameras are not allowed.

The famous Cochiti Corn Dance is performed on July 14, the Feast Day of San Buenaventura. For details, call the pueblo at 465-2244.

COCHITI LAKE
Administered by the pueblo, Cochiti Lake is a 1200-acre impound-ment known for sailing and windsurfing because it is a quiet lake — no motorboats allowed. The lake was created by Cochiti Dam, one of the eleven largest earth-fill dams in the world. Fishing is good here for walleye, bass, channel cats, crappie, northern pike, and rainbow trout. There are boat ramps, RV hookups, a marina, boat rentals, a swimming beach, and food concessions at the lake. Adventurous sailors can navigate up the river into White Rock Canyon. Call 465-2244 for information.

TESUQUE PUEBLO
Just eight miles north of Santa Fe on U.S. Hwy. 84/285, Tesuque Pueblo was formerly a farming community. Settlement here was first made about 1250. A small pueblo of fewer than five hundred persons, Tesuque has some nice two-story dwellings and looks much like it did centuries ago. However, Tesuque has joined the modern world of tourism by operating an RV park (455-2661 and 455-2467), cigarette shop, and a bingo parlor (1-800-85BINGO in New Mexico). Aspen Ranch, a scenic campsite in the Sangre de Cristo Mountains, is available for camping, fish-ing, and picnicking. No state fishing license is needed.

The annual feast day is November 12; photography and sketch-ing are permitted with small fees. **Duran's Pottery** (983-7078) fea-tures traditional Tesuque black and white pottery, red micaceous pottery, and beadwork. For further information on Tesuque pueblo, call the Governor's office at 983-2667.

POJOAQUE PUEBLO
Sixteen miles north of Santa Fe and eight miles north of Tesuque Pueblo on US Hwy. 84/285, Pojoaque is one of the smallest north-ern pueblos. Although the historic village of Pojoaque no longer exists, the native people here work hard to maintain their identity through traditional art forms such as pottery, beadwork, embroi-dery, and silversmithing. They too have entered the modern world of tourism by operating a tourist center featuring traditional crafts and a well-stocked supermarket. For details, stop by or call 455-2278.

NAMBE PUEBLO

Twenty miles north of Santa Fe via US Hwy. 84/285 and right six miles on NM Hwy. 503, Nambe Pueblo is surrounded by the Sangre de Cristo and Jemez Mountain ranges and has its own spectacular attraction: **Nambe Falls Recreational Site,** the location of the July 4 Waterfall Ceremony. Only a few of the original pueblo buildings remain, but the small population of about four hundred still survives by farming, ranching, and employment in nearby cities.

Recently, there has been a revival of interest in traditional Nambe weaving, beadwork, and black-on-black and white-on-red pottery. Feast Day on October 4 honors St. Francis of Assisi and attracts hundreds of visitors for the dances. Permits for fishing, boating, and camping are available at the Governor's office. Sketching, photography, and videotaping are permitted for fees ranging from $3 to $5. For more information, call 455-2036 or 455-7752.

SAN ILDEFONSO PUEBLO

Famous for their black-on-black ware, San Ildefonso potters continue the tradition revived and made famous by the late Maria Martinez, an internationally acclaimed ceramic artist. The pueblo, although small (population about five hundred), is quite progressive, and manages its own visitor center, museum, art studio, and Indian art show. To get to the pueblo, drive about 21 miles north of Santa Fe via US Hwy. 84-285 and turn left on NM Hwy. 502 and go six miles.

The pueblo **Visitor and Information Center** provides free brochures and displays of pottery, ribbon shirts, embroidery, and paintings for sale to visitors. **San Ildefonso Fishing Lake,** a small 4.5-acre impoundment is stocked with catfish and rainbow trout from the Mescalero National Fish Hatchery; daily fishing permits are available at the tribal offices. Picnic shelters, grills, water, and rest rooms are available at the lake. The **San Ildefonso Pueblo Museum** has displays on pueblo history, architecture, and the natural history of the Pajarito Plateau. **Popovi Da Studio of Indian Arts** (455-3332) sells pueblo pottery, paintings, jewelry, baskets, books, and kachinas and has a permanent collection of work created by Maria Martinez and her family. The shop is open by appointment only during Nov.–Dec.

The annual **Eight Northern Indian Pueblos Artist and Craftsman Show** held in mid-July rotates among the pueblos. Call 852-4265 for information. More than three hundred booths display and sell every conceivable Native American art and craft, from squash blossom necklaces to pottery wedding vases the

color of the surrounding red earth. Other booths purvey traditional pueblo foods including mutton stew, fry bread, and red
chile stew. Dancers from both pueblo and Plains tribes perform
Buffalo, Rain, and Eagle dances while craftsmen give pottery-
making demonstrations. This is one of the biggest Indian shows
in New Mexico, on a scale with the Gallup Ceremonial and Santa
Fe's Indian Market. For additional information about San
Ildefonso, contact the Visitor and Information Center at 455-3549.

LOS ALAMOS

This small city of about 11,000, located along the mesa tops northwest of Santa Fe along NM Hwy. 502, probably has the highest
number of Ph.D.s per capita of any community in the country.
Unlike many cities in New Mexico, Los Alamos has not gained its
fame from a long tradition of history, but rather from events which
have occurred during the last few decades. In 1943, the United
States government took over the Los Alamos Ranch School and
transformed it into a laboratory to build the first atomic weapons
in the world. Thus, this community was totally isolated from the
rest of the state and remained cloaked in secrecy. This mammoth
top-secret effort, known as the Manhattan Project, produced the
first atomic bomb, which was tested at Trinity Site on the White
Sands Missile Range on July 16, 1945.

Los Alamos remained a closed city until 1957 and residents were
not allowed to purchase houses there until 1967. The original Manhattan Project laboratories were transformed gradually into Los
Alamos National Laboratories, still a top-secret facility and one of
the premier research labs in the world.

★ ★
ATTRACTIONS

BRADBURY SCIENCE HALL AND MUSEUM
This fascinating museum on Diamond Dr. (667-4444) has an impressive collection of exhibits relating to the dawn of the nuclear
age as well as to the latest research in solar, geothermal, laser, and
magnetic fusion energy. There is an overview of the nation's
nuclear arsenal here and a model of an atomic accelerator.

Films produced at Los Alamos National Laboratory are shown
regularly in the small theater in the museum — subjects range from
historical footage of eminent scientists to the latest computer

graphics. Museum hours are Tues.–Fri. 9 a.m.–5 p.m., and Sat.–
Mon. 1 p.m.–5 p.m.; admission is free.

LOS ALAMOS HISTORICAL MUSEUM

Located downtown on the original grounds of the Los Alamos
Ranch School, at 1921 Juniper Street (662-6272), this museum is
dedicated to preserving, protecting, and interpreting the unique
history of the Pajarito Plateau, which rests at the base of the Jemez
Mountains. Exhibits present the history of the region from prehistoric times through the development of the Manhattan Project.
In the same complex is the **Fuller Lodge Art Center,** a log building
that housed the dining and recreation hall for the Ranch School.
The gallery here features the works of northern New Mexico artists
as well as regional and national traveling exhibits. Admission to the
museum and art center is free; hours are 10 a.m.–4 p.m. Mon.–Sat.
and 1 p.m.–4 p.m. on Sunday, and Thursday evenings until 8 p.m.

BANDELIER NATIONAL MONUMENT

Located about thirteen miles south of Los Alamos off NM Hwy. 4,
Bandelier National Monument is what remains of a large Anasazi
farming village which existed between 1100 and 1500 in remote
Frijoles ("beans") Canyon. After a three-mile drive from the monument entrance, the visitor finds a visitor center and museum, a
snack bar and curio shop, and picnic grounds along Frijoles Creek.
A one-mile, self-guided tour leads from the visitor center into the
ruins. Here are cliff houses carved out of the volcanic rock—
actually rhyolite tuff—which came from the Valles Caldera
explosion.

This short trail is by no means the only hiking route in the monument. There are approximately seventy miles of trails leading to the
Upper and Lower Falls on Frijoles Creek, to the **Ceremonial Cave**
and **Ponderosa Campground,** to **Tyuonyi Overlook,** and to a
number of other sights. The Jemez Mountains, part of Santa Fe
National Forest, are still a wild and rugged area. The area ranks
second in the country for the number of thunder storms, about
75 a year. Only Tampa, Florida, has more—about ninety. Ask for
a map and hiking permit at the visitor center.

Bandelier National Monument, named after famous archaeologist Adolph Bandelier, also has petroglyphs at the Tsirege site and
another interesting ruin at the Tsankawi site.

Operating hours for the visitor's center are 8 a.m.–6 p.m. daily
during the summer and 8 a.m.–4:30 p.m. in winter. The monument
is open during daylight hours, and a $5 per carload entrance fee

is charged. The best reference book about the monument is *A Guide to Bandelier National Monument,* by Dorothy Hoard, published by the Los Alamos Historical Society, and other similar books are available at the visitors center or by mail. For more information on the monument, call 672-3861 or write Bandelier National Monument, HCR 1, Box 1, Suite 15, Los Alamos, NM 87544.

★ ★
LODGING AND DINING

There aren't too many options for lodging and dining in Los Alamos because the city was designed as a high-tech research center, not as a base for tourism. The **Los Alamos Inn,** 2201 Trinity Dr. (662-7211) offers 115 rooms, a restaurant, and a fresh-air facility called the South Forty that is complete with bandstand, picnic tables, and a great view of nearby canyons. The **Hilltop House Hotel,** Trinity at Central (662-2441), has a choice of rooms, mini-suites, or executive suites with full kitchen facilities. There is indoor swimming all year round in the hotel's solarium pool, and the **Trinity Sights Restaurant** is recommended for its Continental cuisine and magnificent mountain views.

Offering international cuisine, **The Blue Window,** 800 Trinity Drive (662-6305) is recommended, as are **The Chili Works,** 1743 Trinity Dr. (662-7591), open for breakfast and lunch only 7 a.m.–3 p.m., Mon.–Sat. and **Boccacio's,** 4244 Diamond Dr. (662-7204), an Italian restaurant with homemade breads and desserts. Bar open 10:30 a.m.–2 a.m., restaurant open 11:30 a.m.–2 p.m., 5:30 p.m.–8:30 p.m. Tues.–Thurs., 5:30 p.m.–9:30 p.m. Fri.–Sat. Closed Sun.–Mon.

ESPAÑOLA

Española is infamous as the "Lowrider Capital of the World" because there are more of these low-slung, radically customized cruisers per capita than anywhere else in the world. A drive through town — actually a slow crawl — at 9 p.m. on Saturday night during the summer will confirm this fact.

On the other hand, Española is a very friendly and progressive town. Hispanics, Native Americans, and Anglos coexist peacefully in this farming community. Even the Sikhs, a religious sect originally from India, have been welcomed in Española, where they have established the **Sikh Dharma,** Rt. 3, Box 1320, Española, NM

87532 (753-9438), an ashram community of two hundred that hosts several international, interfaith events including a Summer Solstice celebration in late June.

The lowriding cars are actually the focus of organized clubs that often assist in community projects. Owners of these custom cars often exhibit in car shows in Albuquerque and Santa Fe, and enter hopping and scraping contests. To hop, a lowrider must have powerful hydraulic systems that, at the touch of a switch, cause the front end of the car to leap as high as three feet into the air!

Española was founded in the 1880s as a stop on the Denver and Rio Grande Railroad and although the railroad has vanished, the town has prospered as the trade center for the Española Valley, which includes many small towns. The town sits at the junctions of US Hwy. 84, the road to Chama, US Hwy. 285, the highway to Ojo Caliente and Santa Fe, NM Hwy. 68, the main route to Taos, and NM Hwy. 76, which, along with NM Hwy. 518, is called "The High Road to Taos."

★ ★
TOURIST INFORMATION

ESPAÑOLA CHAMBER OF COMMERCE
417 Big Rock Center, Española, NM 87532 (753-2831).

BOND HOUSE MUSEUM AND CULTURAL CENTER
Located adjacent to US Hwy. 285, the Northern New Mexico Commemorative Cultural Plaza surrounds a museum, cultural center, and market for native crafts and produce. The **Bond House Museum,** 710 Bond Street, west of the Post Office (753-2377), former home of Franklin Bond, a Canadian-born merchant who achieved great success in Española, is housed in the combination adobe and Victorian structure built in 1887. Exhibits illustrating the tri-cultural heritage of the Española valley are presented here. The museum is open Monday through Friday from 1 p.m.–4 p.m. or by appointment. No admission fee.

★ ★
LODGING, DINING, AND SHOPPING

Unless the visitor is in search of bargain motels, the only place to stay in Española is the **Chamisa Inn and Restaurant,** on the Taos Highway at 920 N. Riverside Dr. (753-7291). The motel features a

heated outdoor pool, two cocktail lounges, mini-suites, an arts and crafts shop, and a nice restaurant.
Ranch O. Casados Restaurant, 411 N. Riverside (753-2837) owned by the Casados family from nearby San Juan Pueblo, is a simple coffee shop with excellent New Mexican dishes—especially the ones utilizing their homemade blue-corn tortillas. Open 8 a.m.–8 p.m. daily. A more luxurious establishment is **Anthony's at the Delta,** 228 Oñate NW (753-4511) on the Chama Highway, open daily 5 p.m.–9 p.m. for dinner only. In addition to the fine steaks and fresh fish, Anthony's offers a wonderful ambience—Spanish Colonial decor, landscaped gardens with a tree-filled courtyard, and a good collection of paintings and sculpture. **Rio Grande Cafe and Liquors,** at Hill Street and the 101 Los Alamos Hwy. (753-2125) open 11 a.m.–7:30 p.m. Mon.–Fri., is a local favorite serving New Mexican food.

★ ★
NEARBY ATTRACTIONS

SANTA CLARA PUEBLO
This pueblo, located just over a mile from Española via NM Hwy. 30 and NM Hwy. 5, has its ancestral home in the **Puye Cliff Dwellings** at the entrance to Santa Clara Canyon of the Pajarito Plateau. According to their legends, the Santa Claras (part of the Tewa language group), emerged from the underworld through a small lake in the sand dunes near Alamosa, Colorado, then migrated to the Puye Cliffs, where they hollowed out caves and existed by farming and hunting.

In the fourteenth century, additional pueblos were built along the slopes and the tops of the mesas, and eventually more than 1500 Indians inhabited this spectacular site. Around 1580, drought caused the Santa Claras to abandon the Puye site and move closer to the Rio Grande, to a site about eleven miles away. In the 1620s the Spaniards established a church at the new pueblo. The church was rebuilt in 1918 on the site of the original structure. Currently, the pueblo has a population of about three thousand.

The original cliff dwellings, now a National Historic Landmark, can be visited by either self-guided tours or a guided tour that includes a pueblo feast and dance performance. There are three trails to the top of the mesa, where stairways connect two levels of cliff dwellings with the 740-room pueblo ruin. Within the ruin is a ceremonial chamber and a "great community house."

There are various shops and tour guide services at the pueblo. **Singing Water Pottery and Tours** on NM Hwy. 30 (753-9663)

features the distinctive, ornately carved, red-and-black Santa
Clara pottery, plus ribbon shirts and silver jewelry.

There are three other galleries and studios of note: **Toni Roller
Pottery and Green Leaves Studio,** on Lower Canyon Road
(753-3003); **The Balloon Butterfly Shop,** two blocks north of the
tribal administration building (753-5657); and **Corn Studio,** at the
north end of the reservation.

The **Santa Clara Canyon Recreation Area** has pond and stream
fishing, hiking, picnicking, and nice camping facilities. It's located
on NM Hwy. 5, three miles south of Española, and fees are charged
for the various recreational activities. No sketching or videotaping
are allowed, but photography is allowed with the proper permits.
For further information, contact the Santa Clara Pueblo Governor's Office, 753-7326.

OJO CALIENTE
This small town, located about 26 miles north of Española on US
Hwy. 285, is famous for its hot springs. **Ojo Caliente Mineral
Springs Company,** P.O. Box 468, Ojo Caliente, NM 87549,
Caliente Springs, off Hwy. 285 (583-2233) offers hotel and motel
accommodations, a restaurant, kitchenette apartments, and bath
houses with trained attendants. The springs here are believed to be
the only place in the world where a combination of five different
minerals bubble out of the ground at the same place. The iron
springs (109 degrees) are fed into a large pool, while the arsenic
springs are piped into individual tubs. The lithia, soda, and sodium
springs are used for drinking.

Apparently, the springs have been utilized by mankind for
millennia. The Pueblo people believed that the springs were sacred
openings into the underworld, and they built pueblos atop the
mesas near the springs. During the seventeenth century, a Spanish
village, including the Church of Santa Cruz, was built at the site.
The church was also used as a fortress against hostile Navajos,
Utes, and Comanches.

The mineral springs were developed as a resort in the 1860s by
Antonio Joseph, New Mexico's first Territorial representative to
Congress, and they were at their height of popularity in the 1940s,
when arthritis sufferers flocked to the springs to soak in their reputedly therapeutic waters. For more information on hot springs and
baths in New Mexico, call the office of New Mexico Economic
Development at 827-0380.

CHIMAYO

This small town in a scenic valley eight miles east of Española on NM Hwy. 76 has often been called "the Lourdes of the Southwest" because it attracts great numbers of the sick, crippled, and aged who believe that the soil here has miraculous healing qualities. The focus of attention for possible miracles is **Santuario de Chimayo,** built in 1816 by Don Bernardo Abeyta after a vision told him to dig in his field to find healing earth. During the Easter season, as many as 30,000 pilgrims descend upon this small church, some making treks on foot for hundreds of miles. The fortunate ones who manage to enter the church reach into "the hole in the holy earth," near the altar, and bring out a small pinch of dirt to rub on their bodies. The walls of the church are adorned with braces, canes, and crutches of those faithful who apparently have been aided or healed by the intense degree of belief of the pilgrims.

Near the Santuario is one of New Mexico's most famous restaurants, **Restaurante Rancho de Chimayo,** one quarter mile north of Santuario on Hwy. 520 (351-4444), which offers New Mexican specialties in a lovely setting complete with a three-level outdoor patio. Open noon–9 p.m. Tues.–Sat., closed Monday. Reservations are almost always necessary. Across the street is **Hacienda de Chimayo,** P.O. Box 11, Chimayo, NM 87522 (351-2222), a bed and breakfast inn with seven guest rooms decorated with turn-of-the-century antiques. Each room opens onto an enclosed courtyard. Another bed and breakfast in the village is **La Posada de Chimayo** (351-4605), which has two separate suites and breakfasts which are, according to owner Sue Farrington, "not for the faint of heart." Call for reservations and directions.

The Chimayo Valley has been a center of weaving for seven generations, and **Ortega's Weaving Shop,** NM Hwy. 76 at NM Hwy. 520 (351-4215), sells authentic Chimayo blankets, rugs, pillows, coats, and vests. Next door is **Galeria Ortega** (351-2288), featuring Hispanic and Native American arts and crafts.

About six miles from Chimayo via NM Hwy. 76 and NM Hwy. 503 is **Santa Cruz Lake,** a popular spot for fishing and camping on the edge of the Pecos Wilderness. About seven miles beyond Chimayo on NM Hwy. 76 is **Cordova,** a small town famed for its wood carvers who fashion native aspen and juniper into *santos*, or carved saints. Two miles further is **Truchas** ("trout"), a former Colonial outpost which has retained many traditional Spanish customs. **Truchas Peak,** which looms over the town, is the second-highest peak in New Mexico at 13,101 feet

SAN JUAN PUEBLO

This pueblo, just three miles north of Española on NM Hwy. 68,
then left on NM Hwy. 74, along the banks of the Rio Grande has
been continuously inhabited since 1300. It was the location of the
first capital of New Mexico, founded in 1598 by Juan de Oñate at
the San Gabriel site. Nearly a hundred years later, a San Juan
Indian named Popé led the Pueblo Revolt against the Spanish.
Today, the ancient and modern sit side by side — two rectangular
kivas are next to the Catholic church in the plazas.

San Juan Pueblo, primarily a farming community, is well known
for its arts and crafts, particularly its distinctive red incised pottery
decorated with geometric designs. The **Óke Oweenge Arts and
Crafts Cooperative** (852-2372) was founded in 1968 to foster the
development of handmade crafts. For sale at the cooperative are
pottery, traditional clothing, embroidery, and jewelry. Paintings,
woodcarvings, and corn dolls are offered at **Aguino's Indian Arts
and Crafts** also located in the pueblo.

Gamblers can try their luck at **San Juan Indian Bingo,** Wed.–Sun.,
located one mile north of Española on US Hwy. 285 (753-3132), while
fishermen can try their luck at **San Juan Tribal Lakes,** just south of
the pueblo. Picnicking is available at the lakes, but camping is not
allowed. However, there is a privately-owned facility with fire
adobe houses complete with kitchens nearby, **Chinguague Compound,** located two miles north of San Juan Pueblo off NM Hwy.
68, P.O. Box 1118, San Juan Pueblo, NM 87566 (852-2194 call for reservations). The **Tewa Indian Restaurant,** in the pueblo, serves authentic San Juan dishes, including fry bread, fruit pies, green chile stew,
and Indian tacos.

During the Feast Day of San Juan, June 24, the Corn Dance is
performed, and the Deer and Butterfly Dances are performed at
other times of the year. Photography, sketching, and videotaping
require permission at San Juan. For more information, contact the
tribal office at 852-4400.

North of San Juan Pueblo, on the way to Taos on NM Hwy. 68,
are several interesting stops. At **Alcalde,** five miles north, the
ancient dance of the Matachines is performed on holidays. Thought
to be of Moorish origin, the dance was brought from Spain with
the earliest settlers of the region. **Velarde,** ten miles north, is the
center of the fruit growing community along the Rio Grande.
Among their various fruit stands here that sell fresh vegetables and
red chile *ristras* is the **Herman Valdez Fruit Stand** (852-2129), which
has an annual wreath festival the last weekend in October. **Dixon**
and **Embudo** are neighboring communities about seventeen miles
north where the Embudo River enters the Rio Grande. Dixon is an
artists' colony which sponsors an annual autumn show.

PICURIS PUEBLO

Located thirty miles north of Española via NM Hwys. 68 and 75, Picuris was the last pueblo to be discovered by the Spanish, and it remains quite isolated today. The pueblo never signed a treaty with any country and it retains its status as a sovereign nation/tribe. Its population of three hundred lives on a remote 15,000-acre reservation surrounded by the Santa Fe National Forest in the Sangre de Cristo Mountains, but the tribe is making a concerted effort to modernize. The publication of the Eight Northern Indian Pueblos compares the pueblo to an emerging Third World nation and observes, "To visit Picuris is to be involved in the dynamic process of change while at the same time reaffirming a culture cemented by time immemorial."

The totally computerized Picuris Tribal Enterprise offers some interesting diversions. **Picuris Pueblo Museum** (587-2519) displays pottery, beadwork, and weavings and has a shop which sells these and other locally produced crafts. **Hidden Valley Shop and Restaurant** offers fishing gear, arts and crafts, and native food. **Pu-na and Tu-tah Lakes** are fishing ponds with picnic facilities. Permits are necessary and may be obtained at the tribal offices or the museum.

The feast day at Picuris is August 10, when the Corn Dance is performed at the San Lorenzo Fiesta. Photography, sketching, and videotaping are permitted for small fees; contact the governor's office at 587-2957.

TAOS

Few towns in the world have a setting as spectacular as this community of forty-five hundred. The towering Sangre de Cristo range, including New Mexico's tallest mountain, Wheeler Peak (elevation 13,161 feet), partially surrounds the town to the north and east. To the west and south, the Rio Grande Gorge, a gigantic tear in the earth 650 feet deep and 1200 feet wide, slices through the plains. The melding of sun, sky, mesas, mountains, and canyons constantly creates a sense of wonderment, so it's not surprising that some of America's greatest artists were inspired to settle here and capture the enchantment of this land on canvas.

Before the white man arrived, Indians had lived in the area for thousands of years; evidence suggests that human activity here may reach back to 3000 B.C. But these people were probably wandering bands of hunter-gatherers and true settlement did not begin until about 900 A.D., when the ancestors of present-day Taos Indians built pit houses. This form of shelter was highly vulnerable to attacks from Plains Indians, who raided the villages in search of food and slaves. To protect themselves, the Indians built the multi-storied Taos Pueblo around 1450, 42 years before Columbus sailed across the Atlantic.

Despite their fortifications, the people could not keep out the Spanish, who first arrived in 1540 and returned in 1598 to settle the region and to convert the Indians to Christianity. In 1617, Fray Pedro de Miranda established the first Spanish colony near Taos Pueblo and relations between the two peoples were peaceful until 1631, when a priest and two soldiers were killed. The first inkling of a revolt occurred in 1650, but the real revolution occurred thirty years later when the San Juan Indian named Popé led the Pueblo Revolt which drove all the surviving Spaniards down to El Paso del Norte.

The Legend of the Lost Aztec or Montezuma Mines originated about this time. Somewhere near Taos, the story went, were the mines that had produced the gold and silver comprising the treasure of Montezuma. Supposedly, the Aztec mines were discovered about 1598 and the early settlers utilized slave labor of Taos Pueblo people to produce millions of dollars worth of gold and silver. It should be noted that despite such legends, the first mining claim in New Mexico was not filed until 1685, and no significant Spanish mines were established until 1722, when Mina del Tiro was worked for lead near Cerrillos. Curiously, many popular history sources state that the use of slaves in these mines was a principal cause of the Pueblo Revolt, and that after the Spanish were driven out, the Taos Indians closed and concealed the mines — which, according to the mining history of New Mexico, did not exist.

In 1693, the Spaniards returned to Taos with a large army, but it took them five years to subdue Taos Pueblo completely. During the early 1700s, peace returned and the village became one of the most important trade centers in New Spain by holding what became known as the "Taos Trade Fairs." But Taos was still vulnerable to raids from the Navajos, Utes, and Comanches and in 1760, fifty women and children were captured before the Spanish soldiers retaliated by killing four hundred marauders.

During the early 1800s, Taos became the headquarters for many of the famous mountain men who trapped beaver and other fur-bearing animals in the surrounding mountains. The town became one of the most important markets for beaver pelts in North America, with trade growing from $15,000 in 1822 to $1.7 million in 1846. Perhaps the most famous of these mountain men was Kit Carson, who lived in Taos for forty years and became a famous scout and fighter against the Navajos.

But beavers were not the only treasure being discussed in Taos during this time. Matthew Field, a journalist who visited Taos, wrote that the Legend of the Montezuma Mines had been revived. Purportedly, the treasure from the mines was buried atop Taos Peak (now Pueblo Peak), but people who attempted to climb the mountain "immediately became lunatics and could never tell what they had seen." Field also reported that a Spaniard arrived from Mexico City and had climbed to the summit in search of the treasure. Some Taoseños accompanied him part of the way, but refused to join him at the top. The Spaniard called down to them that he had found "a magnificent cavern filled with gold and lit into the blaze of day with precious stones." But as fate would have it, the Spaniard was blown over a cliff by a gust of wind and the Taoseños scrambled back down the mountain in terror.

In 1846, the United States declared war on Mexico and the forces of General Stephen Kearny and Colonel Alexander Doniphan quickly drove all Mexican forces from New Mexico. However, they could not prevent a conspiracy between Mexican loyalists and the Indians at Taos Pueblo in northern New Mexico. On January 19, 1847, the conspiracy flared into a battle after several Indians were jailed in Taos. Angry Indians flooded into town and demanded the release of their people, and when their ultimatum was refused, the Indians stormed the house of Territorial Governor Charles Bent. He attempted to reason with the unruly mob, but they responded with violence. They scalped him alive, then shot and killed him and five other important citizens. After the killings, the Indians declared a fiesta, nailed Bent's scalp to a board, and displayed it during a torchlight procession through Taos.

The American military forces were not amused, and about five hundred U.S. Army soldiers and civilian volunteers mounted a punitive expedition to battle about 1500 revolutionaries. In a series of battles that included the artillery shelling of Taos Pueblo, the Americans won decisively, killing 150 Indians while losing only seven of their own men. The revolution was crushed and the law of the United States was established in New Mexico.

The following year, the Kerr brothers arrived in Taos and became the first artists to paint there. In 1880, Joseph Sharp, another artist, sketched in the area and he spread the word back east and in Europe about the beauty of New Mexico. In 1893, he met Ernest Blumenschein and Bert Phillips, two American artists, in Paris and persuaded them to visit the area. They were traveling in a horse-drawn wagon from Denver to Santa Fe when they broke a wagon wheel just north of Taos. By the time the wheel was repaired, the two artists had fallen in love with Taos and decided to stay there. In 1912, Blumenschein became one of six co-founders of the famous "Taos Society of Artists," whose purpose was to enable these artists to exhibit their work as a group across the country.

Thus Blumenschein and Phillips established what became known as the "Taos School" of artists, who relocated from the east and west coasts and settled in the town. The reputation of Taos as a center for the arts was guaranteed by the arrival of Mabel Dodge in·1917, a wealthy patroness of the arts, who attracted some of the most famous artists, photographers, and writers of the time to Taos. The luminaries included Andrew Dasburg, often called the dean of Taos artists, and Dorothy Brett, Oscar E. Berninghaus, Georgia O'Keefe, Ansel Adams, and D.H. Lawrence. Other gifted visual artists who came to Taos were Leon Gaspard, Nicolai Fechin, Marsden Hartley, John Marin, Paul Strand, and Laura Gilpin.

Today, Taos rivals Santa Fe as a center for creative activity and is filled with painters, photographers, sculptors, weavers, jewelers, potters, and writers. Many galleries have been established to trade in the creative arts, and tourists have followed as well. There are two tourist seasons in Taos: the summer, naturally, and the winter when skiers by the thousands invade the town because of nearby Taos Ski Valley, one of the best ski areas in the country.

★ ★
TOURIST INFORMATION

TAOS CHAMBER OF COMMERCE
Drawer I, Taos, NM 87571 (758-3873)

★ ★
HISTORIC SIGHTSEEING

TAOS PUEBLO
This pueblo looks much as it did in 1540, when Captain Alvarado, one of Coronado's officers, was the first European to visit the village. Despite raids from hostile Indians, revolts, and artillery shelling, Taos Pueblo has not only survived, it has managed to retain its culture and religion. The people here choose not to use electricity or indoor plumbing, yet they do not shut out the rest of the world and readily welcome visitors.

The architecture of the multi-storied buildings has long inspired artists and photographers, and because of its nomination by the World Heritage Convention, the pueblo has joined such monumental structures as the Taj Mahal, the Great Pyramids, and Machu Pichu as one of the most significant historical and cultural landmarks in the world.

The pueblo conducts a number of events throughout the year, including a traditional pow wow and arts and crafts fair, July 8–10, Corn Dances in June and July, and the Feast of San Geronimo on September 30, with dances, races, pole climbing, and an arts and crafts fair. It is located two miles north of the town of Taos, just off NM Hwy. 68.

There are a number of shops and studios at the pueblo. **Tony Reyna Indian Shop #1,** on Taos Pueblo Road (758-3835), carries jewelry, sculpture, pottery, and sand paintings. Also on the Taos Pueblo Road are **Native American Creations Guild** (758-2786), with basketry, beadwork, carvings, and shawls; and the award-winning sculpture found at **John Suazo Sculpture Studio** (758-9629).

At Taos Pueblo Plaza are: **Crucita's Indian Shop** (758-3576), with freshly baked Indian bread, jewelry, and beadwork; **Morning Talk Indian Show** (758-1429), offering blankets and paintings; and **Native Arts and Crafts** (758-9519), which sells necklaces, miniature churches, and clothing. There are a half dozen more shops in and around the plaza area.

Photography, sketching, and videotaping are permitted with fees, except in certain areas like the kivas, which are considered sacred. Permits are available from the pueblo offices, 758-9593.

MISSION OF ST. FRANCIS OF ASSISI
Located in the village of Ranchos de Taos, four miles south of town on NM Hwy. 68, this lovely structure—often simply called "the Ranchos church"—is one of the most photographed and painted churches in the world. The mission was started in 1710 and construction took forty-five years and tens of thousands of adobe bricks. It is one of the best examples of early Spanish Colonial mission architecture. The fortress-like mission, with walls four feet thick, has about a half-million dollars worth of paintings, statuary, and other art objects inside, some of which date back to the early 1600s.

In keeping with the New Mexico tradition of superstition, there is a "mystery painting" here, *The Shadow of the Cross,* by Henri Ault, which was first shown at the 1904 World's Fair in St. Louis.

In the daylight, the painting portrays the barefoot Christ, while in darkness the portrait becomes luminescent, outlining the figure while clouds over the left shoulder of Jesus seem to form a shadow of a cross. The mission is open to the public and donations are appreciated. For additional information, call 758-2754. Open Mon.–Fri. 9 a.m.–4 p.m., Sunday mass at 6:45 p.m. at convent chapel, visitors welcome.

THE PLAZA
Located in the center of Taos at Kit Carson Rd. and NM Hwy. 68, the Plaza is the place to begin the exploration of this historic town. Built sometime during the 1700s, the shape of the Plaza has remained the same, but none of the original buildings have survived. Originally, it consisted of single-story homes which faced into the plaza, with no windows or doors on the rear walls in order to protect the buildings from attacks by Navajos and Comanches.

During the early 1800s, the Plaza was the site of the Taos Trade Fairs and wagon trains from Chihuahua and Missouri sold their wares there. A series of fires, with the last ones in the early 1930s, destroyed most of the historic buildings. The west side of the Plaza is the oldest; the east side, including La Fonda Hotel, is the newest. The old jail is now a gallery and beauty salon, while the first gas station in Taos is now Ogelvie's Restaurant. Walking tours of the historic Plaza area depart daily from the Kit Carson House at 10 a.m., June through October. If you'd like a walking tour at another time of the year, make a reservation at 758-4020 one day in advance. Tours are $10 and include museum entry fees.

KIT CARSON MEMORIAL STATE PARK AND
KIT CARSON HOME AND MUSEUM
The small urban park, located just two blocks north of the Plaza, centers upon the graves of Kit Carson and his family. Facilities include picnic areas, grills, rest rooms, a walking path, basketball and tennis courts, and baseball diamonds. No camping is allowed.

The **Kit Carson Home and Museum,** located on E. Kit Carson Rd. about a block from the Plaza (758-4741) is one of three historic homes operated by the Kit Carson Memorial Foundation (and is a National Historic Landmark. Kit bought the house in 1843 as a wedding gift for his bride, Josefa Jaramillo. The Carsons lived in the home until their deaths in 1868.

The living room, bedroom, and kitchen are furnished as closely as possible to the way they were in the mid-1800s. The Carson Room contains exhibits pertaining to the career of Kit and the Early

American Room has old saddles, tools, maps, and firearms utilized by the family. The Spanish Room contains clothing of the era and the Indian Room displays artifacts used by the early Indians of the Taos Valley, some dating back to 3000 B.C. There is also a chapel and a patio containing an *horno*, or outdoor oven.

The Kit Carson House is open every day of the year from 9 a.m.– 5 p.m. daily, and a admission is $2 for adults, and $1.50 for children and seniors. A Taos Walking Tour is available from the Carson Memorial Foundation ($5).

GOVERNOR BENT HOUSE AND MUSEUM
The Bent House is located just north of the Plaza on Bent Street (758-2376). This is the home where the first New Mexico Territorial Governor, Charles Bent, was scalped and killed in 1847. His wife and children, however, escaped by digging a hole in the thick adobe walls with a fireplace poker. Both the hole and the poker have been preserved. Before his appointment as governor, Bent owned wagon trains and trading posts in Taos and Santa Fe and he traded goods with trappers and mountain men in return for animal pelts.

The museum and art gallery here display works by Charles Berninghaus (O.E. Berninghaus' son), Joseph H. Sharp, and other prominent Taos artists as well as artifacts of the period of Governor Bent's demise. The Bent House is open daily 10 to 5 with a small admission charge.

ERNEST L. BLUMENSCHEIN HOME
This beautiful, old (1790) adobe on 222 Ledoux Street (758-0330) was the home of the Blumenscheins from 1919 until 1962, when it was given to the Kit Carson Memorial Foundation for preservation as a memorial. It was designated as a National Historic Landmark in 1966 and today exhibits both the antiques and furnishings of the Blumenscheins as well as displays of Taos and Indian artists.

There is also a permanent display here of the effects of Leon Gaspard, a Russian artist who lived in Taos. The Blumenschein Home is open daily from 9 a.m.–5 p.m. except on holidays.

NICOLAI FECHIN HOME AND INSTITUTE
If ever there was a house that truly reflects the artistry of its owner, this is it. Nicolai Fechin, another renowned Russian artist, moved into this adobe in 1927 and designed and carved the doors, vigas, cabinets, and furniture in it during the late afternoons when natural light filtering through his skylight was too weak to paint by.

The original dining room in the Fechin Home is now a showplace for Fechin's own collection of Far Eastern paintings and Russian icons. Since Fechin disliked artists' houses that looked like museums, his wall and trim effects, furniture placement, and picture-hanging are very un-museum-like.

The Fechin Institute follows that spirit by offering a program of exhibitions, concerts, and summer art workshops in addition to annual exhibitions of Fechin's work. The Fechin Home is located at 227 Paseo del Pueblo Norte, on the north side of Kit Carson Park and can be contacted at 758-1710. Visitors are welcome Wed.–Sun. 1 p.m.–5 p.m., Memorial Day through first week of October, and by appointment during the winter.

Nicolai Fechin advised, "Take care to keep your mind open to all that is wondrous. To love art is necessary, but to become its slave is bad, since you lose your judgment. . . . Art enclosed in itself dies."

LA HACIENDA DE DON ANTONIO SEVERINO MARTINEZ
Located along the banks of the Rio Pueblo two and one half miles from town on Lower Ranchitos Road, this fortress-like building is another historic structure operated by the Kit Carson Foundation (758-1000) and is the last-preserved Spanish hacienda in New Mexico.

The sprawling 21-room house with two placitas is representative of the Spanish Colonial Period and is built in a similar fashion to the original Taos Plaza for a good reason: to fend off attacks by hostile Navajo and Plains Indians. The Hacienda holds an annual trade fair in the fall which re-creates those held in the old Taos Plaza.

Exhibits at Martinez Hacienda tell the story of the government, transportation, and trade in Taos between the years of 1598–1821, with particular emphasis on the family which owned the residence. Don Antonio Martinez was *alcalde* ("mayor" or "magistrate") of Taos and owned caravans of *carretas* ("carts") and pack mules used in the trade between Taos, Santa Fe, El Paso del Norte, and Chihuahua.

The Martinez Hacienda conducts a Spanish Arts Festival in May or June (date varies) where arts and crafts may be purchased and where traditional weavers, *santeros*, and potters give demonstrations. It is open daily from 9 a.m.–4 p.m. for a small admission charge.

HARWOOD FOUNDATION
The public library of Taos and a museum is housed in this nineteenth-century pueblo-like complex at 238 Ledoux Street

(758-3063). At the library is a research room on the Southwest and a collection of books by and about D.H. Lawrence, who lived in Taos for three periods of six to seven months each between 1922 and 1925.

On display in the museum are works by legendary Taos artists Ernest Blumenschein, Bert Phillips, Andrew Dasburg, and Dorothy Brett. Other items of interest include a *santo* collection featuring about eighty *retablos*, religious paintings on wood, and a collection of photographic art that includes many images of early Taos and the surrounding area. Admission is free and the museum is open Mon.–Sat. 10 a.m.–5 p.m., until 8 p.m. on Monday and Thursday evenings.

MILLICENT ROGERS MUSEUM

Oil heiress Millicent Rogers was a contemporary of Mabel Dodge Luhan and acquired one of the finest collections of Southwestern pottery, textiles, basketry, and jewelry in the world. After her death, family members founded the museum in 1953 and moved to its present location, the former ranch of Claude J.K. Anderson, in 1968. The museum is four miles north of Taos, just off NM Hwy. 522 (758-2462).

The museum's displays of Southwestern Native American art include Navajo and Pueblo jewelry, kachina dolls from Hopi and Zuni, paintings from Rio Grande pueblos, and baskets from a wide variety of tribes. The Maria Martinez Family Collection shows an excellent selection of pottery and family memorabilia from the internationally famous potter of San Ildefonso Pueblo.

The Hispanic Collection displays historic *santos*, furniture, weavings, tinwork, and embroidery, along with contemporary painting, sculpture, and weaving. The museum also displays an interesting collection of agricultural implements, domestic utensils, and craftsman's tools from the Colonial era.

The Millicent Rogers Museum is open 9 a.m. to 5 p.m. daily. Admission is $3 for adults and $1 for children six to sixteen and for seniors.

★ ★
GALLERIES

As with Santa Fe, there are more galleries in Taos than can be adequately covered here, so pick up a copy of the Taos section of *The Collector's Guide*, published by Wingspread Communications, P.O. Box 13566-T, Albuquerque, NM 87192 (292-7537). Below is a brief overview of the more prominent galleries.

R. B. Ravens, Ranchos Plaza next to the Mission of St. Francis of Assisi, in Ranchos de Taos (758-7322), offers museum-quality art and Southwestern artifacts such as Navajo and Hispanic textiles.

Stewart's Fine Art, 102 South Plaza (758-0049), first building on right on E. Kit Carson Rd., has paintings by the Taos Founders, second- and third-era Taos artists, and the work of American impressionists and Western realists.

The Mission Gallery, 138 E. Kit Carson Rd. (758-2861), is located in the old Joseph Sharp House and features works by Andrew Dasburg and other great Taos artists.

Stables Art Center, 133 Paseo del Pueblo Norte (758-2052), is the home of the Taos Art Association and presents the work of Taos community artists in a series of exhibitions, as well as an art film series at the Taos Community Auditorium. Open 10 a.m.–5 p.m. Mon.–Sat., and noon–5 p.m. on Sunday.

Established in 1979, **The Variant Gallery,** 135 N. Plaza on the northwest corner of the Plaza (758-4949), represents contemporary and traditional paintings, sculpture, ceramics, glassware, and woodworks.

Burke Armstrong Fine Art, upstairs in the North Plaza Art Center (758-9016), carries works by historic and present-day Taos artists, School of Taos painting by such notables as Dorothy Brett, sculpture, and furniture.

Desurmont-Ellis Gallery, also in the North Plaza Art Center (758-3299), specializes in contemporary art.

E.S. Lawrence Gallery, 132 E. Kit Carson Rd. (758-8229), has one of the largest collections of landscapes by various artists of any gallery in Taos.

El Taller Taos Gallery, 119 A E. Kit Carson Rd. across the street from E.S. Lawrence Gallery (758-4887), specializes in the work of popular Southwestern artist Amado Peña and also carries contemporary sculpture, jewelry, graphics, and weavings by other artists.

Navajo Gallery, 210 Ledoux Street (758-3250 or 776-8313), features the paintings of Navajo women by noted Taos resident R. C. Gorman, who owns this gallery and one by the same name at 323 Romero NW in Old Town, Albuquerque.

There are two arts festivals in Taos. **Taos Spring Arts Celebration** (758-0516), held during the last week of May through mid-June, presents visual, literary, and performing arts at a variety of locations. The **Taos Arts Festival** (758-3873 or 1-800-732-8267), in the last week of September and first week of October, features an arts and crafts fair on the Plaza, special exhibits at local museums and galleries, plus concerts, dances, and special tours.

★ ★
LODGING

Of all the cities and towns in New Mexico, Taos has the best collection of interesting places to stay, including the largest selection of historic houses and bed and breakfasts.

Kachina Lodge, a Best Western motel on 4013 Paseo del Pueblo Norte (758-2275), is set among the trees and has 122 rooms, a dining room, coffee shop,lounge, art gallery, and outdoor pool. The **Cabaret Lounge** here books country/western, rock, rhythm and blues, and reggae groups.

Hotel La Fonda de Taos, on the south side of the Plaza (758-2211), is a family-owned and operated hotel in the European tradition. The hotel features a charming lobby, 24 rooms, three suites, and a private exhibit of the once-controversial paintings of D.H. Lawrence.

Quail Ridge Inn, take NM Hwy. 522 north, turn right one mile on Taos Ski Valley Rd. (776-2211 or 1-800-624-4448), was previously known as a tennis ranch and still offers six courts outside and two inside. There are 110 rooms and suites here with private balconies or patios and fireplaces in all units and full kitchens in some. A giant heated pool, saunas, hot tubs, and four racquetball courts complete the amenities, and the inn also has a restaurant and lounge.

Built in 1929, the **Sagebrush Inn,** located three miles south of town off NM Hwy. 68 on S. Santa Fe Rd. (758-2254 and 1-800-428-3626), is one of the most beautiful inns in the Southwest. The mission-pueblo architecture has graceful portals, outdoor patios, 52 classic rooms, and 41 suites. Amenities include a heated pool, tennis courts, fireplaces in rooms, and furnishings that include Navajo rugs, rare pottery, antiques and Southwestern art. Georgia O'Keefe once lived and painted in a room on the third story of the Sagebrush. The lounge, complete with huge fireplace, is one of the few places in town that could be called a nightclub, and offers a wide variety of entertainment from country-western acts to reggae groups.

San Geronimo Lodge, on Witt Rd. just off E. Kit Carson (758-7117), is situated on four secluded, wooded acres and has nineteen guest rooms plus a covered and heated pool, hot tubs, saunas, and a library. The lodge was built in 1880 and the Witt family added on in 1925 to start the lodge, which soon became a popular meeting place for locals.

The Taos Inn, 125 Paseo del Pueblo Norte (758-2233 or 1-800-TAOS-INN), is a National Historic Landmark with a beautiful lobby and Doc Martin's restaurant (see Dining, below). Its 40 rooms have Taos furniture, handloomed Indian bedspreads, and fireplaces. Other amenities include the Adobe Bar, a library, a greenhouse-jacuzzi room, and a swimming pool.

Historic houses and bed and breakfasts abound in the Taos area. **The Andrew Dasburg House and Studio,** on NM Hwy. 518 four miles south of the Plaza (758-2031), is a magnificent two-hundred-year-old adobe hacienda that was the home and studio of famed painter Andrew Dasburg for 45 years. The house has three bedrooms with fireplaces, a sauna and hot tub, full kitchen, and sleeps eight. A separate studio with living room and kitchen sleeps four. Robert Redford is among the luminaries who have stayed at the Dasburg House. For information write P.O. Box 1813, Taos, NM 87571.

Mabel Dodge Luhan House, E. Kit Carson Rd. (758-9456), is a bed and breakfast with 18 rooms where D.H. Lawrence and other notables have stayed.

La Posada de Taos, two blocks from the Plaza (758-8164), is a bed and breakfast inn with five guest units featuring tiled baths and unique furnishings. Other recommended bed and breakfast inns are **American Artists Gallery House,** P.O. Box 584, Taos, NM 87571 (758-4446), **Two Pipe,** P.O. Box 52, Talpa Rt. (758-4770), **Taos Mountain Outfitters** (758-9292), **Casa Europa Inn and Gallery,** P.O. Box 157, Taos, NM 87571 (758-9798), **Harrison's,** P.O. Box 242, Taos, NM 87571 (758-2630), **Hacienda del Sol,** P.O. Box 177, Taos, NM 87571 (758-0287), and **El Rincon,** 114 E. Kit Carson, Taos, NM 87571 (758-4874).

For additional lodging, see **Taos Ski Valley.**

★ ★
ECLECTIC LODGING NEAR TAOS

During the past decade, there has been an enormous increase in the number of interesting places to stay in Taos. These include: **San Geronimo Lodge,** an adobe lodge in the country, Kit Carson Road (800-828-8267); **Cimarroncita Ranch,** rustic bunkhouse cabins and lodges, Ute Park (376-2376); **Casa de Milagras,** historic adobe house, Kit Carson Road (800-243-9334); **El Monte Lodge,** quaint adobe rooms, Kit Carson Road (800-828-8267); **Chinguague Compound,** guesthouses, San Juan Pueblo (852-2194); **Lara Creek Ranch,** a retreat for women, in La Jara (289-3300); **Ojo**

Caliente Mineral Springs, hot springs and hotel, in Ojo Caliente (583-2233); **The Brooks Street Inn,** near the Plaza (758-1489); **Taos Mountain Lodge,** skiing suites, Taos Ski Valley (776-2229); **The Bed and Breakfast Inn,** adobe estate, Liebert St. (758-7477); **Hondo Lodge,** slope-side at the Ski Valley (776-2277); **Taos Hacienda Inn,** a National Historic Register inn in a park (800-530-3040); **Field's Cottages,** spacious homes by the day or week on the Little Rio Grande (758-9240); **Adobe Inn of Taos,** a century-old hacienda one block from the Plaza (758-1100); **Branham Ranch,** historic ranch house for retreats in San Cristobal (776-2622); and **Adobe & Pines,** a sprawling adobe B&B near Ranchos de Taos (800-723-8267).

DINING

Although there are far fewer restaurants in Taos than in Santa Fe, the quality of these establishments is generally high and there's enough variation among them so that the visitor rarely needs to (but may well want to) dine at the same restaurant twice during a vacation here.

NEW MEXICAN

For classic northern New Mexican cuisine, plus some classic Latin American dishes, the **Chile Connection** is an excellent choice. Located on the Ski Valley Rd. just north of town (776-8787), Richard Vick's restaurant is devoted (as the name implies) to the chile pepper in all its variations. Particularly recommended are the *chiles rellenos* and the *pollo borracho,* a "drunken chicken" marinated in tequila, fruit juices, and hot chiles, then grilled. **Casa de Valdez,** two miles south of the Plaza on S. Santa Fe and Estes Rd. (758-8777), combines New Mexican cuisine with char-broiled steaks and barbecued beef, chicken, and ribs. Open for lunch and dinner, but closed Wednesday.

CONTINENTAL AND AMERICAN

Doc Martin's, at the historic Taos Inn on N. Pueblo Rd. near the Plaza (758-1977), has a wine list so extensive that the *Wine Specta-*

tor magazine named it among the most outstanding wine lists in the world. Also special at Doc Martin's are the housemade bread, salsa, pastries, and ice cream. The entrées are a diverse selection of New Mexican, continental, seafood, and New American specialties. (Open daily for breakfast, lunch, and dinner. Reservations recommended. **The Stakeout**, with a wonderful view of the Rio Grande Gorge, is located eight miles south of Taos just off NM Hwy. 68 (758-2042) in an old, antique-filled adobe house nestled in the foothills of the Sangre de Cristo range. Among the favorite dishes here are grilled Long Island duck, and Alaskan king crab legs. Rack of lamb and a variety of grilled meats and seafood are also excellent. Reservations required dinner only 5 p.m.–10 p.m., 7 nights.

Chef Carlo Gislimberti of **Villa Fontana,** State Hwy. 522, north of town (758-5808) collects and prepares more than seventy different varieties of wild mushrooms that grow in the mountains surrounding his restaurant. Gislimberti, a fungi expert from Merano, Italy, serves northern Italian cuisine liberally dressed with mushrooms, plus seasonal game entrees such as venison, pheasant, and duck. Reservations required, dinner only, 6 p.m.–9 p.m. At the **Brett House** at the intersection of NM Hwy. 68 and Ski Valley Rd. (776-8545), chef/owner Chuck Lamendola serves both American and international specialties prepared entirely with fresh ingredients at his establishment, which is located in the historic home of legendary Taos artist and personality Dorothy Brett. Open for lunch July and Aug., & dinner all year Tues.–Sun., closed Monday. Reservations recommended. Also recommended is **Carl's French Quarter** at the Quail Ridge Inn on Ski Valley Road (776-8319). As the name implies, the restaurant serves Creole and Cajun specialties, as well as fresh seafood, prime steaks, and various continental specialties.

VARIOUS CUISINES

The **Apple Tree Restaurant,** 26 Bent Street (758-1900), serves some New Mexican dishes, as well as pasta, soups, and fresh seafood. Open daily for lunch and dinner. Reservations recommended. **Kitchen** on N. Pueblo Rd. (758-4178) is a coffee shop and bakery justly famous for its breakfasts. Open daily. **Carl's Deli** in Pueblo Allegre Mall (776-8319) has an unlikely but good combination of deli food and Creole/Cajun dishes.

SHOPPING

As is often true of towns where tourism forms a large part of the income base, Taos has an eclectic collection of shops. Many of them reflect the crafts and products of northern New Mexico while others are totally unexpected because they feature imports from many foreign countries.

CRAFTS AND IMPORTS

The oldest Indian arts shop on the Plaza is the **Don Fernando Curio and Gift Shop** (758-3791), which specializes in sculpture, carvings, sand paintings, pottery, and kachinas. **The Market,** 125 Kit Carson Rd. (758-3195), represents Southwestern contemporary craftsmen and offers stoneware, jewelry, crafts, and paintings by internationally known artist Becky Covalt. **Taos Trading Company,** North Plaza (758-3012), has every conceivable craft and souvenir item. At the **Carson House Shop** (117 E. Kit Carson Rd.) there are four rooms filled with a wide selection of crafts ranging from affordable gifts to collectable Indian and folk art. **Tawa,** 108 B Kit Carson Rd (758-4025), means "four" in the Quecha language and this shop specializes in these four categories from around the world: clothing, jewelry, recordings, and folk arts/crafts, including trade beads and masks.

INTERIOR DESIGN

The **Partridge Company,** 131 Bent Street (758-1225), is a charming shop with a nice selection of Southwestern furniture and rugs, plus gifts and a Christmas shop. **Casa Crafts,** on Bent Street (758-8102), sells Navajo and Zapotec Indian rugs, dhurries, pillows, and bedspreads. **La Unica Cosa,** 117 Paseo del Pueblo Norte (758-3065), has a nice collection of Zapotec Indian art as well as handwoven rugs and wall hangings. **Country Furnishings of Taos,** Paseo del Pueblo Norte near the Kachina Lodge (758-4633), sells locally crafted and painted furniture—each piece is unique. Also accessories and gifts. **Coyote Pottery** in Ranchos de Taos (758-3030) is another place which offers chile pepper items including *ristras*, imported pottery, and Zapotec rugs.

CLOTHING AND JEWELRY

One of the most famous clothing operations in Taos is **Overland Sheepskin Company,** Paseo del Pueblo Norte, three miles north of the Plaza (758-8820). Jim and Leslie Leahy oversee an operation that produces some of the finest sheepskin coats and other items in the country. They even have their own flock of sheep. **Martha of Taos,** 202 Paseo del Pueblo Norte (758-3102), has been offering original designs since 1955. Among her designs are hand-pleated calico broomstick skirts and Navajo dresses complete with silver accents. Striking clothing, as well as fine Oriental carpets from Turkey and Afghanistan, can be found at **Afghan Caravan,** 101A Canta Plaza (758-4161). **From the Andes,** on Taos Plaza (758-0485), features fine South American alpaca sweaters and weavings, plus hats, bags, dolls, gloves, and wall hangings. **Taos Mountain Outfitters,** on South Plaza (758-9292), carries the clothing necessary to explore the nearby wilderness and also rents mountain bikes.

BOOKS AND MAPS

The best and most complete book shop in town is **Taos Book Shop** on Kit Carson Rd. about a block from the Plaza (758-3733). This shop specializes in Southwestern titles, art books, and rare books including those by D.H. Lawrence. This store also offers an excellent selection of contemporary fiction and nonfiction titles. **Ten Directions Books,** 228C Paseo del Pueblo Norte (758-2725), specializes in used, rare, and out-of-print books, as well as Southwestern titles. **George Robinson's Old Prints and Maps,** Dunn House, Bent Street (758-2278), has a wide selection of books and prints from the sixteenth to nineteenth centuries.

★ ★
OUTDOOR FUN

Because of its proximity to the mountains and the Rio Grande, Taos is justly famous for a wide variety of outdoor activities including skiing, hunting, fishing, backpacking, river running, hiking, and mountain climbing.

TAOS SKI VALLEY
During the winter, there is a second Taos, a complete village filled with every amenity imaginable for both sportsmen and vacation-

ers. It is, of course, **Taos Ski Valley,** a world-class facility which has been described as "one of the most interesting ski areas in the world, let alone in the Rocky Mountains."

Taos Ski Valley was founded in 1955 by the late Ernie Blake, who had searched the southern Rockies for an ideal ski resort location. His dedication to personal attention and outstanding skier services has proven highly successful. He once stated: "If you give people the best you possibly can, they'll keep coming back."

This ski area has the most challenging slopes in New Mexico but also maintains beginner and intermediate runs. The 71 trails are served by seven chairlifts and two surface lifts, and the total vertical drop for skiing is about three thousand feet — starting from an altitude of 11,800 feet. The slopes here average about 317 inches of snow per year.

On-slope lodging is provided by five lodges and eight condo-cabin operations, enough to provide accommodations for 1171 skiers. There is a ski school here, as well as a huge rental shop, a repair shop, sportswear shop, and pro shop. Numerous restaurants, lounges, and snack bars are located in the Ski Valley.

Taos Ski Valley is located nineteen miles northeast of Taos via NM Hwys. 522 and 150. For additional information and brochures on skiing, lodging, and dining at Taos Ski Valley, call 776-2233 or 1-800-992-SNOW.

SIPAPU

Located 25 miles south of Taos via NM Hwys. 68 and 518, Sipapu is neither as popular nor as spectacular as Taos Ski Valley, but the skiing is quite fine. It offers eighteen trails, two surface lifts, and a chair lift, and averages 110 inches of snow a year. There is on-slope lodging for 186 skiers, a restaurant, and a snack bar. The elevation varies from 9100 to 8200 feet. For more information or reservations at Sipapu, call 587-2240.

RIO GRANDE GORGE STATE PARK

Was this thousand-foot-wide, 650 foot-deep chasm formed by erosion, like the Grand Canyon, or by volcanic activity which ripped the earth apart into a rift valley? The answer is: both. The Rio Grande Gorge is actually a smaller segment of the Rio Grande Rift Valley, which pre-dates the river.

The precise sequence of events is this: more than four million years ago, when New Mexico was highly active volcanically, a huge rift valley opened for nearly the entire length of the state. A layer of gravel and other sediment nearly two miles deep washed into this rift, and further volcanic activity near what is now Taos covered the sediment with volcanic basalt a thousand feet deep.

About 2.4 to 2.8 million years ago, the Rio Grande formed and began cutting though the basalt.

So, although the river did erode the basalt atop the gravel in northern New Mexico, it runs on top of the existing sediment for the rest of its course through the state, and therefore did not "carve" Rio Grande Valley as the Colorado River carved the Grand Canyon. As geologist Vincent Kelley put it: "Instead of the Rio Grande's cutting a valley, it actually has endeavored to fill up a gigantic cave-in of the earth's crust. Imagine what this area would have been like if it had not been filled by sediment brought in by the Rio Grande and its tributaries; the trough would have been larger and more desolate than the Dead Sea!"

Visitors can walk across the Rio Grande Gorge Bridge on US Hwy. 64 north of Taos, but acrophobics should be warned that not only is the view dizzying, the bridge vibrates and sways, especially when large trucks cross it. The trout fishing is superb on the river below, but access is the main problem. There are several camping and picnicking sites accessible on the southern end of the gorge, off NM Hwy. 68 south of Taos, and it is possible to hike upstream to the best fishing spots. Some intrepid adventurers actually climb down the steep slopes of the gorge to reach the river, but such dedication to fishing is not advised.

WILD RIVERS NATIONAL RECREATION AREA
From the Rio Grande Gorge Bridge north to the Colorado border, the Rio Grande is a federally protected wild and scenic river—no dams or development allowed. Near Questa, at the confluence of the Rio Grande and the Red River, the region is now known as the **Wild Rivers Recreation Area** and is administered by the Bureau of Land Management.

Indeed, the area is quite wild and scenic. Twelve miles of trails wander amidst tall ponderosa pines and past ancient Indian petroglyphs and on down to the Rio Grande. Just below the confluence of the rivers, the fishing is particularly good for German brown trout and northern pike.

To reach the Wild Rivers National Recreation Area, drive north on NM Hwy. 522 to Cerro and follow the signs. For more information, call the Bureau of Land Management at 758-8851.

CARSON NATIONAL FOREST AND
WHEELER PEAK WILDERNESS
Approximately 1.5 million acres of Carson National Forest lie within or are adjacent to Taos County, with about 85,000 of those acres designated as wilderness. Throughout the national forest there are

campgrounds and hiking trails of various difficulty. At **El Nogal Campground**, just east of Taos on US Hwy. 64, the El Nogal Nature Trail is an easy one-mile loop along the Rio Fernando. Also starting from this campground are two other more strenuous trails, Devisadero Loop and the South Boundary Trail, which climbs to an elevation of 10,363 feet.

Along Ski Valley Road are several trails that lead to the tops of Gallena and Lobo Peaks, elevation 11,000 to 12,000 feet. The Wheeler Peak Trail, which begins at the upper parking area of Taos Ski Valley, leads to the top of Wheeler Peak, highest point in the state, and to the spectacular views from the Wheeler Peak Wilderness Area. Of course, hikers should be properly equipped before venturing into the wilderness.

Other campgrounds near Taos include **La Vinateria, Las Petacas, Capulin,** and **Taos Wagons West,** all within twelve miles of town on US Hwy. 64 east; **Lower Hondo Canyon, Cuchilla,** and **Ledoux,** all on Ski Valley Road; and **Rio Grande Gorge State Park,** south of Taos on NM Hwy. 68 at Pilar.

For more information, call the Carson National Forest headquarters at 758-6200.

TOURS AND ADVENTURES

There are quite a few companies that specialize in assisting the visitor in the exploration of the great outdoors around Taos. **Central Reservations,** P.O. Box 1713, Taos, NM 87571 (758-9767), assists in securing accommodations. Sightseeing tours and general shuttle transportation are provided by **Pride of Taos,** Box 5271, Taos, NM 87571 (758-8340). **Rio Grande Rapid Transit,** P.O. Box A, Pilar, NM 87571 (758-9700 or 1-800-545-4020), specializes in whitewater rafting, scenic floats, and funyak (two-man inflatable canoe) tours. Two other rafting operations are **Far Flung Adventures,** P.O. Box 707, El Prado, NM 87529 (758-2628 in summer, 800-359-2627 in winter) and **Sierra Outfitters,** P.O. Box 2756, Taos, NM 87571 (758-9556). **Los Rios Anglers,** P.O. Box 4006, Taos, NM 87571 (758-2798), offers a complete fishing program including float trips, wading trips, and can arrange pack trips of one to ten days duration.

RED RIVER

Here is a tourist town pure and simple. Located on NM Hwy. 38 about 35 miles from Taos, Red River caters mostly to Texas families and combines skiing, fishing, and other outdoor activities with an Old West atmosphere complete with melodramas, staged shootouts, and square dances. The resident population of 350 swells during the two vacation seasons, winter and summer, when thousands of vistors determined to have fun descend upon the town.

It wasn't always this way for Red River. Mountain men trapped beaver and ermine in the area's mountains during the early 1800s and they were followed by prospectors who worked claims at nearby Elizabethtown in the 1860s. Red River became a typical boom town as gold, silver, and copper mines operated in the area until 1925. By 1905, Red River had a population of three thousand served by fifteen saloons, a bustling red-light district, four hotels, and two newspapers. But when the mines played out, Red River nearly became a ghost town.

It was saved by another mineral find. Molybdenum was discovered in the lower Red River canyon in 1901 and the first "moly mill" was built in 1921 to mine this metal, which is used to strengthen steel. In the late 1920s and early 1930s, Red River was designated a "mountain playground" by tourists escaping the midwest "dustbowl." In 1928, the first tourist cabins were built on the site which is now the Riverside Lodge and during the years that followed, more lodges, cabins, hotels, and restaurants were constructed to meet the tourist demand.

Because of the proliferation of lodges, shops, and restaurants, it is easy to miss Red River's historic buildings, all of which are in the National Register of Historic Places. The **Red School House,** on E. High Street, was built in 1915. Other interesting buildings include **Pierce-Fuller House** on W. High Street, **Brigham J. Young House** on E. Main Street, and the **Sylvester Mallette Cabin** on River Street.

★ ★
TOURIST INFORMATION

RED RIVER CHAMBER OF COMMERCE
P.O. Box 870, Red River, NM 87558 (800-348-6444)

★ ★
THE GREAT OUTDOORS

Red River Ski Area has the most extensive snow-making equipment in the state, and is able to cover eighty per cent of the slopes with man-made snow, which means that it is often the first ski area to open in New Mexico. The ski area has 41 trails served by two tows and four chair lifts. Some of the trails descend right into town. There are on-slope bars and restaurants, and many lodges adjacent to the ski area. The ski area is open Thanksgiving Day until Easter depending on snowfall. For more information on Red River Ski Area, call 754-2382 or 800-348-6444 or write P.O. Box 900, Red River, NM 87558.

Additional skiing is available at **Ski Rio,** the newest ski resort in New Mexico, located forty-four miles north of Red River via NM Hwy. 38, right on NM Hwy. 522, and right on NM Hwy. 196. This ski area has 64 trails that descend from a bowl called Cinnamon Bear, two tows, three chair lifts, and an on-slope bar and restaurant. The area gets 270 inches of snowfall a year (compared to Red River's 175) and has accommodations for 400 skiers. For more information, call 586-1240.

Enchanted Forest Cross Country Ski Area, located in Bobcat Pass three miles east of town on NM Hwy. 38 (754-2374), has a scenic overlook and a series of trails ranging from easy to most difficult. Its six hundred acres and twelve miles of trails offer some of most spectacular views in Red River. **Snowmobiling** is one of the fastest-growing winter sports and several rental operations on Main Street can provide the equipment and route information, including **Red Dawg Snowmobiles** (754-2721), and **Roadrunner Snowmobiles** (754-6649).

Fishing is excellent along the Red River and its various tributaries, especially near Columbine Creek. There are numerous fishing spots near the campgrounds along Red River between Questa and Red River via NM Hwy. 38. The **Red River Fish Hatchery** (586-0222), located sixteen miles west of Red River on NM Hwy. 38, is the state's largest hatchery, and visitors are always welcome.

Hiking is always popular in Red River, and trail maps are available at the Chamber of Commerce office, downtown at Main Street and Independence Trail (754-2366). The **Red River Chairlift** is an aerial tramway on Pioneer Road (754-2382) that carries sightseers high up the nearby slopes for hikes and nature walks. It runs Memorial Day to Labor Day.

Tours and Trips are conducted by several area guides, including **Blue Skies Outfitters,** P.O. Box 385, Red River, NM 87558

(754-2518), who specializes in pack trips, elk hunts, and fishing trips; **Mountain Top Recreation,** P.O. Box 459, Red River, NM 87558 (754-6402), which also rents four-wheelers, mopeds, and trail bikes in summer, snowmobiles in winter; **Red River Sled Shed,** P.O. Box 217, Red River, NM 87558 (754-6370), which specializes in guided snowmobile tours; and various lodges which offer guide services and rentals.

★ ★
LODGING

There are so many lodges, condominiums, hotels, and cabins in Red River that it would take a separate book just to list them all. The easiest way to decide where to stay is to call **Resort Reservations,** P.O. Box 593, Red River, NM 87558 (754-6415 or 1-800-545-6915), and describe to them your ideal accommodations and price range. A postcard request to the Red River Chamber of Commerce, Box 868, Red River, NM 87558, will bring a deluge of brochures describing the various lodges. Here is just a sampling of recommended accommodations.

Auslander Condominiums (754-2311) on Pioneer Road sits at the foot of the ski area and offers completely furnished apartments. There is a clubhouse here with indoor pool and saunas. **Edelweiss Condominiums** (754-2942 or 1-800-445-6077), at Malette and High Streets, has two-bedroom apartments, each with a kitchen and fireplace, plus a heated outdoor pool. **Eisenhut Condominiums** (754-2326 or 1-800-222-EHUT) on Mallette Trail consists of 26 three- and four-bedroom apartments located three blocks from the ski area. Each apartment has its own fireplace, and the Eisenhut has a heated outdoor pool. **Lifts West Condominium Hotel** (754-2778 or 1-800-221-1859) on Main Street claims that its three-story lobby is "the most dramatic public space in northern New Mexico." Since no one in Red River would ever exaggerate, we must believe them. This hotel is quite nice, perhaps the fanciest hostelry in Red River, and it features apartments with balconies, fireplaces, and kitchens. The complex includes underground parking, a bank, ski rentals, shops, a restaurant, and a bar. Other recommended lodging on Main Street includes **Riverside Lodge and Cabins** (754-2252 or 1-800-432-9999), **Red River Inn** (754-2930), **Redwood Lodge** (754-2951), **Ponderosa Lodge** (754-2988 or 1-800-336-RSVP), and **Bitter Creek Guest Ranch and Stables** (754-2587), which features its own private trout lake.

DINING AND ENTERTAINMENT

Red River's restaurants feature mostly steaks and New Mexican specialties. Recommended are **Brett's Homestead Steakhouse** (754-6136) on Main Street, offering prime steaks and piñon trout; open 5 p.m.–10 p.m. daily except closed during April, May, the last 2 weeks in Oct., and the first 2 weeks in Nov. **Texas Red's Steakhouse** (754-2964) on Main Street, specializing in steaks and smoked pork chops. Open 5 p.m.–9 p.m. seven nights a week.

The **Mine Shaft Theater** at the Red River Inn on Main Street presents a popular melodrama performance during the summer on Wednesday, Thursday, Saturday, and Sunday evenings at 8 p.m. Country-and-western groups play the **Alpine Lodge** on Main Street (754-2952).

SPECIAL EVENTS

The town of Red River has cleverly planned a series of interesting events to fill the entire calendar. **Winter Carnival,** in January, offers dogsled and snowmobile races. February features **Mardi Gras in the Mountains** and March is the time for **Spring Break Bash.** Don't miss the **Easter Egg Scramble** in April or the **motorcycle rally** over Memorial Day Weekend in May. June is the time for **Michael Martin Murphey's Westfest,** with art and music. The **Fourth of July celebration** in Red River is gigantic, while August is rather calm, offering a mere **4-H Horse Show.** But the action picks up in September with the **Top of the World Bike Race** and the **Enchanted Circle Bike Tour** (over 1,000 bicyclists compete). In late September and early October is **Aspencade,** which celebrates the spectacular colors of autumn. Christmas in November features the lighting of the Christmas tree combined with square dancing. In December, of course, Red River goes nuts with Christmas.

EAGLE NEST AND ANGEL FIRE

East and south of Red River along NM Hwy. 38 and US Hwy. 64 are two more resort areas with many attractions. In fact, the route from Taos to Questa to Red River to Eagle Nest to Angel Fire and back to Taos has been dubbed "The Enchanted Circle" because of the spectacular scenery and nature-oriented activities which abound along the route.

Eagle Nest was so named because of the eagles that nested along the banks of the Cimmaron River in the Moreno Valley. In 1916, two men from Iowa, Frank and Charles Springer, began work on a dam near the head of the river in order to create a reservoir. By 1918, the dam was completed and Eagle Nest Lake was formed. However, the dream of a lake providing hydroelectric power and irrigation water was never fully realized. Instead, 1200-acre Eagle Nest Lake became more important as a fishing lake, which in turn created the recreational community of Eagle Nest.

The lake is stocked regularly with Kokanee salmon and three kinds of trout: rainbow, cutthroat, and lake. In addition to fishing and fishing contests, this lake is the site of boat rides, windsurfing regattas, and sailing.

★ ★
TOURIST INFORMATION

EAGLE NEST CHAMBER OF COMMERCE
P.O. Box 322, Eagle Nest, NM 87718 (377-2420)

EAGLE NEST FACILITIES AND ATTRACTIONS
Elizabethtown, five miles north on NM Hwy. 38, is a ghost town that was originally called Virginia City. In 1866, a gold strike near-by cause the expansion of Elizabethtown to the point where it became the first county seat of Colfax County. By 1870 the town had five stores, two hotels and seven saloons and the population soon swelled to six thousand. Between 1866 and 1902, $6 million worth of gold had been mined, but soon the lodes played out and a fire destroyed the business district in 1903. Today only the walls of the old Mutz Hotel are standing.

Laguna Vista Lodge (572-8500 or 1-800-821-2093), located on US Hwy. 64 in the center of town, is the nicest place to stay. It offers satellite TV, a restaurant and deli, and a saloon with live entertainment. **Horseshoe Motel and Cabins** (377-6961) on US Hwy. 64 is a motel-and-cabins establishment complete with a bunk-bed dorm for large groups of kids. Nearby is the **New Eagle Nest Marina** (377-6941) with rental boats and a tackle shop. **Mickey's Boat Rentals** (377-2501) on US Hwy. 64 east of town has bait and tackle in addition to rentals.

Tour Guides include **Eagle Nest Outfitters,** P.O. Box 66, 87718 (377-6941), **The Fish Eagle,** P.O. Box 211, Eagle Nest, NM 87718 (377-3359).

ANGEL FIRE FACILITIES AND ATTRACTIONS
Angel Fire is a resort first started in 1954 with a golf course and ski area. In 1972 it was purchased by the Arizona Land and Cattle Company and since then has gone through a series of owners. The name was coined by Franciscan friars who first called the mountain "the place of the fire of angels." Later, according to legend, Kit Carson named the peak Angel Fire because of the reflection of the sun on frozen dew in the early morning.

The resort features a ski area and one of the nation's highest golf courses, a par-72, eighteen-hole facility that meanders though spruce trees and ponderosa pines. There is also fishing on Monte Verde Lake, a 37-acre facility that is always stocked. Other fun-filled activities available at the resort include horseback riding, hiking, jeep tours, hunting, swimming, tennis, boating, and game-sighting safaris.

Angel Fire Ski Area has six chair lifts servicing 53 trails of which two-thirds are beginner and intermediate levels. The area receives 140 inches of snow a year that is supplemented by snowmaking equipment on sixty per cent of the trails. Lodging is available at **The Legends Hotel and Conference Center,** Drawer B, Angel Fire, NM 87710 (377-6401 or 1-800-633-7463), which has 157 rooms, or at more than twenty other lodges, condos, chalets, apartments, camps, and bed-and-breakfast places.

The DAV Vietnam Veterans National Memorial, a chapel shaped like a gull's wing, is just off US Hwy. 64 and is a shrine to those who died in that tragic conflict. The site includes a visitor's center. **Music From Angel Fire** is a music festival held August–September, featuring internationally known artists performing chamber music, jazz, and bluegrass, with 13 concerts at Angel Fire, Red River, Taos, and Raton. Information is available by calling 377-6353 or 377-3233 or write P.O. Box 547, Angel Fire, NM 87710.

CIMMARON

Located between Taos and Raton on US Hwy. 64, Cimmaron is a fascinating town with a past that reads like a *Who's Who* of the wild west. In fact, *Cimarrón* means "wild" or "untamed" in Spanish, and this is an apt description of Cimmaron's history. It was a major stopover point on the Santa Fe Trail and thus attracted both desperadoes and heroes. Kit Carson built a ranch here in 1849, and the town served as the headquarters for Lucien B. Maxwell's Land Grant—the largest single land holding in the United States, 67 square miles!

The guest list at the St. James Hotel included the likes of Buffalo Bill Cody, Annie Oakley, Black Jack Ketchum, Frederick Remington, Lew Wallace, and Zane Grey. Davy Crockett, the grandson of the Alamo hero, was gunned down here a few months after he shot three soldiers from Fort Union.

★ ★
TOURIST INFORMATION

CIMMARON CHAMBER OF COMMERCE
P.O. Box 604, Cimmaron, NM 87714 (376-2417)

★ ★
HISTORIC SIGHTSEEING

The **Old Mill Museum,** located in the Cimmaron Historic District is all that remains of Lucien Maxwell's ranch. It was built in 1864 as a grist mill and now houses an interesting collection of early photos, memorabilia, mining equipment, and cowboy gear. Admission is $2 for adults.

If there are bullet holes in the ceiling, then you must be inside the **St. James Hotel,** a magnificently restored building that was built as a saloon in 1873 by Henri Lambert, Abraham Lincoln's chef. The bullet holes reputedly are from the pistol of the notorious gunman Clay Allison, who danced on the bar while firing. Legend holds that 26 men were killed within the walls of the hotel. Fortunately, things are more peaceful at the St. James these days. Fifteen of the original rooms have been restored to their Victorian splendor, and the dining room is the best restaurant in town, located off Hwy. 64 on Collison Rd. Visitors may stay in the restored rooms or in the modern hotel annex. Reservations can be made by calling 376-2664.

The **Philmont Museum and Seton Library** is located four miles south of town on NM Hwy. 21 at Philmont Scout Ranch. In 1938 Oklahoma oil baron Waite Phillips donated 137,493 acres (215 square miles) to the Boy Scouts of America. About 23,000 scouts camp here each year, making Philmont the largest private camping facility in the world. Statistics freaks will be pleased to learn that these scouts consume 15,000 pounds of buffalo meat and 450 gallons of picante sauce served on 250,000 paper plates each season, and use up 22,000 rolls of toilet paper. The **Philmont Museum** offers exhibits on the history of Philmont and the surrounding area, and the **Seton Memorial Library** houses the library and personal art and natural history collections of Ernest Thompson Seton, world famous author, naturalist, artist, and first Chief Scout of the Boy Scouts of America. Admission to the museum and library is free, and tours of nearby **Villa Philmonte,** the Spanish Mediterranean style mansion of Waite Phillips, can be arranged there through the library. For information on the Philmont Complex, call 376-2281.

Just south of Philmont Ranch is the **Kit Carson Museum** at Rayado (376-2281), built in the style of nineteenth-century Mexican haciendas. The rooms of the museum are decorated with furniture of the period when Kit Carson lived there. This museum is open June through August and admission is free.

Fifteen miles north of Cimmaron on US Hwy. 64 is the semighost town of **Colfax,** which boomed in the 1890s during the coal mining activity at Dawson. Remains of the old hotel still stand here in testimony to changing fortunes.

★ ★
LODGING

In addition to the St. James Hotel mentioned above, other lodging in Cimmaron includes the **Kit Carson Inn** on US Hwy. 64 (376-2288), and the **Pine Ridge Motel** on US Hwy. 64, twelve miles west of town in Cimmaron Canyon (376-2960). For additional information on historic Cimmaron, contact the Cimmaron Chamber of Commerce at 376-2417, P.O. Box 604, Cimmaron, NM 87714.

★ ★
NATURE AND WILDLIFE

Cimmaron Canyon State Park (377-6271), located between Eagle Nest and Cimarron along US Hwy. 64, is part of a state wildlife area and is managed in cooperation with the New Mexico Department of Game and Fish. Camping fees are waived here, but campers must possess a current New Mexico hunting or fishing license. Trout fishing is excellent along the Cimarron River, and the park is ideal for hiking and wildlife watching. Along the river are crenelated granite formations called the "Palisades" that are popular with rock climbers. Campgrounds, drinking water, and rest rooms are available at the park.

More campsites can be found at **Valle Vidal** in Carson National Forest; the entrance to the Valle is located four miles north of Cimmaron on County Road 204, but the campground is 36 miles beyond that point. The Valle Vidal is a great place to observe elk, deer, bobcat, mountain lions, and many species of birds. Fishing is also available at **Shuree Ponds,** and **Costilla** and **Comanche Creeks** in the middle of the **Valle Vidal,** and at **Maxwell Lakes,** ten miles east of Cimarron. The best northern pike fishing in the state is found at **Springer Lake,** twenty miles southeast of Cimmaron via NM Hwy. 58.

Kiowa National Grasslands, (374-9652) southeast of Springer via US Hwy. 56 and NM Hwy. 39, contains about one hundred thousand acres of grasslands administered by the Cibola National Forest. Camping is available at **Mills Canyon,** just off NM Hwy. 39. Another unit of Kiowa is located along NM Hwys. 402 and 406 near Clayton. **Chicosa Lake State Park,** near Mills off NM Hwy. 39 (485-2424), is a small natural lake that was a watering stop for the great herds of longhorn cattle driven north out of Texas along the Goodnight-Loving Trail. The park has historical exhibits, a small herd of longhorns, and a chuckwagon. Chicosa Lake offers fishing, camping and picnicking sites, rest rooms with showers, and a playground.

RATON

No one seems to know or care why the name of this town of 9400 can be translated as "mouse" in Spanish, although some rodent experts speculate the name has something to do with the long-tailed kangaroo rats that abound in nearby Raton Pass. Originally named Willow Springs, Raton is located on I-25 just a few miles south of the Colorado border. The town began in 1880 when the Atchison, Topeka, and Santa Fe Railroad decided to locate its repair shop at the base of Raton Pass. Within a few years the town population grew to three thousand as coal deposits and ranching added to the prosperity which accompanied the railroad.

Soon Raton was a stop on the theatrical circuit of the late 1880s, and it even boasted of an opera house. Like Cimmaron, Santa Fe, and Las Vegas, Raton had its share of frontier violence, but that was tempered by education when the first high school in New Mexico Territory opened in Raton in 1884. Today, five blocks of Raton's original townsite have been named the **Raton Downtown Historic District,** with about seventy buildings listed on the National Register of Historic Places. These Victorian-and Mission Revival-style buildings have changed very little in the past sixty years and are an excellent place to start the exploration of the Raton area.

TOURIST INFORMATION

RATON CHAMBER OF COMMERCE
P.O. Box 1211, Raton, NM 87740 (445-3689)

HISTORIC SIGHTSEEING

The **Santa Fe Depot** at the railroad tracks at the end of Cook
Street was built in 1903 to replace the earlier frame structure, which
witnessed as many as sixty trains a day passing through Raton in
the early years. The depot, built in Spanish Mission Revival style,
serves today as the Amtrak depot. Another Mission Revival style
building is the **Wells Fargo Express Company** on First Street, built
in 1910.

The elaborate **Shuler Theater** on Second Street was completed in
1915 and housed the opera house, the fire station, and the city
offices. Built in the European Rococo style and remodeled in the
1970s, the theater has nearly perfect acoustics. Today the Shuler is
still utilized for theatrical performances and community events.
The **Swastika Hotel** on Cook Street, now the International State
Bank, was built in 1929 and decorated with the swastika, a symbol
of good luck to some Native American tribes. During World
War II, the name of the hotel was changed to the Yucca Hotel because the German Nazi party had adopted the swastika as its logo.

The **Raton Museum** on First Street was originally the **Coors
Building,** owned by the brewing company in Colorado. The building shared a common wall with the **Haven Hotel,** which agreed to
serve Coors Beer in perpetuity in return for the wall-sharing ar-
rangement. The neo-classical **Arthur Johnson Memorial Library** on
Cook Street was originally the US Post Office and now houses a
fine collection of Southwestern art.

The **Palace Hotel** at the corner of First and Cook Streets was built
in 1986 by three Smith brothers, immigrants from Scotland. It was
the first three-story building in Colfax County .

LODGING AND DINING

Unfortunately, none of the old hotels in the Raton Historic District
are still open for business, so the visitor must resort to rather stan-

dard chain motels. Recommended are the **Holiday Inn,** I-25 and Clayton Road (445-5555 or 1-800-255-8879), which has an enclosed courtyard and pool; **Melody Lane Motel,** 136 Canyon Drive (445-3655 or 1-800-421-5210) with in-room saunas; and the **Sands Manor Motel,** 300 Clayton Road (445-2737), a Best Western facility.

I recommend **El Matador,** 445 S. Second Street (445-9575), with excellent New Mexican cuisine, open 7:30 a.m.–8 p.m. Tues.–Sat., closed Monday.

★ ★
NEARBY ATTRACTIONS

LA MESA PARK RACETRACK
New Mexico's oldest privately owned track has been racing for more than forty years and is located one mile south of downtown Raton off I-25 (445-2301). Private pilots may fly in to bet at La Mesa Park, since the Raton Airport is adjacent to the racetrack. The track presents about forty days of racing on weekends between June and September. Facilities include a full food and beverage service, a Grandstand, Clubhouse, Turf Club, and Jockey Club. The Roadrunner Futurity is held in early September.

SUGARITE CANYON STATE PARK
Located fourteen miles north of Raton via NM Hwy. 72 and NM Hwy. 526, Sugarite Canyon is one of New Mexico's newest state parks. An innovative visitor center has displays on the colorful coal mining history of the canyon. The park itself has two fishing lakes — **Alice** and **Maloya** — but gasoline-powered motors are not allowed. There are excellent hiking and cross-country skiing trails here where deer, turkey, and other wild game can be observed. There are camping and picnicking sites as well as rest rooms available. For information call 445-5607.

CAPULIN VOLCANO NATIONAL MONUMENT
Travelers should not miss this fascinating example of New Mexico's legacy of Vulcan, one of the few places in the world where mankind can walk into a volcano. Capulin is a near-perfect cinder cone located thirty miles east of Raton via US Hwy. 64/87 east 28 miles to Capulin, turn left two miles north on NM Hwy. 325.

A visitor center at the monument has instructive displays about volcanism in New Mexico and explains how Capulin was formed 10,000 years ago. The cinder cone has nearly perfect symmetry because it was not breached by lava overflowing the rim. Rather, the molten rock flowed from secondary vents at the western base of the cone.

The **Crater Rim Trail**, a one-mile walk, is a self-guiding trail around the top of the volcano, which rises about one thousand feet above the surrounding plain. Along the trail are signs that identify the native vegetation covering the cone—grasses, piñon pine, Gambel oak, mountain mahogany, squawbush, and chokecherry, or *capulin* in Spanish. Bird watchers will have a literal field day spotting warblers, grosbeaks, gold finches, and many species of hawks. Wildflowers along the rim include lupine, golden pea, penstemon, verbena, and paintbrush.

The Barella, Raton, and Johnson mesas visible from the rim are capped with lava—an example of what geologists call an "inversion of relief." The previously lower areas where lava once flowed are now higher because the uncapped land has eroded away, creating the mesas. To the southeast, Sierra Grande is visible. This million-year-old shield volcano is more than forty miles around the base, making it the largest mountain in North America that is not part of a range.

For more information on Capulin Volcano National Monument, contact the monument at 278-2201.

FOLSOM

In 1925 in tiny Folsom, New Mexico (NM Hwy. 72 between Raton and Clayton), a cowhand named George McJunkin made a discovery that shocked the world of archaeology and caused a re-evaluation of all previous theories about early man in North America. In an arroyo, McJunkin spotted some unusual white bones poking out from the bank and along with those bones, he found a finely crafted flint point too large to be an arrowhead. An acquaintance of the cowhand took to the bones to Jessie Figgins of the Colorado Museum of Natural History in Denver, who identified them as belonging to an extinct bison. He believed the flint point to be the first evidence of paleo-Indians in the New World—a heretical idea at the time because archaeologists firmly believed that Indian cultures could be no older than five thousand years.

Figgins launched the first official dig at Folsom in 1926 and found several more points in the same strata along with more bones of the extinct bison. But, despite his proof, other experts were not convinced about Figgins' theory and reminded him that the bones and flints could have been brought together by other means, such as flooding. But Figgins never gave up, and the following summer he uncovered more solid evidence which he did *not* excavate, but rather left in place. He then invited archaeologists to come see the undisturbed find for themselves. In the words of famous archaeologist Frank H. H. Roberts, "There was no question but there was evidence of an authentic association. The point was still imbedded in the matrix between the two ribs of the animal skeleton."

Now there was no doubt that paleo-Indians had killed a Pleistocene bison beside a small lake in what is now northern New Mexico, and the find pushed back the date of the earliest American to between 10,000 and 11,000 years ago. The **Folsom Museum,** in the former Doherty's Mercantile building in Folsom (278-2155), has displays of bison bones and Folsom points found nearby.

MAXWELL NATIONAL WILDLIFE REFUGE
Located 25 miles from Raton and fifteen miles from Springer just off I-25, Maxwell National Wildlife Refuge was established in 1966 as a sanctuary for migratory waterfowl. There are about 3500 acres of grassland here, and more than two dozen irrigation impoundments. **Lake 13** is the largest of these ponds and fishing is permitted in season. More than 153 species of birds have been spotted at this refuge which is open to the public. For more information on Maxwell National Wildlife Refuge, call 375-2331 or write P.O. Box 276, Folsom, NM 87728.

CLAYTON
Tucked away in the far northeastern corner of New Mexico at the intersection of US Hwy. 87 and US Hwy. 56/64, Clayton is the seat of Union County and a town of about five thousand population. It is primarily a cattle ranching town, but the discovery of gigantic carbon dioxide deposits in the Bravo Dome has led to the development of that industry. Carbon dioxide is injected into oil wells to increase the recovery percentage of the oil, and Bravo Dome has the world's largest and purest known natural carbon dioxide deposits.

The history of Clayton is typically wild West. The nearby Rabbit Ear Mountains were the site of the bloodiest confrontation between the Spanish and the Comanche Indians. In 1717, a volunteer army of five hundred Spaniards from Santa Fe attacked the Comanches and killed hundreds while taking seven hundred prisoners. The resulting truce made the eastern plains much safer for settlers, though the Comanches still occasionally raided wagon trains. The town was also along the route of the Cimarron Cut-Off of the Santa Fe Trail, and some of the nineteenth-century wagon ruts are still visible north of town.

In 1901, the infamous train robber Black Jack Ketchum was hanged in Clayton in one of the most unusual public executions in the West. Black Jack was a large, heavy man and the drop from the gallows was an unusually long seven feet. His body was yanked so hard by the rope that Black Jack was decapitated and his head bounced into the applauding crowd!

★ ★
TOURIST INFORMATION

CLAYTON CHAMBER OF COMMERCE
P.O. Box 476, Clayton, NM 88415 (374-9253)

★ ★
HISTORIC BUILDINGS AND NEARBY ATTRACTIONS

Perhaps the most interesting building in Clayton is the old **Eklund Hotel,** an elegant Victorian structure which has been restored and is now the **Eklund Dining Room and Saloon** at 15 Main Street (374-2551), open 10:30 a.m.–9 p.m. daily.

CLAYTON LAKE STATE PARK
Located fifteen miles north of Clayton on NM Hwy. 370, this state park is set amidst the grasslands that once supported huge buffalo herds. Clayton Lake is stocked with bass, trout, and channel catfish and has a boat ramp and small courtesy dock for limited boating. Also available are campgrounds, modern rest rooms with showers, and a playground.

Bison were not the only large animals that once roamed this area. From the park's headquarters (374-8808), a short trail leads to an interpretive pavilion overlooking a trackway of dinosaur footprints. These tracks, or traces as paleontologists call them, were not discovered until 1982 when the New Mexico officials arrested vandals who were attempting to remove them. The traces, estimated to be 100 million years old, include a set of hand prints from a pterodactyl, a soaring dinosaur that apparently was in the process of taking off from a mud flat. Other tracks include those of therapods and hadrosaurs.

Additional information on this state park and other attractions around Clayton is available from the Clayton–Union County Chamber of Commerce, 374-9253.

TUCUMCARI
There is no doubt that Tucumcari was named after nearby Tucumcari Mountain (actually a butte), but the actual origin of this un-

usual name is in question. Fanciful legend relates the story of two Apache lovers, Tocom and Kari, and their tragic love affair, but this town is located in Comanche territory, not Apache. A more reasonable etymology is found in *New Mexico Place Names:* The Comanche word for a lookout spot is *tukamukari,* and the butte nearby was an excellent vantage point for Comanche raiding parties.

Despite such evidence, the town continues to promote the myth of the Apache lovers, even to the point of crowning Prince Tocom and Princess Kari each year during the Piñata Festival in June. Beauty contest competitors should note that this competition is limited to four- and five-year-old children.

Located on I-40 about forty miles west of the Texas border, Tucumcari was originally called Six Shooter Siding and began as a railroad town in 1901. Today it is still a railroad, ranching, and farming town that earns significant additional revenue from tourism. In fact, there is one motel room for every four residents — about two thousand rooms total.

★ ★
TOURIST INFORMATION

TUCUMCARI CHAMBER OF COMMERCE
P.O. Drawer E, Tucumcari, NM 88401 (461-1694)

★ ★
LODGING AND DINING

Tucumcari's 26 motels are designed for the Interstate motorist rather than for long-term visitors. Recommended are: **Apache Motel,** 1106 Tucumcari Blvd. (461-3367); **Comfort Inn** 1023 E. Tucumcari Blvd. (461-0360 or 1-800-228-5150); **Royal Palacio Motel,** 1620 E. Tucumcari Blvd. (461-1212); and the **Safari Motel,** 722 E. Tucumcari Blvd. (461-3642).

Recommended restaurants include: **Dean's Restaurant,** 1806 E. Tucumcari Blvd. (461-3470) with good New Mexican dishes, open 6 a.m.–9 p.m. daily; **Dale's Restaurant,** 1202 E. Tucumcari Blvd. (461-1740), featuring steaks, open 11 a.m.–9 p.m. Mon.–Sat., closed Sunday; **The Headquarters,** 200 E. Estrella (461-0750), open 6 a.m.–10 p.m. every day; and the **Pow Wow Restaurant,** 801 W. Tucumcari Blvd. (461-2587), open 6 a.m.–10 p.m. daily.

NEARBY ATTRACTIONS

Tucumcari Historical Museum, 416 S. Adams (461-4201), is a two-story brick building with an eclectic collection of artifacts, including early Indian items, gems, minerals, and reconstructions of an early school room and sheriff's office. Fencing enthusiasts and wire collectors will delight in the museum's barbed wire collection. Open 9 a.m.–5 p.m. Mon.–Sat., 1 p.m.–6 p.m. and on Sundays only in winter.

Ladd S. Gordon Wildlife Area, just east of town off Tucumcari Blvd., is a 770-acre reserve for migratory waterfowl and other wildlife. Boating and fishing are available on **Tucumcari Lake.**

Caprock Amphitheatre, located ten miles south of Tucumcari at San Jon (exit 356 off I-40), is the site of an outdoor drama entitled "The Real Billy the Kid," which is performed Friday and Saturday nights July through late August. A Barbecue is also served. For ticket information, call 461-1694.

UTE LAKE STATE PARK
This lake on the Canadian River is 23 miles northeast of Tucumcari via US Hwy. 54 and left two miles on NM Hwy. 540. The fishing for walleye is excellent here, and other game fish in the lake include white and largemouth bass, crappie, and channel catfish. Park facilities include camping and picnicking sites, rest rooms with showers, boat ramps, and a marina. More information is available by calling 487-2284.

CONCHAS LAKE STATE PARK
Another dam on the Canadian River has created Conchas Lake, a 25-mile-long reservoir (nine thousand acres) about 34 miles west of Tucumcari via NM Hwy. 104. The state park here is one of the best-equipped facilities in the state, offering (at two separate sites) a nine-hole golf course, a paved and lighted air strip, a marina, and a 38-room lodge with lounge, a restaurant, and a general store. The park has two campgrounds with utility hookups and rest rooms, and is considered excellent for waterfowl hunting in the winter and fishing for walleye, bass, and crappie during the spring and summer. For reservations and information, call 868-2270.

SANTA ROSA
This small community of three thousand just off I-40 about 54 miles west of Tucumcari is called "The City of Natural Lakes" because of

the abundance of water in the area. The **Blue Hole,** a ninety-foot-deep, bell-shaped opening into a subterranean river flowing at a rate of three thousand gallons per minute, is the best location in the state for scuba diving. Also in the center of town is **Park Lake,** a small swimming lake with other recreation facilities. **James-Wallace Memorial Park,** south of town, offers free camping on the shores of its lake, which is regularly stocked with rainbow trout and is also populated with bass and channel catfish. Located north of town, **Tres Lagunas** has camping, hiking, and fishing facilities.

★ ★
TOURIST INFORMATION

SANTA ROSA CHAMBER OF COMMERCE
486 Parker Ave., Santa Rosa, NM 88435 (472-3763)

★ ★
LODGING AND DINING

Recommended motels are the **Holiday Inn,** at the I-40 east interchange (472-5411), and the **Best Western Adobe Inn,** I-40 at exit 275 (472-3446). The **Adobe Inn Restaurant** (472-3446) is one of the best in town. For New Mexican specialties, try the **Club Cafe,** 561 Parker Ave. (472-3631), open 6 p.m.–9 p.m. every night, or **Joseph's Restaurant,** 865 Will Rogers Dr. (472-3361), open 6 a.m.–9 p.m. daily.

MORE WATER

SANTA ROSA LAKE STATE PARK
The first of two man-made lakes on the Pecos River near Santa Rosa, Santa Rosa Lake State Park (472-3110) is located seven miles north of town off I-40 on the edge of the *Llano Estacado,* or Staked Plains where Comanchero traders bartered with the Comanches during the eighteenth and nineteenth centuries. Catfish, bass, and walleyes inhabit this lake, which has a boat ramp, utility hookups, rest rooms with showers, and camping and picnicking sites. **Sumner Lake State Park** (355-2541), 25 miles south of Santa Rosa via US Hwy. 84 and then right on NM Hwy. 203, is a large lake with virtually identical facilities.

LAS VEGAS

This city of about 15,000 is located about sixty miles north of Santa Fe just off I-25. Founded in the early 1800s, it was a Spanish stopover on the Santa Fe Trail until 1846, when General Stephen W. Kearny took possession of New Mexico by issuing a proclamation in Las Vegas Old Town Plaza. He declared, "We are your protectors, not your conquerors." Sure thing!

The arrival of the Santa Fe Railroad in 1879 pumped more than one million dollars a year into the economy of Las Vegas, and started a boom that would make this the largest city in the state by 1900. But this boom also brought problems for Las Vegas. By the early 1880s it was considered the wildest town in the Wild West. In fact, the ten years between 1880 and 1890 were called "The Deadly Decade" in New Mexico, and much of the violence was concentrated in Las Vegas. In 1880, a gun duel between the Tom Henry Gang and deputy marshall "Mysterious Dave" Mather resulted in the death of Henry and three of his gang members, and town marshall Joe Carson. That same year, famous lawman Bat Masterson shot it out with bartender Charley White.

In 1882, a famous poster appeared on Las Vegas' street corners and in the town's saloons. "Notice to Thieves, Thugs, Fakirs, and Bunko-Steerers," it read, "if you are found within the limits of this city after 10 o'clock p.m. this night, you will be invited to a Grand Neck-Tie Party."

Las Vegas was sarcastically referred to as "Elbow City" because of the number of citizens who rested their elbows on saloon bars. "The town of Las Vegas had been taken over by murderers, thieves, and prostitutes," wrote historian Carlos C. De Baca, "their drunken brawls were the order of the day. The barking of .45 guns were as common to the ears then as the honking of auto horns in our present day."

After the violence of the Deadly Decade, Las Vegas settled down and became a railroad and commercial center for the state. Teddy Roosevelt's Rough Riders made Las Vegas their headquarters and in 1912 the town hosted the world championship boxing match between Jack Johnson and Jim Flynn. The financial boom, which lasted for decades, did not end with a sudden bust as it did in the mining towns. Rather, it just faded away and Las Vegas gradually became a town dependent upon ranching, light industry, and tourism.

★ ★
TOURIST INFORMATION

LAS VEGAS CHAMBER OF COMMERCE
P.O. Box 148, Las Vegas, NM 87701 (425-8631)

★ ★
HISTORIC SIGHTSEEING

Las Vegas boasts of more than nine hundred buildings on the National Register of Historic Places. The **Historic District** of Las Vegas consists of **New Town** and **Old Town Plaza**. The **Hotel Casteneda**, Lincoln at Railroad Ave., was built in 1898 and was part of the famous Fred Harvey chain of railroad hotels. It is still utilized during **Rails 'n' Trails Days** in early June.

The **Plaza Hotel** (see the Lodging section below), on the Plaza, is one of the most famous buildings in town and was built in 1881. The **Charles Ifield Company** headquarters and the **Louis C. Ifield Law Office**, both on the Plaza, are notable structures. The **Las Vegas Chamber of Commerce**, 721 Grand Ave. (425-8631), will provide a map of the historic buildings upon request.

The **Rough Riders Museum**, 727 Grand Ave. (425-8726), contains memorabilia of the Teddy Roosevelt's campaigners during the Spanish-American War (free admission). **Montezuma's Castle**, five miles west of town on NM Hwy. 65 was formerly a 343-room hotel owned by the Santa Fe Railroad and it hosted such notables as Teddy Roosevelt, Ulysses S. Grant, and Japan's Emperor Hirohito. Now it is the American Branch of Armand Hammer's **United World College** (454-1461).

★ ★
LODGING AND DINING

There are a number of motels in Las Vegas, but visitors in search of history have but two choices. The **Best Western Plaza Hotel**, 230 Old Town Plaza (425-3591) was restored to its former glory in 1983 and has 39 rooms and suites within its three stories. The dining room is probably the best restaurant in town, offering both continental and New Mexican specialties. Plaza Hotel guests of the 1880s included Doc Holiday and Pat Garrett, and in the early 1900s, western silent movie star Tom Mix made the hotel his headquarters.

Another historic district hostelry, the **Carriage House Bed and Breakfast**, 925 Sixth Street (454-1784), is a three-story Victorian house with five bedrooms. Since the owner is an antiques dealer, all of the furnishings in the Carriage House are for sale and visitors can spend a night or two in the hotel and then buy the bed they slept in.

Recommended restaurants include **Spic and Span Bakery Cafe**, 713 Douglas Ave. near the Plaza (425-6481), open 6 a.m.–6 p.m.

daily, with wonderful pastries and New Mexican cuisine; and
Estella's Cafe, 148 Bridge Street (454-0048) with New Mexican
dishes served in an historic building. Open 11:30 a.m.–7 p.m.
Mon.–Sat., closed Sunday.

★ ★
NEARBY ATTRACTIONS

FORT UNION NATIONAL MONUMENT
Located 28 miles north of Las Vegas just off I-25. Turn left on (new)
NM Hwy. 161 at exit 366 and drive eight miles. This national
monument consists of the ruins of old Fort Union, built between
1851–61 to protect the Santa Fe Trail from Indians, and later,
Denver from the Confederates. This fort was the largest military
post in the Southwest but was abandoned in 1891 because the
Indian Wars had ended.

The visitor center details the history of the fort and there is a self-
guided, interpretive trail through the ruins with audio stations that
tell the story of the early days. A half-mile portion of the original
Santa Fe Trail, complete with original trail ruts, runs north of the
monument.

Picnicking facilities, rest rooms, and drinking water are available
here, but camping is not permitted. For more information, contact
the monument staff at 425-8025.

STATE PARKS AND WILDLIFE

The Las Vegas area, close to the Santa Fe National Forest as well
as the eastern plains of the state, is blessed with a number of recreational facilities. **Storrie Lake State Park,** six miles north of Las
Vegas via NM Hwy. 518 towards Mora (425-9231), has a visitor
center with exhibits detailing the history of Santa Fe Trail and Las
Vegas. Other visitor facilities include camping sites with utility
hookups, a boat ramp, and excellent trout fishing. Located 31 miles
southwest of Las Vegas via I-25 and NM Hwy. 3, **Villanueva State
Park** (421-2957) is situated along the scenic Pecos River. Camping
and sightseeing are the main activities here, although some campers
fish for trout along the river.

Coyote Creek State Park, fourteen miles north of Mora on NM
Hwy. 434 (387-2328), has a picturesque setting in the foothills of
the Sangre de Cristo range beside a stream with beaver ponds. Fishing for rainbow and German brown trout is the main activity here,
and camping sites and rest rooms are available. Four miles south
of Mora via NM Hwy. 94 is **Morphy Lake State Park,** a primitive-

use area accessible only by backpacking or four-wheel-drive ve-hicles. Campsites and toilets are present here, but no drinking water. Morphy Lake is stocked with trout, but fishermen should note that boating is permitted with oars or electric motors only. For information, call (387-2328).

Las Vegas National Wildlife Refuge, six miles southeast of Las Vegas via NM Hwy. 104 and right four miles on NM Hwy. 281, has a varied habitat — marshland, grassland, and timber. Its eight thou-sand acres provide a sanctuary for some 220 species of wildlife. Especially interesting to observe are both bald and golden eagles, and the rare prairie falcon.

McAllister Lake, one of five lakes in the refuge, is noted for its excellent trout fishing. Restricted boating is permitted during the fishing season, as is camping. For additional information, call 425-3581.

PART III

Las Cruces and the Southwest Quadrant

LAS CRUCES AND MESILLA

Most popular accounts attribute the origin of the name "the crosses"—Las Cruces—to massacres of travelers by Apache Indians. In 1787, and again in 1830, the story goes, oxcart drivers from Taos were on their way to Chihuahua along the Camino Real when they were ambushed and killed. Passersby buried the dead and marked the graves with crosses. The site became known as "La Placita de las Cruces," later shortened to Las Cruces. It was certainly an inauspicious beginning for a town, but neither the name nor its origin have prevented Las Cruces from becoming New Mexico's second-largest metropolitan area and one of the ten fastest growing cities in the country.

Early Spanish settlements in the area did not begin at the Las Cruces site. The little town of Doña Ana, north of Las Cruces, was settled first, in 1839. Ten years later, the first buildings were erected in Las Cruces and Mesilla, south of Las Cruces, was founded shortly afterward because of a set of unusual circumstances.

In 1846, the United States declared war on Mexico and claimed New Mexico as its own. When American troops moved into the Mesilla Valley in 1848, half the populations of Doña Ana and Las Cruces founded Mesilla, which was still in Mexico because it was then across the Rio Grande. Mesilla remained in Mexico and Las Cruces in the Territory of New Mexico until 1854, when Mexico sold 30,000 square miles of land to the U.S. as a part of the Gadsden Purchase. On July 4, 1854, the purchase was celebrated in the Plaza at Mesilla, but many of the residents missed it because they had moved even further south in order to remain Mexican citizens.

Mesilla flourished despite the departure of many of its citizens and soon became a booming town of five housand — larger than both Las Cruces and El Paso. In fact, for a while, Mesilla was the largest city west of San Antonio. Part of its success was due to the fact that Mesilla was chosen as a major station along the 2800-mile-long Butterfield Stage route from St. Louis to San Francisco.

Mesilla briefly became the capital of the Confederate Territory of Arizona in 1861 and was headquarters for the rebels' military governor of the Southwest, Lt. Col. John Robert Baylor. But the town was retaken by Union forces from California thirteen months later. In 1863, nature played a cruel trick on Mesilla as the Rio Grande shifted course and turned the town into an island.

During the 1870s, Mesilla was occasionally the scene of violence. In 1871 rival Democratic and Republican factions started a bloody riot on the Plaza, leaving nine dead and fifty wounded, and in 1880 Mesilla was the site of the first trial of Billy the Kid. He was found guilty of murder and sentenced to hang, but escaped and later participated in the Lincoln County War (see listing for Lincoln).

When the Santa Fe Railroad selected Las Cruces, rather than Mesilla, for its route in 1881, Mesilla declined in importance as a territorial city. Las Cruces soon became the commercial center of the Mesilla Valley, which was a fertile agricultural region. Farmers grew pecans, onions, alfalfa, vegetables, and of course, the famous New Mexico chile peppers.

In 1888, the founding of the New Mexico College of Agriculture and Mechanical Arts ushered in a new era for the Las Cruces area. The college, which later became New Mexico State University with the world's largest campus (6250 acres), not only assisted in bringing Las Cruces into the modern age by educating the youth of New Mexico, its researchers assisted local growers with the latest techniques in horticultural science.

One of the most significant achievements from the College of Agriculture was the development of the modern strains of chile peppers. In 1907, Fabian Garcia of the Agricultural Experiment Station at the college began to standardize chiles into easily recognizable varieties so that farmers could determine which strains to grow. Until that time, there was no way to tell how hot the chiles might be, or how much fruit they would produce. The now-famous "No. 9" strain was one of fourteen varieties produced by Garcia, and once the growers had dependable seed, the chile crop gradually became the most important food crop of the Mesilla Valley.

Chile peppers are so ingrained in New Mexico agriculture and diet that virtually all that are grown here are either consumed in New Mexico or canned and frozen for export to other states, which are now beginning to appreciate the pungent pods. Between 1979 and 1986, chile production in New Mexico increased 96 per cent, and in 1987 growers harvested 36,972 dry-equivalent tons of chiles.

Chile peppers became the basis for a cuisine that is now called "New Mexican" in order to distinguish it from "Mexican food," which has dozens of variations both in Mexico and the United States. New Mexican cuisine originated from a collision between the corn-dominated foods of Chihuahua and Sonora and the New Mexican varieties of chile peppers, rather than the *ancho* ("wide") chiles that are the most popular in Mexico, or the jalapeños that have conquered Texas. It is important to remember that although New Mexico chiles can be either green (immature) or red (mature), they are not separate varieties.

The basic dishes in New Mexican cuisine are easy to remember. *Enchiladas* are corn tortillas filled with meat or cheese or both, and then smothered in chile sauce. *Carne adovada* is pork that has been marinated in red chile, baked until it nearly falls apart, and then served covered with red chile sauce. *Tamales* are created when pork mixed with red chile is wrapped in *masa*, a dough made with corn meal, secured with corn husks, and then steamed. Green chile stew is a combination of pork or beef, green chiles, and sometimes tomatoes and potatoes. *Chiles rellenos* are whole green chiles that have been stuffed with cheese, dipped in a batter, deep-fried, and then served with green chile sauce.

Another important fact to remember about New Mexican cuisine is that corn tortillas can be either yellow, which is more common, or blue, when they are made from traditional Indian blue corn. Ordering enchiladas at a New Mexico restaurant involves a virtual quiz from the waiter or waitress, who will ask: "Red or green? Blue or regular? Stacked or rolled? Cheese or meat? Fried egg?" A true chile enchilada aficionado knows the answers to these questions before they are even asked, and will order the dish to personal specifications such as: "blue corn stacked enchiladas with meat and cheese, red chile sauce, topped with a fried egg."

The Las Cruces area, which along with nearby Hatch, touts itself as the "chile pepper capital of the world," is a perfect place to try all the delicious New Mexico specialties, but first some sightseeing is in order.

★ ★
TOURIST INFORMATION

LAS CRUCES CONVENTION AND VISITORS BUREAU
311 N. Downtown Mall, Las Cruces, NM 88001 (524-8521)

LAS CRUCES CHAMBER OF COMMERCE
P.O. Drawer 519, Las Cruces, NM 88004 (524-1968)

★ ★
HISTORIC, SCIENTIFIC, AND ARTISTIC SIGHTSEEING

In celebration of the American Bicentennial, city fathers of Las Cruces found a log cabin in the Black Range in southwestern New Mexico and moved it to Main Street at the north end of the **Downtown Mall,** a multi-million-dollar renovation of the central downtown area. The **Bicentennial Log Cabin,** as it's now called, dates from approximately 1879 and has authentic furnishings and artifacts. It is closed during the winter.

The **Old Armijo House,** on Lohman Avenue (522-3300), is more than 120 years old and has been restored and stocked with original furnishings (the building now houses Pioneer Savings and Trust). Another famous site is the **Amador Hotel** at Amador and Water Streets, one of the earliest buildings in town, built in 1850 by Don Martin Amador and used as a hotel, post office, jail, and courthouse. As a hotel, the Amador hosted such luminaries as Pat Garrett, Billy the Kid, and the Mexican president Benito Juarez. The building now houses the Doña Ana County offices, but special rooms upstairs have been restored with period furniture and artifacts.

The **Branigan Cultural Center,** 106 West Hadley (524-1422), houses artifacts from Fort Selden (see below) and produces shows by local artists and craftspeople. The center also presents lectures, concerts, and performing arts. The facility has a gallery, museum, and an auditorium. Two other interesting sights downtown at Water and Lohman Avenues are **El Molino,** a grinding wheel from an 1853 flour mill that commemorates the work and hardships of the early settlers, and **Our Lady at the Foot of the Cross Shrine,** which is a reproduction of Michaelangelo's "Pieta."

Within the campus of **New Mexico State University,** south of

University Avenue, are several museums and galleries worth visiting. The **University Museum,** in Kent Hall (646-3739) has displays of artifacts from prehistoric and historic Native American cultures of the region, plus traveling shows and art exhibits. The museum is open 10 a.m.–4 p.m. Tues.–Sat. and 1 p.m.–4 p.m. Sun. The **University Art Gallery,** in Williams Hall (646-2545), offers monthly exhibits of historic and contemporary art, plus a permanent collection of prints, photographs, and folk art. It is open 10 a.m.–4 p.m. Mon.–Fri., 1 p.m.–4 p.m. Sunday, closed Saturday. The heavens are the focal point of the **Clyde Tombaugh Observatory,** which is open to the public one night a month. Call University information at 646-2711 for details or call the Astronomy Dept. at 646-4438.

Visitors interested in the latest advances in science and technology will be interested in the **Southwest Residential Experiment Station,** which has eight working solar photovoltaic prototypes on display. There is a visitor center and guided tours can be arranged by calling 646-1049. Located at 1505 Payne and I-10.

Mesilla, also called **La Mesilla** and **Old Mesilla,** is a charming village that retains much of the feel of Spanish colonial days. A major tourism center much like Albuquerque's Old Town, Mesilla (located southwest of Las Cruces on Avenida de Mesilla) has restaurants, shops, galleries, and a museum. Restaurants are covered in a separate listing below, but there are several other places the visitor should not miss.

The Plaza, site of both celebrations and riots, has been well preserved over the years and serves as the center of town. The **San Albino Mission,** with its twin towers, adjoins the Plaza. It was founded in 1851 by Fray Ramon Ortiz. The **Gadsden Museum** on Barker Road (526-6293) has displays of artifacts and relics relating to the turbulent history of Mesilla. Hours vary, but the museum is usually open daily 9 a.m.–11 a.m. and 1 p.m.–3 p.m.

The **William Bonney Gallery,** #3 Calle de Parian (526-8275), was once the jail of the old territorial courthouse, so it's appropriately named since Billy the Kid once escaped from it. The gallery features the works of outstanding Western and Native American artists, bronze sculptures, woodcarvings, and pottery from many New Mexico pueblos. The collection is rounded out by Hopi kachinas, Navajo weavings, and a fine display of turquoise and silver jewelry. It is open daily Mon.–Sat. 10 a.m.–6 p.m., Sun. noon–5 p.m.

One of the finest book stores in New Mexico, **Bowlin's Mesilla Book Center** (526-6220), is located on the Plaza. The store's collection of Southwestern titles and Americana is outstanding. It is open Tues.–Sat. 11 a.m.–5:30 p.m., Sun. 1 p.m.–5 p.m. Closed Monday.

Among the excellent gift and specialty shops in and around the Plaza are **Del Sol** (524-1418) with rugs, baskets, and tapestries, open 10 a.m.–6 p.m.; **La Tienda** (524-2513), with Indian jewelry, and **La Bonita Gifts and Glass** (526-6229). Clothing boutiques in Mesilla include **The Purple Lizard** (523-1419) and the **Chile Country Boutique** (524-3227). There are some excellent food shops in Mesilla, including **Chile Gourmet** (525-2266) with farm fresh produce in season and frozen green chiles; **Adelina's Pasta Shop** (527-1970) with green chile and jalapeño pastas; and **Going Nuts** in Mesilla (525-9555), with a great assortment of locally grown and imported nuts. Try their chile-flavored pecans and pistachios.

★ ★
LODGING

Las Cruces and Mesilla offer a fine selection of more than thirty lodging establishments, from large modern hotels to small bed and breakfast inns. Recommended facilities follow.

HIGH COUNTRY INN
A secluded courtyard with a heated swimming pool is the highlight of this 120-room motel. It is located at 2160 W. Picacho (524-8627).

HOLIDAY INN DE LAS CRUCES
An actual stagecoach, perhaps a survivor of a career on the Old Butterfield Trail, is on display in the lobby of this nicely landscaped motel. An indoor pool set in a tropical garden is popular with guests, as are the on-site dining and drinking places, which are named after local banditos such as Pancho Villa (cantina), and Billy the Kid (saloon). The 110 rooms here have Southwestern decor, and the Holiday Inn is the closest motel to New Mexico State University at 201 E. University Ave. (526-4411).

LAS CRUCES HILTON
The most impressive lodging establishment in town, the seven-story Hilton is located across from the large Mesilla Valley Mall at 705 S. Telshor Blvd. (522-4300). It offers 207 deluxe guest rooms, some with wonderful views either of the Organ Mountains or of the valley below. Two restaurants, a nightclub, and a gift shop welcome guests.

LUNDEEN'S INN OF THE ARTS
This unusual bed and breakfast inn is located in a territorial style hacienda adjoining the Linda Lundeen Gallery. Each of the seven

rooms here expresses the work and personality of a famous American artist. The inn is located at 618 S. Alameda Blvd. (526-3327).

MESON DE MESILLA
Located at 1803 Avenida de Mesilla (NM Hwy. 28), this bed and breakfast inn has thirteen rooms, a swimming pool, and a restaurant. It is within walking distance of Mesilla Plaza and can be reached by calling 525-9212.

LA QUINTA INN
This inn is near Mesilla at 790 Avenida de Mesilla (524-0331 or 1-800-531-5900). Thirty of the one hundred guest rooms here have spa tubs, and the motel provides a complimentary continental breakfast and newspaper. Other amenities include a heated swimming pool and cable TV.

MESILLA VALLEY INN
Another motel quite close to Mesilla, this Best Western operation at 901 Avenida de Mesilla (524-8603) has 170 rooms, a heated pool, and cable TV. **Eddie's Bar and Grill** here serves, ribs, steaks, and seafood.

MISSION INN
Another Best Western motel, the Mission Inn at 1765 S. Main St. (524-8591) has 72 rooms, a large, landscaped heated pool, and refrigerators available in some rooms.

PLAZA SUITES
For visitors with families, or travelers staying for several days, this three-story complex at 301 E. University (525-5000) has one- and two-bedroom mini-suites, most with kitchenettes. Amenities include a free continental breakfast seven days a week and a free happy hour on weekdays. There is a landscaped central courtyard with a swimming pool here, as well as a piano bar inside.

★ ★
DINING

Nearly every major cuisine is represented in some manner at the restaurants in Mesilla and Las Cruces. Excellent dining is also available in El Paso and Ciudad Juarez, about forty miles southeast via

I-10. Below, arranged by type of cuisine, are the recommended restaurants.

NEW MEXICAN

Without question the most famous restaurant in the area is **La Posta,** just off the Plaza in Mesilla (524-3524). Originally built as a stage station along the Butterfield Overland Mail Route, this building is more than 175 years old and has been a restaurant since 1939. In fact, it is the only way station on the entire stage route still serving visitors. The rest were burned to the ground by Apaches. Several dining rooms in the sprawling complex feature authentic New Mexican foods served amidst plants, tropical birds, and stage- coach artifacts. Because it serves so many tourists, its chile special- ties tend to be milder than usual, so chileheads should request their sauces extra-spicy. La Posta is open 11 a.m.–9 p.m. Sunday–Thurs- day; Friday and Saturday 11 a.m.–9:30 p.m.; closed Monday.

Another highly recommended New Mexican restaurant around the Plaza in Mesilla is **Peppers** (523-4999), with unique entrees such as *chile molido,* spit-roasted chicken, and, believe it or not, Mexican won tons. And don't overlook banana enchiladas for dessert. The restaurant is open 11 a.m.–10 p.m. Mon.–Sat. and noon to 9 p.m. Sunday.

Las Cruces also has excellent New Mexican restaurants, in- cluding **My Brother's Place,** 334 S. Main (523-7681), which serves mesquite-grilled steaks in addition to the fine chile-oriented specialties, open 11 a.m.–9 p.m. Mon.–Thurs.; 11 a.m.–10 p.m. Fri. and Sat.; closed Sunday. **Nellie's Cafe,** 1226 W. Hadley (524-9982) is popular with the locals because of the authenticity of its homemade chile dishes. Open 8 a.m.–8 p.m. daily, closed Sunday. **Chope's Bar and Cafe** is sixteen miles south of town on NM Hwy 28 in La Mesa (233-3420). Chope's is a small cafe in a tiny town, but it's justly famous for its chile cuisine and home- spun atmosphere. It is a very popular restaurant and visitors should be warned that it is open for exactly one and a half hours for lunch, starting at twelve noon, and for dinner from 6 p.m.–8:30 p.m.—that's it, no excuses or tardiness permitted.

Also recommended are **La Ristra,** 939 East Main (523-0991), with homemade gorditas; **Roberto's,** 908 E. Amador (523-1851), which has been selling tortillas since 1968; and **The Spanish Kitchen,** 129 E. Madrid (526-4275), with fine red chili con carne enchiladas.

STEAKS AND SEAFOOD

Another very famous restaurant on the Plaza in Mesilla is the **Double Eagle** (523-6700), located in a restored adobe that is on the National Register of Historic Places. Here the visitor will enjoy Victorian-era elegance amidst antiques, Baccarat chandeliers, gold-leaf ceilings, and huge French mirrors. The large hardwood bar in the saloon is magnificent, as is the Maximilian Room. The Carlotta Room is famous for the ghost of Carlotta, the Jilted Maid, which supposedly spooks the patrons—especially loud and obnoxious ones. Ask the bartender to exhibit the polaroid pic of the she-ghost in action. Of course, the Double Eagle has dining in addition to the splendid surroundings. Specialties include tournedos of beef Oscar, *chateaubriand bouquetiere,* and salmon Hollandaise. Open 11 a.m.–10 p.m. daily.

The **Cattleman's Steak House** on US Hwy. 70 east (382-9051) features charbroiled steaks, prime rib, and barbecued pork ribs. It is open 11 a.m.–2 p.m. and 5 p.m.–10 p.m. weekdays. Sat. 5 p.m.–10 p.m. Sun. 11 a.m.–10 p.m.

CONTINENTAL AND SPECIALTIES

The **Meson de Mesilla,** in the bed and breakfast inn of the same name at 1803 Avenida de Mesilla (525-2380) is an intimate restaurant specializing in continental dishes prepared from fresh ingredients. For Asian food, check out **Tatsu,** 930 El Paseo Rd. (526-7144), a superb Japanese restaurant that often wins awards in restaurant shows, open 11 a.m.–10 p.m. daily; and the **Ming Palace,** which serves fiery Szechuan entrees at 2801 Missouri (526-8384).

Hamburger fans will be delighted with **Henry J's,** 523 E. Idaho (525-2211), which serves "gourmet burgers" with a background of nostalgic rock 'n' roll from the '50s and '60s. It is open daily for lunch and dinner. For barbecue, the best place in Las Cruces is **Big John's,** 810 S. Valley (523-9347), which prepares real pit-cooked Texas-style barbecue, including brisket, ribs, ham, sausage, and chicken. Big John's is open daily from 11 a.m.–8:30 p.m.

Also recommended for breakfast is **Pancake Alley,** 2146 W. Picacho (527-0087), open 5:30 a.m.–9 p.m. daily; for excellent desserts, try the **Dessert Company,** 1702 El Paseo (523-1572), open Tues.–Fri. 3 p.m.–11 p.m., Sat. and Sun. 1 p.m.–11 p.m., closed Monday.

★ ★
JUST FOR THE FUN OF IT

SUNLAND PARK

Because for decades Texas refused to allow parimutuel betting, it was only natural that enterprising entrepreneurs should build a race track in Sunland Park, New Mexico, just a couple of miles from downtown El Paso. Sunland Park offers more than one hundred days of racing from October to May and important races include the Sunland Park Handicap, the Riley Allison Futurity, and the Tri-State Thoroughbred Futurity. The recently renovated Turf Club and grandstand area provide excellent seating, and the Turf Club now offers individual TV monitors and remote wagering terminals that allow patrons to place bets from their seats.

Wednesday is Senior Citizen's Day and Friday is Ladies' Day, and both days offer special admissions. Sunland Park is located near its own exit off I-10, forty miles south of Las Cruces. For additional information, call the track at 589-1131.

CIUDAD JUAREZ, MEXICO

This large and funky border town is a lot of fun. No passports or visas are necessary to cross the Rio Grande into Mexico over any one of several bridges, including the International Bridge off I-10, and the downtown bridges near the Civic Center. There is excitement at the bullfights and with horse and dog racing, or shopping at the PRONAF Center, Avenida Juarez, and the traditional Centro Mercado. Take some time to see the Spanish missions, the museums, or to dine at one of the many fine restaurants. Visitors may bring up to $800 worth of merchandise per person back into the United States without paying any duty. For more information on visiting Ciudad Juarez, contact the El Paso Convention and Visitors Bureau at 915-534-0600 or 800-351-6024.

★ ★
SPECIAL EVENTS

Las Crucans love to party, as you can see when you count the number of special events and celebrations hosted by the city. The **Southern New Mexico State Fair,** held the fourth Tuesday through the fourth Sunday in September at the fairgrounds off west I-10, features a rodeo, midway, exhibitions, and entertainment. For details, call 526-1106.

By far the biggest event of the year is the **Whole Enchilada Fiesta,** a three-day celebration of regional cuisine held the first weekend in October at the Downtown Mall. Hundreds of food and entertainment booths are set up for some 250,000 participants who enjoy the food, the music, and the making of the world's largest enchilada, some seven feet in diameter. For information, call 524-1968.

For additional information on these events and the entire Mesilla Valley, contact the Las Cruces Convention and Visitors Bureau at 524-8521.

★ ★
NEARBY ATTRACTIONS

ORGAN MOUNTAINS RECREATION LANDS
To the east of Las Cruces are the spectacular peaks of the Organ Mountains, so named by early settlers because of a resemblance to a pipe organ. The highest peak, Organ Needle, is 9012 feet above sea level.

The Organ Mountains Recreation Lands consist of about 27,000 acres managed by the Bureau of Land Management. There are three life zones that occur in the area, the Upper and Lower Sonoran Zones and the Transition Zone. Despite the arid conditions, wildlife abounds, including eighty species of mammals, 185 species of birds, and sixty species of reptiles and amphibians. The vegetation ranges from grasses and mesquite in the lower elevations to oak, juniper, and Ponderosa pine in the higher regions.

Aguirre Spring Campground is located on the east side of the Organ Mountains and entrance to the campground is by way of an access road that turns south off US Hwy. 70. There are two group areas here and a total of 55 camping and picnicking units with tables and fireplaces. Toilet facilities are available, but no drinking water. At the campground are the trailheads for two trails that are restricted to hiking and horseback riding. The **Baylor Pass Trail,** about six miles long, leaves the campground and ends up on the west side of the mountains. The **Pine Tree Trail** is a loop about four and a half miles long that begins and ends at the campground.

The Organ Mountains Recreation Lands are located 23 miles east of Las Cruces via US Hwy. 70. For more information, call the Bureau of Land Management in Las Cruces at 525-8228.

STAHMANN FARMS
Located in the center of the world's largest pecan grove (about four thousand acres) along NM Hwy. 28, Stahmann Farms is six miles

south of Mesilla Plaza. A number of pecan food products – as well as the raw nuts themselves – are available at **Stahmann's Country Store,** which is open during the summer season from 9 a.m.–5:30 p.m. Mon.–Fri. and 11 a.m.–4 p.m. on Saturdays and Sundays. Tours of the pecan groves are available by reservation only. Call 525-3470 for details.

HATCH
The small town of Hatch, named after Gen. Edward T. Hatch, the ineffectual fighter against the Apaches, calls itself the "chile capital of the world" and is the site for the **Hatch Chile Festival.** This celebration, held every Labor Day weekend at the small airport on NM Hwy. 26, attracts thousands of chile fans who gorge themselves on various chile dishes, wander through other food and artisan booths, compete in contests, and listen to fiddlers. Hatch is located about thirty miles north of Las Cruces near its own exit off I-25, and the Chamber of Commerce can be reached by calling 267-4243, or writing P.O. Box 38, Hatch, NM 87937.

FORT SELDEN STATE MONUMENT
Located about fourteen miles north of Las Cruces at the Radium Springs exit off 1-25, the ruins of this old fort provide an interesting stop. Fort Selden was established in 1865 to protect the settlers of the area from both Apaches and desperadoes. Its design was typical of other frontier forts: a central parade ground surrounded by flat-roofed adobe buildings. The installation consisted of barracks for enlisted men, a kitchen with a bake shop, officers' quarters, a ten-bed hospital, store houses, a stone guard house, corrals, and an ordnance magazine with walls three feet thick. In 1884 it was the boyhood home of General Douglas MacArthur, whose father Arthur McArthur was post commander.

Across the Rio Grande west of the fort, on the summit of Mount Robledo are the ruins of a heliograph station that was used to transmit flashing messages in code to Fort Bliss at El Paso. Fort Selden was abandoned in 1879 but reoccupied when the audacious Apache chiefs Victorio, Nana, and Geronimo went on the warpath and terrorized New Mexico because they had been displaced from their traditional lands and forced onto inadequate reservations in Arizona. The fort was also the base of the famous Buffalo Soldiers, black volunteers who fought the Apaches in the nearby mountains.

Even though Fort Selden was again abandoned in 1891, the grounds of the fort were used for cavalry maneuvers by Army units stationed at Fort Bliss during World War I. In 1963, through the efforts of the Doña Ana Historical Society, the fort was named a

State Monument. There is a visitor center here which re-creates the appearance of the original buildings thought photos and displays. Self-guided trails wind through the ruins and signs identify the historic features of the post. Camping and picnicking are available at nearby Leasburg State Park, and more information on Fort Selden is available by calling the monument at 526-8911.

LEASBURG DAM STATE PARK
This rather small facility (140 acres) is located on the banks of the Rio Grande near the Leasburg Diversion Dam, which was built in 1908 to provide irrigation water to the upper Mesilla Valley. Fishing and boating with canoes and kayaks provide most of the outdoor recreation here. Camping and picnicking facilities with electrical hookups are provided, as are rest rooms with showers. Leasburg Dam State Park can be reached by taking the Radium Springs exit off I-25 or by calling 524-4068.

DEMING
Deming is a railroad town recently made famous by a duck race. In fact, this town's new slogan is, "Home of Pure Water and Fast Ducks." Here's how it all happened:

The town was founded in 1881 at the spot where two railroads — the Southern Pacific and the Atchison, Topeka, and Santa Fe — met and completed the second transcontinental rail line across the United States. It was named Deming after Mary Deming, the wife of one of the Southern Pacific officials.

In addition to the railroad, which was the principal reason for Deming's existence, settlers soon learned that there was a vast underground lake beneath the town that was fed by the Mimbres River. This lake provided ample irrigation water and soon farmers were raising lettuce, onions, cotton, and chiles. Nearby mountains proved rich in minerals, so mining of zinc, gold, silver, and manganese was another attraction for the area.

The people of Deming were content with their agrarian existence for nearly a century. Then, suddenly, they reached out for national and international fame. They weren't the first small town residents in New Mexico to attempt to gain such publicity (see Truth or Consequences listing below), but they were the first to do it with ducks.

In 1980, some local townspeople were conducting a brainstorming session in a Deming bar when someone — nobody in town seems to remember precisely who it was — suggested that the town could promote a duck race to put Deming back on the map. So they decided to rename Luna County Courthouse Park as "Deming

Duck Downs," raise money for race purses, and promote the event all over the state. They were astonished when 184 ducks were entered and thousands of people descended on their town.

Since the first race, the event has been a gigantic success. During the fourth weekend in August, crowds of up to 50,000 waddle into Deming for "The World's Richest Duck Race," plus other events such as the Best Dressed Duck Contest and the Great American Duck Ball. There is a parade, plenty of booths serving chile, and a hot air balloon rally.

The duck race has achieved its objective of publicizing Deming beyond the citizens' wildest expectations. Stories about the event have appeared in all fifty states and in many foreign countries, even though no one has figured out why New Mexicans get so excited about ducks. And believe it or not, the Bosque Farms man whose ducks have won the most races at Deming is named . . . Robert Duck.

★ ★
TOURIST INFORMATION

DEMING CHAMBER OF COMMERCE
P.O. Box 8, Deming, NM 88031 (546-2674)

★ ★
SIGHTSEEING

However, there is more to Deming than ducks. A stop at the **Deming Welcome Center**, 800 Pine Street (546-2674), which can't be missed because of the locomotive parked outside, will orient the visitor to the attractions in the area.

DEMING-LUNA MIMBRES MUSEUM
Located at 301 S. Silver in the old National Guard Armory, this museum is operated by the Luna County Historical Society, which has done a great job assembling the exhibits. In Ruebush Hall is a large, authentic chuckwagon on display. This "traveling kitchen" sets the scene for the "Way It Was Room," which reflects the pioneer days of Luna County with antiques, relics, and memorabilia.

The Gilmore Quilt Room contains an impressive collection of beautiful quilts dating back to 1847, and the Louise Baumgartner Southerland Doll Room has an assortment of some five hundred costumed dolls. Because of the local interest in rocks and minerals, the museum has a Gem and Mineral Room that showcases hundreds of samples. The Military room contains mementos of early Fort Cummings, the Pancho Villa raid on Columbus (see listing below), and the Deming Army Air Field from World War II. The pre-Columbian Mimbres Indians are the center of attention in the Indian Gallery, which displays relics, pots, and baskets of this culture. There is also an Art Gallery and a Transportation Annex.

The museum and museum store are open daily from 9 a.m.– 4 p.m. and Sundays from 1:30 p.m. to 4 p.m. For more information, call 546-2382.

ROCK HOUND STATE PARK
This park is the only one in New Mexico where visitors are urged to take part of it home with them. Located twelve miles south of Deming off NM Hwy. 11 in the foothills of the rugged Little Florida Mountains, this 240-acre facility is dedicated to rocks and minerals. Rock hounds may collect up to twenty pounds of rock and mineral specimens, including quartz crystal, black perlite, agate, onyx, and opals. A particular favorite with rock hounds are the "thunder eggs," a variety of spherulite with agate or opal inside. Some twenty years of rock collecting by visitors has not significantly changed the appearance of the park.

In addition to rocks, the park has camping and picnicking facilities with hookups, rest rooms with showers, hiking trails, and a playground. Two miles south of the park headquarters is the Spring Canyon area with additional camping sites, spectacular views of the desert mountain landscape, and exotic wildlife such as the Persian ibex, which were introduced into the area in the early 1970s. For additional information on Rock Hound State Park, call 546-1212.

Rock hounds of all ages will be interested in the **Annual Rock Hound Roundup,** which is a national rock show held in early March at the Southwestern New Mexico Fairgrounds in Deming and which attracts nearly five hundred participants. Details are available by calling 546-6209.

CITY OF ROCKS STATE PARK
Located 28 miles northeast of Deming via US Hwy. 180 and NM Hwy. 61, this park stands out on the plain like the skyline of a city. This skyline is not composed of skyscrapers but of 25-foot-tall boulders composed of welded tuff, which is compacted volcanic ash. After a volcano deposited the ash here 33 million years ago, wind and water erosion created these formations that eerily resemble a city complete with "streets" and "office buildings."

There are 56 camping sites here (no hookups), plus picnic tables, rest rooms with showers, and a playground. All of the water and electricity for the campground is provided by solar and wind power. Hiking trails wind through the rock formations and state park officials have created an impressive cactus garden. Rock climbing is an obvious attraction here and visitors are warned to wear rubber-soled shoes and to bring protection for the hands and legs which can be scraped raw from the rough volcanic rock.

Wildlife abounds in and around the park. At least 35 species of birds have been identified, and although rattlesnakes are common, bites from them are not. For some obscure reason, Easter weekend is the busiest time of the year at City of Rocks as hundreds of people arrive to view the rocks that some deranged tourist brochure copywriter has called "Stonehenge of the Southwest." City of Rocks State Park can be reached by calling 536-2800.

COLUMBUS

This small town on the Mexican border 32 miles south of Deming on NM Hwy. 11 is famous because it was raided in 1916 by Mexican bandit-politician Pancho Villa. The raid marked the only time in history that the United States was invaded by foreign armed forces. However, it should be pointed out that Villa was acting on his own and not as a representative of the Mexican government.

Columbus was a flourishing village in those days because it was a depot of the El Paso and Southwestern Railroad and was the site of a U.S. army base, Camp Furlong. It boasted of a school with seventeen teachers, a Coca-Cola bottling plant, three hotels, and a theatre. The size of the town made it a tempting target for Pancho Villa.

Villa, called a cattle thief and bank robber by his opponents, was on the run from General Alvaro Obregon, who had defeated Villa's forces in five previous battles after Villa had fallen out with the Mexican president, Venustiano Carranza. Although no one really knows why Villa chose to attack Columbus and its nearby Army base, the most common explanation given is that Villa was trying to embarrass President Woodrow Wilson, who had recently given recognition to Carranza as Mexican president.

At about four in the morning on March 9, 1916, about a thousand of Villa's men cut the boundary fence separating the two countries and attacked Columbus and the 13th Cavalry at Camp Furlong. Although surprised and outnumbered three to one, the soldiers rallied and drove the Mexicans back into town. There, Villa's men made the mistake of setting fire to a block of buildings including the Commercial Hotel.

The light of the flames made perfect targets of the raiders, and

the soldiers opened up a withering barrage of gunfire. Villa ordered
his men back across the border with the American soldiers in hot
pursuit. American casualties were seventeen civilians and soldiers
killed and twelve wounded. Mexican casualties were far more
severe: 142 killed in the United States and perhaps another hundred
killed during the pursuit into Mexico.

The following day, President Wilson ordered a punitive expedition against Villa commanded by General John J. Pershing. This
expedition would mark the first time in American history that
motorized vehicles and aircraft would be used in warfare. However, the trucks and biplanes were of limited value because of harsh
desert conditions. Pershing did succeed in chasing Villa more than
five hundred miles into Mexico and defeating several of his bands
of troops in battle, but he did not capture the revolutionary leader.

The advent of World War I caused President Wilson to withdraw
Pershing from Mexico in February, 1917, but Villa kept on battling
the Mexican Army forces until he was assassinated in 1923.

Today Columbus is a quiet little border town (population four
hundred) and New Mexico's only international port of entry. The
two main attractions here both owe their existence to Villa's raid.
The **Columbus Historical Museum,** located in the old Southern
Pacific Railroad depot on Pacific Ave. (531-2620), has photographs, relics, and other material pertaining to Villa's raid. The
museum is open daily 10 a.m.–4 p.m.

It might seem strange to name a state park after a foreign
invader, but New Mexico did just that when it opened **Pancho Villa
State Park** in 1959 "in interest of preservation of the memory of the
unique, historical occasion of the last hostile action by foreign
troops within the continental United States." The park is located on
the site of old Camp Furlong just south of Columbus.

The park features an outstanding museum at the visitor center
with exhibits of artifacts, photographs, and a documentary film on
the raid and its aftermath. There are 61 campsites with water and
electricity, two group shelters, rest rooms with showers, and hiking
trails. About five thousand different varieties of cacti and desert
plants are on display at the botanical garden which is part of the
state park. For additional information, call 531-2711.

★ ★
LODGING AND DINING

Deming has more than six hundred rooms for visitors and every
one of them is in a roadside motel. Recommended are the **Best**

Western Chilton Inn, US Hwy. 70/80 east (546-8813 with the **Branding Iron Restaurant**); **Holiday Budget Inn,** exit 85 on I-10 to Motel Dr. (546-2661), with a swimming pool, restaurant, and lounge; and the **Grand Motor Inn** on US Hwy. 70/80 east (546-2632), with a heated pool, restaurant, and lounge.

It's hard to go wrong by ordering New Mexican food in Deming. Recommended restaurants include **Cactus Cafe,** 218 W. Cedar (546-2458), open 6:30 a.m.–9 p.m. daily; and **La Fonda,** 601 E. Pine (546-0465), open 6 a.m.–9 p.m. daily.

LORDSBURG

Named after railroad engineer Delbert Lord, Lordsburg was established in 1880 during the construction of the Southern Pacific Railroad. The route for the railroad was chosen because of previous trails in the area, an Apache trail that prospectors followed to California, and the Butterfield Stage Trail, which was established in 1858.

The stage company established a relay station nineteen miles west of present-day Lordsburg in Doubtful Canyon. The ruins of this station at Steins Pass have been restored because of the station's tumultuous history — attacks from both bandits and Apaches. The notorious Black Jack Ketchum roamed the area preying upon both stages and trains, and once raided Separ, just south of Deming and robbed the town's entire population — a total of thirteen people. This event became the only time in New Mexico's frontier history that an entire town was victim to holdup men.

The Steins Pass station was also the scene of an Apache attack that started a legend known as the Treasure of Doubtful Canyon. On the eve of the Civil War in 1861, a band of Apaches led by Cochise attacked a trail of six wagons belonging to the company of George Giddings, which held the mail delivery contract of the San Antonio-San Diego Stage Line. The attack took place in Doubtful Canyon near Steins Station, and the Indians eventually killed all of the drivers but one and burned the wagons and the stage station.

According to some sources, the wagon train, led by George Gidding's brother James, was engaged in closing all the stage stations because of Apache violence. The wagons had been moving from El Paso to San Diego, closing stations as they went and transporting any valuables west. By the time they reached Steins Station, they were carrying about $30,000 in company gold, which they buried somewhere in Doubtful Canyon during the Apache attack.

Of course no one has found the gold, despite hundreds of

searches. It is even doubtful that any gold was ever buried here, because in his claim for damages against the government for the burned wagons and stations, Giddings did not list any gold, cash, or valuables. Treasure stories such as this one are numerous in southwestern New Mexico, as you shall see.

Today Lordsburg depends upon agriculture, tourism, and mining for its financial base. Annual events include the Lordsburg Windsail Races held on a dry lake bed in late March or early April, and the Hidalgo County Fair in late August.

★ ★
TOURIST INFORMATION

LORDSBURG-HIDALGO CHAMBER OF COMMERCE
P.O. Box 699, Lordsburg, NM 88045 (542-9864)

★ ★
SIGHTSEEING

The first stop in Lordsburg should be at the **Lordsburg Museum,** at 205 Main Street. Here are relics of early frontier life and a display of Charles Lindbergh's 1932 visit to Lordsburg in the "Spirit of St. Louis" when he dedicated the town's airport.

SHAKESPEARE
This restored village is now being billed as the "The West's Most Authentic Ghost Town," whatever that means. Located two and one-half miles south of Lordsburg, the town is a good example of the boom-and-bust cycles of mining towns.

Founded as a stage station in the 1850s, Shakespeare was first called Mexican Springs, then, after the Civil War, the name was changed to Grant. The name was changed again to Ralston after the discovery of silver in the 1870s; because William Ralston, founder of the Bank of California, financed most of the mining operations.

Ralston soon became a rip-roarin' mining town complete with hotels, saloons, and houses of ill repute to service the miners. The population of the town soared to three thousand, but the silver boom was short-lived. As the ore began to play out, Mr. Ralston salted some of the mines with diamonds in 1872. After word spread about diamond mines in Ralston, more miners flocked into town and Ralston sold stock in his diamond mines to investors from all over the United States and Europe. The hoax was finally uncovered and Ralston was ruined. Fearing for his life, he fled his eponymous hometown and returned to San Francisco, where he committed suicide.

Embarrassed at having their town identified with a suicidal swindler, citizens changed the name again in the late 1870s to Shakespeare – after the Shakespeare Gold and Silver Mining Company, which had bought up all the claims in the area. There was just one little problem: The town's population had dwindled to only a few hundred.

The coming of the railroad in the early 1880s kept the town alive as a supply camp, and silver and copper mini-booms in the 1890s, 1920s, and 1940s also helped. But the population of Shakespeare continued to dwindle away to almost nothing.

Rita and Frank Hill bought the entire town in 1935 as the headquarters for their cattle ranch and eventually discovered that tourism could also be a source of income. The Hill family conducts tours of the town on Saturdays and Sundays during the summer for $2 per person. For more details and directions, call the town at 542-9034.

RED ROCK EXOTIC GAME PRESERVE
Located about thirty miles north of Lordsburg on NM Hwy. 464, this refuge is the home of Persian gazelles, Mexican bighorn sheep, and other exotic game animals that will be transplanted into the Big Hatchet and Florida Mountains. Late afternoons and early mornings are the best times to see the game. There are no facilities whatsoever at this preserve. Southeast of Lordsburg via I-10 and NM Hwy. 146 is the **Big Hatchet Wildlife Refuge,** about twenty miles south of Hachita. There are no facilities here either – just a wild expanse of rugged mountain and desert terrain.

★ ★
LODGING AND DINING

Lodging in Lordsburg is similar to that in Deming. Recommended motels are the **American Motor Inn,** 944 E. Motel Dr. (542-3591), a Best Western facility with a pool, restaurant, and lounge; **Holiday Motel,** 512 E. Motel Dr. (542-3535), which has an Olympic-size pool, a restaurant, and a lounge; and **Desert West Motel,** seventeen miles west of Lordsburg off I-10 at its intersection with US Hwy. 80 (542-8801) with a pool, lounge, restaurant, and a mini-mall across the street.

A recommended restaurant is **El Charro,** 209 S. P Boulevard (542-3400), open 24 hours daily.

SILVER CITY

This city has a particularly appropriate name. In 1870, Capt. John Bullard of La Cienega de San Vincente ("St. Vincent's marsh"), as the site of Silver City was known then, traveled to Shakespeare to prospect the area because of the silver mines that had opened up. During his prospecting he recognized some of the ore. He is reported to have said, "If that's silver ore, we know where there's plenty of it."

He returned to his farm at La Cienega and picked up some ore samples which assayed at $60 to the ton — not great, but promising. He promptly founded the Bullard Mining Company, and the strikes at Chloride Flat, as it was later called, became a major silver-producing district in New Mexico, generating nearly $3 million in silver.

The boom town was renamed Silver City to reflect its newly found wealth and soon it became the center of trade for the area, and eventually the leading city in the southwestern part of the state. One witness to the peak of the gold and silver boom in Silver City wrote of gold bricks and silver bars stacked like cordwood on the sidewalks outside shipping offices. Unfortunately, John Bullard did not live very long to enjoy his new-found wealth. One year after he discovered silver he was shot and killed by Apaches, who claimed title to all the land around Silver City.

The silver boom in Silver City lasted until 1893, when the national crash in silver prices, combined with the fact that the Chloride Flats ore was played out, caused the end of silver mining in the area. But unlike many other towns totally dependent upon mining, Silver City survived the bust because it had begun to diversify its income base.

There were several factors that helped Silver City to survive the decline of mining. Since the coming of the railroad, the town became a major center for the shipping of cattle and lumber. The discovery of gold in the Mogollon Mountains, of iron at Fierro, and of copper at Santa Rita all helped to keep Silver City as a central commercial center. Also, a major health care boom occurred in the early 1900s when many easterners moved to Silver City to take cures for tuberculosis at sanatariums established for that purpose.

In 1895, a severe flood struck the town as water washed down from the denuded hills around Silver City. A twelve-foot wall of water rampaged down Main Street, carrying everything with it and creating a thirty-foot-deep ditch where the street had been. A second flood in 1903 made the ditch 25 feet deeper, and the citizens learned they had to live with occasional floods. So they changed the name of the thoroughfare from Main Street to Big Ditch, and life went on. In 1936, the Civilian Conservation Corps lined the Big Ditch with masonry, and in 1980 the city declared the ditch a park. It is now a sort of river walk, complete with shade trees and waterfalls.

★ ★

TOURIST INFORMATION

SILVER CITY CHAMBER OF COMMERCE
1103 Hudson Street, Silver City, NM 88061 (538-3785 or 1-800-548-9378)

★ ★

HISTORIC SIGHTSEEING

Much of the downtown area is part of the **Silver City Historic District,** which is on the National Register because of the quality of the buildings that preserve the look and feel of the town's silver boom days. Visitors wishing maps and detailed historical information should visit the **Silver City Chamber of Commerce,** 1103 Hudson Street (538-3785 or 1-800-548-9378).

BULLARD STREET
Named after the founder of Silver City, John Bullard, this street has many buildings dating from the 1880s. On the northwest corner of Bullard and Broadway is the 1882 Meredith and Ailman Bank with its original cast-iron front. Although legend holds that Billy the Kid killed his first man on this street, the story cannot be substantiated.

However, naming of the **Billy the Kid Jail Site** is historically accurate. The U.S. Forest Service warehouses at 304 N. Hudson are on the site of the jail where The Kid was incarcerated in 1875 for stealing from a Chinese laundry. He escaped by climbing up the jail's chimney—he was a very skinny boy of fifteen then.

WESTERN NEW MEXICO UNIVERSITY MUSEUM
Located at the end of Alabama Street on the university campus (538-6386), the Fleming Hall Museum has an eclectic collection of artifacts, folk art, and material pertaining to the mining, military, and natural history of the Southwest. The **Eisele Collection** is en-

titled "People of Mystery: The Ancient Mimbres Culture" and consists of an outstanding collection of ancient Mimbres artifacts in the country. Containing more than three hundred ceramic pieces with startlingly beautiful animal and geometric designs, this collection has been featured in publications such as *National Geographic* and displayed at the New York Metropolitan Museum of Art. The Mimbres people, who lived at the Gila Cliff Dwellings (see listing below), occupied this area between 900 and 1150.

The **Robert Miller Collection** features an excellent assemblage of Nigerian folk art donated to the University by science faculty member Robert Miller. The collection includes drums and other musical instruments, religious ritual objects, and ceremonial artifacts. Hundreds of pocket and wrist watches comprise the **J. H. Taylor Collection of Watches and Timepieces**. Most are in working order and some date from as early as 1750.

The museum also has extensive collections of early photographs. It is open Mon.–Fri. from 8 a.m.–4:30 p.m. and Sundays from 1 p.m.–4 p.m. There is no admission charge.

Also on the campus of WNMSU is the **Francis McCray Gallery** (538-6386), with a collection of Southwestern art on display.

THE GRAVE OF BILLY THE KID'S MOTHER

The Silver City Cemetery on US Hwy. 180 north of town at Memory Lane is the site of this touching memorial to Katherine Antrim, who died of tuberculosis in 1874 and thus never survived to witness the fame — and infamy — of her son. Her headstone may or may not be present, depending upon the whims of history buff vandals. Four graves to the north lies the final resting place of John Bullard.

SILVER CITY MUSEUM

This 1881 mansion of silver tycoon H. B. Ailman at 312 W. Broadway (538-5921) has been transformed into a museum that reflects the history of Silver City with exhibits of mining memorabilia, furnishings of early houses, and an excellent collection of Mimbres and Casas Grandes artifacts. There is also an exhibit featuring the mining town of Tyrone (see listing below) as well as a large annex with other regional displays. The museum is free, open 9 a.m.–4 p.m. Mon.–Fri, and 10 a.m.–4 p.m. on weekends.

OLD TYRONE (Phelps Dodge Mine)

Located ten miles southwest of town via NM Hwy. 90, this pre-planned company town has now been enveloped by the huge Phelps Dodge open-pit copper mine, one of two such mines in the area. In 1912, the mining company hired famous architect Bertram Goodhue, who had designed the San Diego Exposition, to build a Mediterranean-style company town.

The town was ready for occupation by 1915, complete with hospital, shopping center, railroad station, and luxurious houses, but a drop in copper prices caused Tyrone to be abandoned—hence the nickname, the "million dollar ghost town." From 1928 to 1941, Tyrone was a dude ranch, but when the mine started up again in 1966 as an open-pit operation, the town was sacrificed to make way for the huge pit and tailings that are seen today. A new townsite— modern Tyrone—was built seven miles north of Old Tyrone.

LODGING

Because Silver City's engaging history and a present population of 25,000 in the surrounding area, visitors might expect to find a wide range of lodging facilities, including restored hotels. But such is not the case in Silver City, where excepting the establishments listed below, the accommodations are disappointing. Additional lodging facilities are listed under the listing headed "Nearby Attractions."

BEAR MOUNTAIN GUEST RANCH
Located on Bear Mountain Road (538-2538), this bed and breakfast operation also conducts nature and archaeology tours of the nearby Gila National Forest and ghost towns. There are fifteen rooms and more than just breakfast—three meals are served daily. Mailing address is P.O. Box 1163, Silver City, NM 88062.

COPPER MANOR MOTEL
Adjacent to the Red Barn Steak House (see the listing below) at 708 Silver Heights Blvd. (538-5392), the Copper Manor has an indoor pool with jacuzzi, a restaurant, a lounge, and offers cable TV.

THE DRIFTER MOTEL
This oddly named establishment at 711 Silver Heights Blvd. (538-2916) offers a pancake house, heated pool, a lounge with entertainment, and also offers cable TV.

HOLIDAY MOTOR HOTEL
The area's largest lodging facility is located on US Hwy. 180 East (538-3711) and features a restaurant and lounge, a large swimming pool, and cable TV.

ECLECTIC LODGING NEAR SILVER CITY

Get into the boonies at **Bear Mountain Guest Ranch,** a B&B near the wilderness area (538-2538). **The Carter House** is a large Edwardian home in the historic district (388-5485) while the **D-Bar Guest Ranch** is a mountain lodge on a working cattle ranch in Mimbres (772-5563).

DINING

Silver City has its fair share of good restaurants, with most of them devoted to New Mexican specialties or steak and seafood.

NEW MEXICAN

New Mexican foods are served up in hot style by Silver City dining emporiums, including the **Jalisco Cafe,** 103 S. Bullard (388-2060), where all the food is prepared fresh daily using non-processed ingredients. Open 11 a.m.–8:30 p.m. Mon.–Sat., closed Sunday. Also recommended are **Mi Casita,** 2340 Bosworth Dr. (538-5533), and **Matias,** 1007 North Pope (388-1343). Both are open 8 a.m.–8 p.m. daily).

STEAKS AND SUCH

Perhaps the most interesting restaurant in the area is not in Silver City, but in nearby Pinos Altos. The **Buckhorn Saloon and Opera House,** six miles north of Silver City on NM Hwy. 15 (538-9911), features an occasional dinner theatre and is set amidst an atmosphere straight from the 1860s. There are huge stone fireplaces and pine log ceilings, and the saloon is exactly what one would picture from the gold mining days, complete with paintings of fleshy nude women on the walls. Oh, yes—the steaks, seafood, and prime ribs are excellent. The bar opens at 3 p.m., and the restaurant starts serving at 6 p.m. Closed Sunday.

Also recommended is the **Red Barn Steak House** on US Hwy. 180 East (538-5666) with steaks and seafood, open 11 a.m.–10 p.m. daily.

SHOPPING

There are some interesting shops and galleries here for the visitor, including the **Kiva Trading Company,** 510 W. US Hwy. 180 (538-5852), a gallery with Indian turquoise and silver jewelry, Navajo and Zapotec weavings, and prints by Southwestern artists; the **Western Heritage Gallery,** on Alabama and Cottage San Rd. (538-9640), with originals and limited-edition prints.

★ ★

THE GREAT OUTDOORS

Approximately one-third of the entire southwest quadrant of New Mexico is blanketed by national forest lands, making the area a true recreational paradise. Visitors should be advised, however, that much of the region is true wilderness, completely devoid of any amenities for human interlopers.

GILA NATIONAL FOREST
This three-and-one-half-million-acre forest is typical of other national forests in New Mexico, in that it encompasses a variety of life zones ranging from Upper Sonoran to arctic conditions and elevations from 4300 to 10,900 feet. However, due to the variety of habitats and the proximity to Arizona and Mexico, the Gila has a very diverse collection of wildlife. Primary game animals include deer, elk, pronghorn antelope, javelina, black bear, bighorn sheep, and the highest population of Merriam's turkey of any national forest. There is also quite a variety of smaller birds and mammals, including the tassel-eared squirrel, Mearn's quail, and the band-tailed pigeon. There are more than four hundred miles of trout streams in the Gila.

Two wilderness areas are included in the Gila National Forest, the Aldo Leopold Wilderness Area and the Gila Wilderness Area, which was the first National Wilderness, so designated in 1924. Only foot or horseback travel is permitted in the wilderness areas.

One portion of the Gila is less than fifty miles from the Mexican border, but the main unit is just north of Silver City and is about 75 by one hundred miles in area. The Continental Divide winds for about 170 miles through this spectacular canyon country which was the stronghold of Apache warriors such as Victorio, Nana, Cochise, and Geronimo. Centuries before the Apaches, the ancient Mimbres culture inhabited these mountains, leaving only the ruins of structures they abandoned, such as the Gila Cliff Dwellings (see listing below).

The mountain ranges in the Gila include the Mogollons, Tularosas, Diablos, and the Black Range. One of the easiest ways to view those mountains is to take the 75-mile loop drive from Silver City to Santa Rita via US Hwy. 180 and NM Hwy. 152, then up the Mimbres Valley on NM Hwy. 35 to Sapillo Creek, and then back to Silver City on NM Hwy. 15.

There are about thirty camping sites in the Gila. Near Silver City, the most popular are **Mesa,** thirty miles northeast via NM Hwy. 15 and 35, **Little Walnut,** six miles north of town on Little Walnut Rd., and **Scorpion Corral,** 45 miles north via NM Hwy. 15. Fishing is good along the branches of the Gila River and Willow and Negrito Creeks. Fishing is prohibited in some areas to protect the endangered Gila Trout, which is native to the area. There is also fishing at **Bill Evans Lake,** 25 miles northwest of Silver City via US Hwy. 180.

For maps and additional information, contact the Gila National Forest at the Silver City Ranger District at 538-2771 or 388-8201.

★ ★
NEARBY ATTRACTIONS

PINOS ALTOS
Just six miles north of Silver City on NM Hwy. 15 is the restored ghost town of Pinos Altos ("tall pines"). Originally called Birchville, the area was the site of a gold discovery in 1837 and the boom was on. By 1867 the population of the town was seven hundred and there were saloons dancehalls, and brothels designed to separate the miners from their gold.

But the Apaches had different ideas about the white man's lust for gold and in 1861, a force of about five hundred warriors led by Mangas Coloradas attacked Pinos Altos, killing many miners and soldiers. Sporadic attacks continued until peace was made with the Indians. The truce called for peace as long as a white cross was visible on a nearby mountain.

Sam and Roy Bean operated a general store and sold liquor here before moving to Texas to become "the law west of the Pecos." Pinos Altos was the original county seat of Grant County before the success of Silver City, and one of its most prominent citizens was George Hearst, father of William Randolph Hearst, who later built a newspaper empire with the gold mined by his family.

In addition to the Buckhorn Saloon and Opera House, mentioned above, there are other interesting sights here, including the **Hearst Church,** built in 1898, which now houses the Grant County Art Guild. The **Santa Rita del Cobre Fort and Trading Post** is a three-quarter scale reproduction of the original fort built at the Santa Rita mine in 1804 to protect the area from Apaches. The **Pinos Altos Museum** is housed in a log cabin which was Grant County's first school house, probably built around 1866. The museum's collection includes pottery and old household items and memorabilia of the early settlers and of the first copper works. For information call 388-1882.

There are various arts and crafts shops in Pinos Altos, plus the **First Courthouse** (1871) with the legendary "hanging tree" out front. Surprisingly, there is also lodging available here at **Bear Creek Motel and Cabins** on NM Hwy. 15 (388-4501). Mailing address is P.O. Box 82, Pinos Altos, NM 88053.

CHINO MINES COMPANY COPPER MINE

The gigantic open-pit copper mine is located fifteen miles east of Silver City at the former townsite of Santa Rita on NM Hwy. 152 and is the oldest active mine in the Southwest. It was worked as early as 1800 by Col. Jose Carrasco from Mexico. Convicts worked in the mine, which was a shaft operation in those days. Mule trains carried the ore down the Janos Trail to Chihuahua.

An adobe fort was built near the mine, along with smelters and other buildings, but it was ineffective and the mine was abandoned to the Apaches. A replica of this fort can be seen in Pinos Altos. In 1851 the fort was taken over by the U.S.-Mexican Boundary Survey and the next year it was named Fort Webster and became the first military post in the area.

In the 1890s the mine was reopened and in 1910 it became an open-pit operation that consumed the fort and the entire town of Santa Rita. The mine is operated now by Phelps Dodge and Mitsubishi and huge shovels scoop copper ore from the pit and load it on 175-ton trucks, which then take it to a reduction mill. The pit is a mile and a quarter across and more than one thousand feet deep.

MIMBRES VALLEY

The Mimbres Valley extends from City of Rocks State Park near US Hwy. 180 between Deming and Silver City up to Lake Roberts, and NM Hwys. 61 and 35 follow the entire valley. It is a picturesque trip with many small villages along the way. At **Faywood,** also called **Dwyer** for some unknown reason, there are many orchards producing apples, pears, apricots, and peaches. Roadside stands such as **Mimbres River Fruit** sell the fruit, other produce, and cider. **San Lorenzo**, off NM Hwy. 152 just east of NM Hwy. 61, is a small village first settled in 1869 that still retains the flavor of the nineteenth century.

The town of **Mimbres** was booming in 1875 when the Georgetown Milling Company was operating. About 1.5 million dollars in silver was produced here, and the ore was reduced at Mimbres. An old adobe building still stands at the dirt road turnoff to the ghost town of **Georgetown;** it was the mess hall for the mill workers. The population of Georgetown and Mimbres exceeded 1200 at this time. In Mimbres are several places to stop and visit, including **Mimbres Valley Cafe** with New Mexican food (536-2857); the **Mimbres Trading Post** with rocks and gifts (536-9300); and **El Mimbreño** (536-9432), featuring T-shirts with Mimbres Indian designs on them. Lodging is available at the **Mimbres Valley Country Inn** at 8544 NM Hwy. 35 (536-3600).

Just north of Mimbres on NM Hwy. 35 is the entrance to **Bear Canyon Dam,** which retains a 35-acre lake for fishing and the **Bear Canyon Campground.** Information about these sites and the Gila National Forest is available at the **Mimbres Ranger Station** (536-2250), which issues wilderness camping permits.

The Mimbres Valley terminates at **Lake Roberts,** a 72-acre lake 25 miles northeast of Silver City via NM Hwys. 15 and 35. There is fishing for trout, bass, and catfish here, plus a nature trail that leads to a Mimbres Indian site. The **Lake Roberts General Store** (536-9929) has food, fishing and camping supplies, and cabins. Just north of the lake off NM Hwy. 35 is an abandoned meerschaum mine, the only one in the U.S., which produced the sea foam used in European pipes in the 1890s.

GILA CLIFF DWELLINGS NATIONAL MONUMENT
These ancient homes built into cliffs were first discovered by non-Indians in the early 1880s, and in 1884, the famed anthropologist Aldoph Bandelier first wrote about them. In 1907, President Theodore Roosevelt signed legislation designating the site as a national monument. The monument is located 44 miles north of Silver City at the termination of NM Hwy. 15.

The Gila Visitor Center features exhibits on the prehistoric inhabitants of this valley, as well as information on Gila National Forest. In the parking lot outside the center, rangers present evening programs during the summer. Topics vary from week to week but include presentations on food preparation, tool making, archaeology, wilderness ethics, and forest ecology.

A trail leads from the visitor center to the cliff dwellings, and visitors can take the trail and follow information provided in the park service brochure which describes this ancient culture.

The earliest ruin in the monument is a pithouse of a type constructed between A.D. 100 and 400. People of this period, a part of the Mogollon Culture, lived in these underground chambers, surviving by growing corn and beans or hunting game. These people also made a primitive, plain brown pottery.

The pithouses eventually gave way to square houses built above ground around A.D. 1000. Some sources speculate that influence from the Anasazis in Chaco Canyon was responsible for this change in lifestyle. About this time the Mogollan people began making a new type of pottery decorated with white and black designs. Late in the twelfth century, these people began to construct cliff dwellings for protection as well as pueblos on the terraces overlooking the West Fork of the Gila River.

Although the cliff dwellings are the most spectacular of these ancient Indian houses, they are also the most rare. Most of the population lived in the open pueblos such as the two-acre ruin behind the visitor center. The pottery continued to improve, and most of the classic vessels with animal designs were made at the time the cliff dwellings were occupied.

Five caves contain the ruins of the Gila cliff dwellings, which contain a total of about forty rooms. Walls of the dwellings were constructed of stone quarried from the cliffs, and the timbers in the dwellings are all original. By utilizing dendrochronology—tree ring dating—scientists have placed the construction of the cliff dwellings through the 1280s.

These Native Americans, often called Mimbreños, a branch of the Mogollon Culture, were primarily farmers whose fields were spread along the river and also on the mesa tops. They raised squash, corn, beans, and probably tobacco and amaranth, and also gathered wild berries and nuts from the forest. They trapped and hunted game, and fished for trout to supplement their farm crops.

The Mimbreños abandoned the cliff dwellings shortly before 1400, a fact that has led to the same type of speculation that surrounds the Anasazis (see listing for Chaco Culture National Monument). However, there is no real mystery about the abandonment of the cliff dwellings; ancient Indian peoples commonly abandoned their settlements and moved to other regions. The usual causes of such migrations were drought or attacks from their enemies, the

Mescalero Apaches. In fact, after the Mimbrenos left the area, nomadic bands of Apaches made it their homeland.

Near the national monument is **Scorpion Campground,** which is the principal entry point to the Gila Wilderness. For further information on the cliff dwellings, call the national monument at 536-9461.

A few miles south of the national monument is the small community of **Gila Hot Springs** with the **Grapevine Campground** which boasts, according to one source, of the World's Largest Grapevine. Nearby is the **Heart Bar Wildlife Area,** a ranch operated by the New Mexico Department of Game and Fish for the development of elk herds and for studying mountain lions. The **Gila Hot Springs Vacation Center** on NM Hwy. 15 (536-9551) has lodging, snacks, groceries, horseback riding, and an outfitting service for hunting and fishing trips into the Gila Wilderness. Oddly enough, that facility also has the **Faerie Land Museum** with a collection of miniature dolls and towns.

GLENWOOD
Located about 68 miles northwest of Silver City on US Hwy. 180, this small mountain community of about 450 is at the junction of Whitewater Creek and the San Francisco River. Hunting, fishing, and exploring are the major attractions here. A half mile outside of town is the **Glenwood State Hatchery** (539-2461), which supplies trout for stocking in the Gila National Forest. Visitors are welcome at the hatchery. Adjacent to the hatchery is a large pond where fishing is permitted.

One of the most famous attractions in the Glenwood area is the **Catwalk** through Whitewater Canyon, five miles east of Glenwood on NM Hwy. 174. The Catwalk is a metal walkway with four-foot-high wire mesh sides fastened to the sheer walls of the cliffs about thirty feet above the stream. In places the canyon is so narrow that the hiker can almost touch both sides simultaneously. The Catwalk follows the route of an old pipeline built to supply water to an ore mill and is about two and one-half miles long. Not all of the Catwalk is metal; in places the walk is constructed of timbers or cut out of the rock. In addition to catwalking, visitors can picnic at the site, take photographs, watch nature at work, or play in the stream. Overnight camping is not permitted.

Lodging is available at **Los Olmos Guest Ranch** in Glenwood (539-2311), which bills itself as the "biggest little resort in Southwest New Mexico." The ranch has individual cabins, a dining room, swimming pool, and fishing.

MOGOLLON

Located nine miles off of US Hwy. 180 on the winding and often precipitous NM Hwy. 159, this semi-ghost town was named for a former governor of the Spanish Province of New Mexico in the early 1700s. Mogollon boomed for more than fifty years after the gold strike of 1878 when wagonloads of gold, silver, and copper were hauled out of mines called Little Fanny, Confidence, and Deep Down. It was a typically wild New Mexico boomtown, and attracted such notables as Butch Cassidy, who headquartered there for a while, and Apaches led by Victorio periodically raiding. More than five million dollars worth of gold was produced between 1885 and 1900 alone, and the population of this town — precariously perched on the mountain slopes — topped two thousand.

Today Mogollon is sparsely inhabited, but the population grows during the summer tourist season. There are arts and crafts galleries here, the **Mogollon Museum** with displays of mining memorabilia, and a restaurant and theatre. The motion picture "My Name is Nobody" with Henry Fonda and Terrence Hill was filmed here. For information call 539-2481.

East of Mogollon along unimproved NM Hwy. 159 are **Willow Creek Campground** and **Snow Lake,** two rather primitive camping areas on the edge of the Gila Wilderness. The scenery is some of the finest in this part of the state, and Snow Lake is a one-hundred-acre impoundment with good trout fishing.

RESERVE

This small town about a hundred miles from Silver City via US Hwy. 180 and NM Hwy. 12 was founded in the 1860s by Mormon ranchers. Originally there were three towns here, Upper, Middle, and Lower San Francisco Plazas. Reserve was wild and wooly in those days, and is mostly famous for a gunfight that produced a true New Mexico folk hero, Elfego Baca.

In 1884, Middle San Francisco Plaza was the site of one of the most one-sided battles in all six-shooter history. The nineteen-year-old, self-appointed deputy sheriff, Baca, held off eighty Texas cowboys for 36 hours; killing four and wounding eight in a firefight that used up four thousand rounds of ammunition — or so the legend goes.

Some historians who have studied the incident have concluded that although the shootout did occur, only one Texan was killed by Baca and reports of eighty cowboys and four thousand rounds of ammo are greatly exaggerated. The legend was enhanced by a movie entitled "The Nine Lives of Elfego Baca," made by Walt Disney Studios in the late 1950s. Incidentally, Baca was tried for murder at Socorro, was acquitted, and later became a school superintendent and a district attorney.

SOCORRO

The name of this city at the intersection of US Hwy. 60 and I-25 means "help" in Spanish, but it refers to giving assistance, not asking for it. In 1598, the exhausted travelers of the Juan de Oñate expedition gave that name to the pueblo here because the Indians gave food and shelter to these explorers who eventually established a Spanish colony near what is now Santa Fe. By 1627 the Spanish had established a mission at Socorro to serve not only the local Indians, but also travelers on El Camino Real — the Royal Road — between Santa Fe and Chihuahua.

During the Pueblo Revolt of 1680, the residents of the Socorro Pueblo did not join their brothers to the north but rather fled south to El Paso with the Spanish and most of the Indians at Ysleta Pueblo. They never returned, which is the reason that there are settlements today near El Paso called Socorro and Isleta.

Socorro remained empty and in ruins for the next 136 years. Finally, in 1815, the governor of New Mexico issued a grant for the settlement of the town and the first settlers arrived the next year. Because of the fertile land and a large spring at the base of the mountains, the settlers were successful and by 1850 the population of Socorro was about six hundred.

The arrival of the Santa Fe Railroad in 1880 caused the population of Socorro to jump to four thousand in just a year or two. Smelters in the town processed the ore from nearby gold and silver mines, and farming, ranching, and mercantile interests provided the town with a diversified income base. In 1889, the New Mexico School of Mines was founded, and the first students attended classes in 1892. The college is now known as the New Mexico Institute of Mining and Technology — New Mexico Tech for short.

Today Socorro is an interesting blend of the old and new. Visitors who arrive from I-25 might have the impression that Socorro is comprised only of gas stations, motels, and restaurants along California Street. However, the historic section of town near the old Plaza has some beautiful examples of both adobe and California mission–style architecture.

★ ★
TOURIST INFORMATION

SOCORRO CHAMBER OF COMMERCE
103 Francisco de Avondo, Socorro, NM 87801 (835-0424)

★ ★
HISTORIC SIGHTSEEING

The Plaza area, just off California via Manzanares, contains most of the historic buildings in Socorro. Of particular interest is the **Hilton Block** on the east side of the Plaza, which was built by relatives of hotel magnate Conrad Hilton, who was born in nearby San Antonio. Nearby, around the northeast corner on Abeyta Street, is the **J. N. Garcia Opera House,** built in 1886 and now a National Historic Site.

Socorro is unusual for New Mexican cities and towns in that the mission church is located three blocks away from the Plaza instead of directly facing it. No one seems to know why. **San Miguel Mission,** north of the plaza off Bernard Street, was built about 1820 on the site of the original church that was burned to the ground during the Pueblo Revolt.

On the southeast corner of the Plaza is the **Capitol Bar,** which undoubtedly served Illinois Beer brewed at the **Hammel Brewery** on 6th Street. Another National Historic Site, the Hammel operation was the largest brewery and ice plant in New Mexico until Prohibition cut off beer production. The plant continued to bottle soft drinks until the 1950s when it closed permanently. The Socorro County Historical Society is in the process of converting the brewery building into a museum.

Along Manzanares Street east of the Plaza are a number of historic buildings, including the former **Val Verde Hotel,** which was built in 1919 in the California mission revival style. It was a sixty-room operation catering to travelers along Route 60, the "Ocean to Ocean Highway." The Val Verde was remodeled in 1985 and now houses shops, offices, and a restaurant. Further from the Plaza on Manzanares is the original **Atchison, Topeka, and Santa Fe Railway Depot,** built in 1880.

Park, Church, and McCutcheon Streets, south of the Plaza, are known as the "French Quarter" because of the Queen Anne and Italianate architectural elements on the houses. A rare New Mexico earthquake in 1906 caused the owners of some of these houses to reinforce them with steel rods. Details of all these historic houses, and a walking tour map are available courtesy of the Socorro County Historical Society at the Chamber of Commerce offices, 103 Francisco de Avondo (835-0424).

MINERAL MUSEUM

Because New Mexico Tech was founded as a mining college, it is only natural that it should have a museum such as this one. Located on School of Mines Road, the Mineral Museum has displays of more than 10,000 specimens, including invertebrate and vertebrate fossils, minerals of foreign countries, minerals of the United States, and minerals of New Mexico.

Of particular interest are a mastodon jaw found nearby, beautiful gypsum crystals, and minerals representing all the mining districts in New Mexico. The Dana Reference Collection, a compilation of 475 mineral species identified by chemical analysis and x-ray crystallography, is so complete that prospectors often drop by to compare ore samples they have collected in the field in order to identify them correctly. The museum maintains a set of New Mexico minerals for sale or trade and is open Monday through Friday from 8 a.m.–5 p.m. (835-5420). Admission is free.

★ ★

LODGING

Unfortunately, the Val Verde no longer accepts guests, so the only lodging available in Socorro is at standard motels—every one of which is on California Street. All of the following recommended motels have a swimming pool, restaurant, and cable TV: **El Camino,** 713 California (835-1500); **The Economy Inn,** 400 California (835-4666); the **Best Western Golden Manor,** 507 California (835-0230 or 1-800-528-1234); and the **Vagabond,** 1009 California (835-0276).

★ ★

DINING

At least half of Socorro's restaurants serve New Mexican specialties exclusively, so fiery food aficionados will have no problem here.

NEW MEXICAN

Visitors can take their pick from the following recommended restaurants: **Armijo's,** Hwy 85 (835-1686), open 11 a.m.–9 p.m. daily and Fri. and Sat. 11 a.m.–10 p.m. **El Sombrero,** 210 Mesquite (835-3945), open 11 a.m.–9 p.m. daily.

STEAKS AND SUCH

Perhaps the most famous restaurant in the area is the legendary **Owl Bar,** located nine miles south of Socorro on US Hwy. 380 in San Antonio (835-9946). The green chile cheeseburgers here have been written up in dozens of magazine and newspaper articles, and the Owl is a very popular (and refreshing) stop for travelers. The vehicles in the parking lot reveal the diversity of the clientele: a BMW parked next to a pickup parked next to a Harley. The adjoining steakhouse is open for dinner. Travelers should be warned that the Owl Bar is closed on Sundays. It is open 8 a.m.–9:30 p.m. Mon.–Sat. The **Val Verde Steak House,** 203 Manzanares (835-3380), is located in the remodeled, former Val Verde Hotel. It offers steaks, chicken dijon, shrimp dijon, steak tampico, and some New Mexican entrees. Open Mon.–Fri. 11 a.m.–2 p.m. and 5 p.m.–9:30 p.m., Sat. 4 p.m.–10:30 p.m., and Sun. noon–9 p.m.

★ ★
NEARBY ATTRACTIONS

SITE OF NEW MEXICO'S BEST CLOSE ENCOUNTER UFO CASE
In Socorro, California Street extends south to the small municipal airport. There, in 1964, Socorro police officer Lonnie Zamora was chasing a speeding black Chevy when he ticketed a much stranger craft. After losing the speeder somewhere in the desert, he heard an odd noise in the sky and then spotted the UFO.

"Object was oval in shape," Zamora wrote in his police report. "It was smooth — no windows or doors. As the roar started, it was still on or near the ground. Noted red lettering of some type. Insignia was about two-and-one-half feet wide, guess. Was in the middle of object, like a drawing. Object still like aluminum — white."

The egg-shaped object that Zamora encountered had occupants. He wrote that he "saw two people in white coveralls very close to object. One of these persons seemed to turn and look straight at my (police) car and seemed startled. Those persons seemed normal in shape — but possibly they were small adults or large kids."

Zamora's experience was quite brief. After spotting him, the occupants scrambled aboard the egg-shaped craft and took off, leaving behind a smoking bush and four imprints of landing gear. Zamora radioed for assistance and got far more than he bargained for—more than a thousand media people contacted him, and the story went national.

The Socorro UFO is a "nuts and bolts" case in UFO investigation circles, a case that suggests a real and quite terrestrial craft malfunctioning during a test flight and narrowly escaping public detection. A quick look at pictures of experimental military aircraft would convince even the most hardened skeptic that they could easily be mistaken for alien craft.

Although this episode is regarded as a classic in UFO literature, skeptics have continued to attack Zamora's account as a fabrication. If that is true, what was Zamora's motive? He certainly was not looking for publicity, for he shunned that. And he never made any money off the UFO sighting. It is likely that this New Mexico mystery will never be solved.

MAGDALENA

Settled in 1884, Magdalena soon became one of the most important cattle shipping points in the Southwest—perhaps because of its central location at US Hwy. 60 and NM Hwy. 169, about 27 miles west of Socorro. Ranchers could drive their cattle along the Magdalena Livestock Driveways, which utilized the Plains of San Agustin, a huge treeless prairie one hundred miles long, ten wide and surrounded by seven mountain ranges.

From Magdalena, a railroad carried the cattle to Socorro and the main line. Named after a fanciful rock formation in the shape of the head of Mary Magdalene, Magdalena was held by legend to be immune from Indian attacks because of the protective influence of the religious image on the mountain.

One of the oddest gunfights in New Mexico history occurred at the Hilton Saloon in Magdalena. Four men were playing poker when a dispute broke out over the cards dealt. Each man slid his chair back simultaneously, reached for his revolver and shot the man directly across from him. All four bullets found their mark and all four men fell to the floor, killed instantly. The guns had been fired from beneath the gaming table, so four bullet holes were left in it. The table was proudly displayed in the saloon for years after the incident.

Today Magdalena is a sleepy little town that comes alive during its annual Old Timers Reunion (835-0424) held at various locations in town every July, or when the piñon nuts are plentiful in the nearby mountains.

KELLY

Located two miles southeast of Magdalena on NM Rd. 107, Kelly is another mining ghost town. After its founding in 1870, Kelly grew very quickly to a population of three thousand because the Magdalena mining district was in the process of producing more than $28 million worth of lead-silver ore over the next quarter century. The mines had imaginative names such as the Graphic, Hardscrabble, Ambrosia, Legal Tender, and Vindicator.

During its boom years, the town boasted seven saloons, and two each of the following: dance halls, hotels, and churches. Kelly is well known for its feuds with Magdalena as the miners raided and shot up the cowboy's town and vice-versa.

Today the remains of a mine, a few crumbling adobe walls, and a dilapidated church are all that's left of Kelly.

VERY LARGE ARRAY RADIO TELESCOPE

Located between Magdalena and Datil just off US Hwy. 60 (watch for signs) is the world's most powerful and most sensitive radio telescope. Travelers are often startled by such a high tech wonder on the lonesome Plains of San Agustin. It is an astronomical observatory funded by the United States government via the National Science Foundation. It is named the Very Large Array (VLA) because of its 27 dish-shaped antennas that are 82 feet in diameter and which weigh 270 tons each. Weak radio waves from celestial sources are collected by each antenna and then sent to a central location where they are recorded. These signals are stored as numbers in a supercomputer that performs tens of millions of operations a second to form and analyze these images.

By using many antennae, which can be focused by moving them into certain patterns, the VLA can make detailed pictures of extremely faint objects in the radio image of the sky. The VLA is also utilized in the national Search for Extra-terrestrial Intelligence (SETI)—the antennae attempt to find intelligent radio patterns amidst all the galactic static. So far the SETI search has failed to match the success of the Starship Enterprise.

There is a visitor center here with displays on radio astronomy and the operation of the VLA. It is open from 8 a.m. to sundown. The self-guided walking tour sounds like something out of "Star Trek." There are stops at the Whisper Gallery, the Aperture Synthesis, the Variable Resolutions, and finally at Central Electronics Room next to the Control Room. Readers will be skeptical of the name of the last stop on the tour, but it's true: the Transporters.

Visitors to VLA are not allowed to leave designated pathways, enter buildings, or climb up the antennae (sorry, kids). The VLA brochure warns that "poisonous snakes are sometimes found in this area," but it doesn't state whether or not the snakes use the designated pathways. For additional warnings, write the VLA at public

information room at P.O. Box O, Socorro, NM 87801 or call
772-4255.

DATIL AND QUEMADO

Datil is a former well site along US Hwy. 60 about 37 miles west
of Magdalena that has been a watering hole for humans and
livestock since 1885. Today it is just a small, wayside stop for sleep
and refreshments. Located here is **Eagle Guest Ranch** on US Hwy.
60 (772-5612), with an eight-unit motel, a restaurant, and a lounge.
Just south of town is the **Datil Well National Recreation Site,** a
campground with shelters, a water supply, 22 picnic tables, and
rest rooms.

Quemado, a town devoted primarily to hunting and fishing, is
located 45 miles west of Datil on US Hwy. 60. The name means
"burned" and supposedly it originated from the fact that settlers
burned the underbrush where Apaches might lurk. Information
about recreational activities in the area can be obtained from the
Largo Motel on US Hwy. 60 west of Quemado (773-4686) or at the
El Serape Cafe on US Hwy. 60 (773-4620)., open 11 a.m.–9 p.m.
Mon.–Fri, closed Sat.–Sun. About eighteen miles south of town on
NM Hwy. 32 is **Quemado Lake,** a popular trout fishing spot.

Quemado is the town nearest to the legendary **Adams Diggings,**
the site of a classic New Mexico treasure tale. In 1864, the story
goes, a man named simply "Adams" and his men were led to a box
canyon by an Indian named Gotch-Ear. They found lots of gold in
a stream, which they mined despite threats from the Apache chief
Nana. The Indians attacked the miners and killed them all except
Adams and a man named Davidson. Unfortunately, the men had
to abandon the bags of gold they had mined and they barely escaped with their lives and a single gold nugget — which Davidson
sold for $93.

Years later, Adams led two expeditions in an attempt to find his
box canyon, but he was terrible with directions. After becoming
lost and traveling in circles, Adams' men accused him of deliberate-
ly leading them astray. At least five other expeditions failed to find
the Adams Diggings, and one in 1914 cost the life of Captain Mike
Cooney, who fell off his horse and froze to death even though his
horse survived.

In 1928, a party of six treasure hunters led by the famous
Western novelist Zane Grey also failed to find the box canyon of
gold. Nevertheless, the Adams Diggings have been the subject of
dozens of magazine articles and books on treasures, and the story
simply will not die.

BOSQUE DEL APACHE NATIONAL WILDLIFE REFUGE

In 1936, the Bosque del Apache Land Grant was purchased by the government and established three years later as "a refuge and breeding grounds for waterfowl and other wildlife." This lovely refuge is located two miles south of San Antonio on NM Hwy. 1, which runs parallel to I-25 south of Socorro. (Take exit 139.) The refuge's 57,191 acres are a paradise for birds and animals. Water is diverted from irrigation canals or pumped from underground wells to create temporary marshes amidst the bosque. During the winter months, migratory birds such as snow geese, ducks, and sandhill cranes seek refuge here from the arctic storms of their breeding grounds. Mallards make up most of the duck population, but pintails, shovelers, and teal are also common. Other birds also abound in the winter, including fish-eating mergansers, red-tailed hawks, and bald eagles.

During the summer, most of the temporary ponds are drained, but enough water is left for fish, egrets, and rails. Other animals found here include mule deer, rattlesnakes, soft-shelled turtles, and porcupines. In all there are 295 species of birds and more than four hundred different mammals, reptiles and amphibians found in the Bosque del Apache.

The endangered whooping cranes winter at this refuge due to a unique experiment with the sandhill cranes, a type of crane related to the whooper. Since 1967, Canadian and U.S. scientists have removed whooping crane eggs from nests and placed them with sandhill cranes. The sandhills have raised the whoopers, thus creating a new flock of whooping cranes with a shorter migratory route — from Gray's Lake National Wildlife Refuge in Idaho to Bosque del Apache. Visitors should remember that whooping cranes are the most famous of American's protected birds and even attempting to harm them is a federal offense.

Picnicking, backpacking, camping, hiking, and nature study are permitted here, but motorized vehicles are allowed only on designated roads and are definitely not allowed in the wilderness areas of the refuge. Fishing with a New Mexico permit is allowed here, and hunting for deer and certain waterfowl is permitted in season. Hunters must check in at the Refuge Headquarters. There is a twelve-mile driving loop tour with two observation towers and markers that are keyed to an informative brochure on the natural features and inhabitants of the refuge. During the winter, the flocks of thousands of snow geese or sandhill cranes make an impressive and beautiful sight, so visitors should bring a good camera with a zoom lens.

For more information, call the refuge at 835-1828.

TRUTH OR CONSEQUENCES

In a state renowned for the odd names of its communities, T or C is the all-time champ. And it's not the name itself that makes it the oddest, because "Truth or Consequences" has sort of a threatening Western law-and-order ring to it. No, it's the oddest name because of the circumstances surrounding its choice.

The great name change began in 1950 when the town was called Hot Springs. According to the Chamber of Commerce, "Hot Springs was plodding along slowly and fairly comfortably, much the same as hundreds of other small resort cities. Tourist trade constituted practically the only industry, but recreation was not developed to its full potential. The town was lost among hundreds of other little 'Hot Springs' scattered all over the United States; the name indicating nothing more significant than that there were probably some hot springs in or near the city."

To the rescue came Ralph Edwards, host of an enormously popular radio quiz show. He made a startling promotional announcement, promising that if some town or city would change its name to that of his show — "Truth or Consequences" — not only would the citizens be able to promote their town, he would personally visit their town every year for a parade and festival.

Hot Springs jumped at the opportunity. The manager of the Chamber of Congress, State Senator Burton Roach, negotiated the deal with Edwards and then handled the politics of such a startling move. On April 1, 1950, the name change was official: Hot Springs was now Truth or Consequences.

To promote the name change, NBC brought the entire cast of the radio show to Truth or Consequences for a live, coast-to-coast broadcast from the fiesta. About 10,000 people — a huge crowd in New Mexico in those days — lined the streets of the town to watch the Ralph Edwards Parade complete with all eighty members of the sheriff's posse on horseback.

As part of the celebration, a bottle of mineral water was smashed over the head of Burton Roach, the guy who put the name-change deal together. Edwards went back to Hollywood realizing that not only had the promotion worked, this town named after his show was a lot of fun. He wrote back to Roach, "Arrived home with enchilada in one hand and wife in other. Thanks to America's most gracious city. You will always be in our hearts and on our tongues."

Indeed. Ralph Edwards has returned to Truth or Consequences for the fiesta named after him, at this writing, for the last 37 years. The **Truth or Consequences Fiesta** is held in early May each year.

Since the name change, Truth or Consequences has received more national publicity via radio and TV than any other city of its size in the United States, which accounts for its success as the site for the largest resort area in New Mexico – **Elephant Butte State Park.**

Before the name change, Hot Springs was the home of Doc Noss, the man who created New Mexico's greatest treasure hunt. He was a slippery character who moved to New Mexico about 1930. Allegedly a foot doctor, he was arrested for practicing medicine without a license and threatening a waitress with a gun. While living in Hot Springs in 1937, Noss claimed to have discovered a treasure inside Victorio Peak, about 45 miles southeast of town, across the **Jornada del Muerto,** the extremely harsh desert valley between the Caballo and San Andres mountain ranges that is accurately described as the translation of its name, "journey of the dead man."

According to a report from the Museum of New Mexico, which investigated the treasure story, "Noss reportedly discovered a cave or crevice at the top of Victorio Peak in the San Andres Mountains through which he said he was able to descend 187 feet. He then proceeded along a passage to a room 2700 feet long. The room, he claimed, contained a large treasure consisting of several stacks of Spanish-made gold bars, chests of jewelry, Spanish armor, swords, crowns, the statues of several saints, and Wells Fargo chests. Noss also reported there were 27 skeletons in the room and he later brought one out to prove it."

The Victorio Peak Treasure is a catch-all legend encompassing elements of the most famous New Mexico treasure myths from Montezuma to Doubtful Canyon to the Adams Diggings. At one time or another each one of them was thought to be the source of the Victorio Peak treasure supposedly found by Noss.

For more than a year after the find, Doc Noss supposedly removed more than eighty gold bars from Victorio Peak and hid them on a number of slopes in the area. He hired an engineer in 1939 to help him enlarge the shaft to remove the rest of the treasure more easily, but they used too much dynamite and the shaft caved in, sealing off the treasure.

Doc raised money from investors and sold gold bars to pay for the excavation of the shaft, and by December 4, 1941, he told his partners they were within two weeks of reaching the gold. Three days later, the Japanese bombed Pearl Harbor and White Sands Proving Grounds was declared a restricted federal range. Access to Victorio Peak was denied to Noss. But the Doc managed to regain control after World War II and again staked his claim. Excavations resumed but Noss never saw them successfully completed: He was shot dead by one of his partners after he failed to produce the gold bars to exchange for $25,000 in cash.

Hundreds of amateur treasure hunters roamed the San Andres after the story hit the press. They found no gold. Nor did several later expeditions including a 1961 effort that was abandoned after finding a cave-in, the 1963 Museum of New Mexico exploration with its simultaneous archaeological, seismic, and gravity surveys — which lasted thirty days and discovered a few "rubble-filled cracks" but no treasure, and Operation Goldfinder in 1977.

Operation Goldfinder was an joint effort of the Museum of New Mexico and Expeditions Unlimited, a Florida treasure salvage company. It lasted only thirteen anti-climactic days but was covered by representatives from at least fifty media organizations, including the *New York Times*, *Time*, *Newsweek*, and CBS's news program "60 Minutes." Despite the media blitz, Operation Goldfinder was a flop.

To this day the Victorio Peak treasure — whether it existed or not — is still a big story in New Mexico because various claimants keep the pressure on U.S. Army officials to open Victorio Peak for yet another expedition. But the Army is not likely to yield. What is likely is that the New Mexico tradition of treasure stories will continue as long as the people have romance — and a little greed — in their souls.

The real treasure in the area of Truth or Consequences is outdoor fun. Since the creation of Elephant Butte Lake in 1916 and the name change in 1950, the town's facilities catering to vacationers have grown so much that over the Fourth of July weekend, it becomes New Mexico's second largest city, with more than 100,000 temporary inhabitants.

TOURIST INFORMATION

TRUTH OR CONSEQUENCES CHAMBER OF COMMERCE
P.O. Box 31, Truth or Consequences, NM 87901 (894-3536)

ELEPHANT BUTTE LAKE STATE PARK
Built primarily as an irrigation lake, Elephant Butte Reservoir is now equally important as a fishing and boating impoundment. The name originated with a volcanic cone which protrudes from the southern part of the lake and resembles the head and back of an elephant. After its completion in 1916, the lake was the largest body of impounded water in the world.

Elephant Butte is still New Mexico's largest lake, with a capacity of more than two million acre-feet of water — about 40,000 surface acres — which means that it extends up the Rio Grande for more than forty miles and has more than two hundred miles of shoreline. The state park comprises 17,000 surface acres and five thousand acres of land around the southern section of the lake. It can be reached by its own exit off I-25 about seven miles north of T or C.

The rule of nature which states that the largest fish live in the largest ponds applies at Elephant Butte. More than twenty species of sport fish can be caught here, including northern pike, blue catfish, channel catfish, white bass, striped bass, largemouth and smallmouth bass, black crappie, and walleye pike. The biggest fish caught are channel cats and striped bass, both of which can top forty pounds. Huge specimens of carp and large-mouth bass have also been caught, and Elephant Butte has been voted one of the ten best bass lakes in the United States.

The park headquarters at **New Hot Springs Landing** on NM Hwy. 195 (744-5421) is the main entrance to the park, where visitors receive information, have their boats checked, and pay necessary fees. A camping area below has hookups, rest rooms with showers, and picnic shelters with grills. A large boat ramp serves the public here, and nearby are three large commercial marinas for serious boaters on the lake and the river below.

Elephant Butte Resort Marina (744-5486), on NM Hwy. 195 a quarter-mile north of Hot Springs Landing state park entrance, offers a 162-slip marina, rental fishing and water skiing boats, a restaurant, bar, grocery store, tackle shop. **Rock Canyon Marina** (744-5462), just a bit further north, has a new fishing dock, boat and ski rentals, a marina store, and gas station. The **Damsite Recreation Area,** five miles east of the 3rd Street traffic light, features a fine restaurant and lounge (894-2073) serving steak, seafood, and New Mexican specialties in a lake-view setting, plus a complete marina (894-2041), cabins, and a RV trailer park.

Fishing expeditions are conducted by **Desert Bass Fishing Guide Services,** 744-5314. Golfers will be pleased to learn that there are two eighteen-hole courses in T or C, the **Municipal Golf Course** at 700 Marie Ave. (894-2603) and the **Oasis Golf Course** off NM Hwy. 195 (744-5224).

★ ★
LODGING

Most visitors to T or C stay aboard their boats or camp out in RVs and tents. However, there are good lodging facilities here.

ACE LODGE
This bargain motel at 1014 N. Date Street (894-2151), located next to the Los Arcos Steak House (see below), has 38 units and a heated swimming pool.

BEST WESTERN HOT SPRINGS INN
The newest motel in T or C is located at 2700 N. Date Street (894-6665 or 1-800-528-1234) near I-25. It has forty rooms and sports an outdoor pool but few other amenities.

ELEPHANT BUTTE RESORT INN
One of the largest motels in the area, this establishment has 48 rooms, overlooks the lake, and offers a landscaped pool, two tennis courts, and a restaurant and lounge. It is located on NM Hwy. 195 north of T or C (744-5431).

RIO GRANDE MOTEL
Located at 700 Broadway (894-9769) in Williamsburg, just south of T or C, this motel has fifty rooms (some with kitchenettes), a swimming pool, and a restaurant nearby. It is midway between Elephant Butte Lake and Caballo Lake (see below).

There are also more than fifteen RV parks in the area, including a large **KOA Campground** at the NM Hwy. 152 interchange south of T or C (743-2811). A complete list is available at the T or C Chamber of Commerce, 894-3536.

LODGING AND SOAKING
Despite the name change, the hot springs are still here. In fact, T or C is situated directly above thermal waters with a temperature range of 98-115 F. The principal "mineral" in these waters is sodium chloride—common salt—but significant amounts of potassium, magnesium, and calcium salts are also present. The town sports nine bath houses to soak up visitors. These are not particularly elegant facilities, but take a look at the **Artesian Bath House and Trailer Park,** 312 Marr (894-2684), with hot mineral baths, RV hookups, only a short walk from downtown; **Charles Motel and Bath House,** 601 Broadway (894-7154), a refurbished and quaint 1940s motor court which looks like it should be a set for a period black-and-white film.

★ ★
DINING

Perhaps the best all-around restaurants at the Butte are the **Los Arcos Steak House,** 1400 North Date Street (894-6200), with steaks broiled over mesquite wood and New Mexican entrees, open Sun.–Thurs. 5 p.m.–10:30 p.m., Friday and Saturday 5 p.m.–11 p.m., and for brunch on Sunday, 11 a.m.–2 p.m.; and the **Elephant Butte Inn Restaurant** (744-5431), which specializes in seafood and overlooks the lake, open 6 a.m.–2 p.m. and 5:30 p.m.–9:30 p.m. daily. **Rocky's Bar** is located at 315 Broadway (894-2217). The restaurant is open 11:30 a.m.–3 p.m., while the bar is open from 8 a.m.–1:30 a.m.

★ ★
LOCAL ATTRACTIONS

GERONIMO SPRINGS MUSEUM
Dedicated in 1972 during the T or C Fiesta, this museum at 211 Main Street (894-6600) was truly a community effort. Local civic clubs and businesses donated money, materials, and time to build the museum and its collections. The present museum occupies four adjoining buildings on Main Street, and an attractive stone block facade was built to unify the fronts of all four buildings.

Permanent exhibits tell the stories of the mining camps and army forts in the area, the construction of Elephant Butte Dam, and both prehistoric and more recent Indian culture. The **Ralph Edwards Wing** contains memorabilia from the many T or C fiestas and from the radio show. The **Cultural Heritage Wing** has historical murals and other displays which explain the history and culture of the region.

The museum is operated by the Sierra County Historical Society, which maintains a gift shop and book store on the premises. The museum is open 9 a.m.–5 p.m. daily.

CABALLO STATE PARK
Caballo Lake, another large impound, is located fourteen miles south of Truth or Consequences. It was built by the Bureau of Reclamation as part of the same project that included Elephant Butte, which began in 1902. The lake is long and winding, with about 12,000 surface acres of water—roughly one-third the size of Elephant Butte Lake.

The state park, located just off I-25 at exit 59 (743-3942), has a marina, camping sites with RV hookups and rest rooms with showers, interpretive exhibits, hiking trails, and a playground. The fish in the lake are the same species that roam Elephant Butte Lake, with pike, catfish, panfish, and the various species of bass being the most common.

Caballo Lake Trading Post, on NM Hwy. 187 across from the
state park entrance (743-2939). This facility has groceries, tackle,
bait and beer, plus the adjacent restaurant and lounge called
Sportsman's Paradise.

PERCHA DAM STATE PARK
Located 21 miles south of T or C just off 1-25 and NM Hwy. 187
(267-9394), Percha Dam State Park has a lovely setting amidst the
towering cottonwoods in the bosque along the Rio Grande. There
is stream-side fishing here near a dam which diverts water for irrigation purposes, plus sandy beaches. Park facilities include camping and picnicking sites with hookups, rest rooms with showers, a
playground, and hiking trails.

NEARBY ATTRACTIONS

HILLSBORO
The first of a cluster of mining towns that are now ghost or semi-
ghost towns along NM Hwy. 152, west of T or C, Hillsboro is
about 32 miles from Ralph Edwards' favorite city. First settled in
1877, Hillsboro became the center of a rich gold and silver mining
region. Mines called Bonanza, Ready Pay, Snake, and Wick's
Gulch provided the $6 million treasure that turned Hillsboro into
a boomtown complete with gambling, outlaws, and shootouts.

Although listed as a ghost town, today Hillsboro is a lively little
community of artists, writers, retirees, and shopkeepers. There are
gift and antique shops, galleries, and restaurants here now, but
most are open only during the summer months. During the first
weekend in September, the town hosts the **Black Range Art Exhibit,**
which is part of the **Hillsboro Apple Festival** and its large street
sale, street dances, and food booths. Information on this event is
available from **Sue's Antiques** (895-5328).

Interesting lodging is available at the **S-X Motel and Saloon** (*sic*),
which is located on NM Hwy. 152 eighteen miles west of exit 63
off I-25 (895-5222). This quaint motel in the foothills of the Black
Range has seven rooms, bar, and a restaurant.

KINGSTON
Nine miles west of Hillsboro on NM Hwy. 152 is Kingston, a similar old mining town. The **Percha Valley Bank Museum** still stands

today as evidence of the riches of Kingston in its heyday. Rich silver strikes in 1882 set another mining boom town—perhaps the thirstiest—in motion. Kingston, which eventually had a population of seven thousand, also had more than twenty saloons, which was so many that a brewery was built here to supply them all. The Kingston Brewery sold beer all over the Southwest before the bottom fell out of the gold and silver markets and the beer drinkers moved away.

Sadie Orchard became New Mexico's most famous madam in Kingston. Her brothel on Virtue Avenue dispensed what she referred to as "male social services," and was so successful that she opened a branch brothel in Hillsboro and a stage line to carry customers from Lake Valley. Sadie and her girls raised more than $1500 to build the first church in Kingston.

Today Kingston has perhaps twenty full-time residents remaining from those boom times and is a tiny community of mostly summer homes.

LAKE VALLEY TO THE MIDDLE OF NOWHERE

Between 1882 and 1888, nearly $5 million worth of silver was extracted from mines such as the famed Bridal Chamber at Lake Valley, seventeen miles south of Hillsboro on NM Hwy. 27. The mines surrounding the town eventually proved to be some of the richest pockets of silver found anywhere in the world. The silver from the Bridal Chamber was so pure that it was sawed into blocks instead of being blasted out of the ground. One account from those days said, "The ore body is so rich and porous that at many points a candle flame will melt it into silver globules."

The silver panic of 1893 was the ruin of Lake Valley, and its population of miners soon drifted away. Today, there are a few houses and dilapidated buildings here, and locals hold a dance in the old school house the first Saturday of every month.

The road leading south out of Lake Valley, NM Hwy. 27, is one of the loneliest and most beautiful stretches of road in the state. There is virtually no traffic, and hence, no city noises at all. Visitors often can stop their cars, admire the vistas for a half-hour, and never be disturbed.

About 34 miles south of Hillsboro, NM Hwy. 27 intersects with NM Hwy. 26 at a crossroads called **Nutt**, population two. Visitors to Nutt should be sure to stop at the **Middle of Nowhere Bar and Cafe,** which is owned by both residents of town, Sally and Terry Cosgrove. They can describe the sights in the area and answer any questions. A sign on the wall at the Middle of Nowhere Bar gives the rates for such services: "Answers, $1. Answers Which Require Thought, $2. Correct Answers, $4."

PART IV

Roswell and the Southeast Quadrant

ROSWELL

This city of about 50,000 on the eastern plains of New Mexico owes its existence to gambling. In the early 1860s, the site where Roswell sprawls today was a campsite at the junctions of the Pecos and Hondo Rivers where Texas cattlemen John Chisholm, Charles Goodnight, and Oliver Loving frequently rested the herds they were driving to Fort Sumner. The campsite was fairly primitive, consisting of a corral, a small house, and an adobe building that served as a hotel. But the outpost was attractive to professional gambler Van C. Smith, who purchased it in 1869.

Smith had big plans for his settlement, which he named after his father, Roswell Smith. In 1870 he built a post office, general store, and guest house where Fourth and Main streets now intersect, and made certain that Main Street was wide enough to handle the vast herds of cattle that still rumbled through his town. The street was also wide enough to serve as a race track, and soon Smith was conducting horse races between his store and the Hondo River. Before long, Roswell was a gambling center and it attracted many settlers to the area.

In 1875, John Chisholm, the "Cattle King of the Pecos," established his Jinglebob Ranch at South Spring, six miles south of

Roswell. Chisholm soon became a major political and commercial force in the region and his ranch, amazingly enough, stretched 200 miles along the Pecos River from Fort Sumner to the Texas border.

Another famous cattleman, Captain Joseph C. Lea, built a ranch northwest of town in 1877 and then purchased Van Smith's property, thus making Lea the sole owner of the little town of Roswell. He also owned one of the largest cattle ranches in history, with an estimated 40,000 head of cattle. His cattle holdings were surpassed only by Chisholm, who reputedly had 100,000 head by 1878.

Lea is often called the "Father of Roswell" because his influence turned the town into a important trading center. He was also instrumental in the establishment of New Mexico Military Institute and the incorporation of Roswell as a town in 1891. That same year, the discovery of artesian wells near Roswell led to the digging of irrigation ditches, which in turn led to the growing of alfalfa, cotton, and corn. At one time, as much as eight million gallons of water a minute flowed from those wells and the ground was so fertile that one farmer remarked, "You can stick a fence post in the Pecos Valley dirt, water it, and the darned thing will grow."

The arrival of the railroad between 1894 and 1899 connected Roswell to Carlsbad and Amarillo and created a spurt of growth that saw the town's population increase six hundred percent in just a decade. By 1916 Roswell had more than 1500 houses and more than seven thousand residents, and town leaders, ever eager to expand the population, touted the town to tuberculosis doctors back east as the "best prescription for your patient." Thus many retirees chose Roswell as their home, and added to the town's growth.

Roswell has survived two potentially disastrous blows to its economy during this century. Drought and the Depression struck in the early 1930s and the artesian wells dried up, forcing strict conservation measures, and bringing severe unemployment to Roswell. However, the Works Progress Administration assisted with the construction of Bitter Lakes National Wildlife Refuge and the Roswell Museum and Art Center (see below). The second economic blow to Roswell was the closing of Walker Air Force Base in 1967, which resulted in the departure of 15,000 residents (46 per cent of the work force) and one-half of the financial capital.

Despite such difficulties, Roswell bounced back. Business and community leaders founded the Roswell Industrial Development Corporation, which purchased the former air force base and turned it into the Roswell Industrial Air Center. The resulting industrial and commercial development helped the city recover in dramatic fashion.

"Everybody felt sorry for Roswell when we lost the air base," commented Mayor Bill Brainerd. "But that turned out to be the greatest opportunity and the greatest assest we could have hoped for." Roswell's recovery was so dramatic that it was named an "All-American City" in 1979 and serves as a model for other cities seeking to prosper in the face of reversals.

Today, Roswell is nicknamed the "Can-Do City" and thrives because of its diversified economy. No longer do the residents depend on one large employer such as the air base. Instead, agriculture, oil and gas, industrial development, and retail facilities such as the new Roswell Mall all contribute to the financial base of the community.

★ ★
TOURIST INFORMATION

ROSWELL CONVENTION AND VISITORS BUREAU
131 W. Second Street, P.O. Drawer 70 (623-5695), Roswell, NM 88201

★ ★
HISTORIC SIGHTSEEING

ROSWELL MUSEUM AND ART CENTER
Visitors to Roswell are often pleasantly surprised that a city of such modest size has such a fine museum. The Roswell Museum and Art Center, 100 W. 11th Street, opened in 1937 as a result of a combination of the efforts of four organizations: the Works Progress Administration, the City of Roswell, the Chaves County Archaeological and Historical Society, and the Roswell Friends of Art. In 1937 the museum had but one gallery and an office. Today it is sixteen times the size of the original structure and boasts seventeen galleries, eight offices, a museum store, and several classrooms.

The **Southwestern Collection of Paintings, Prints, and Sculpture** was established under the direction of the first president of the board of trustees, noted author Paul Horgan. Artists whose works are displayed in this collection include Ernest Blumenschein, Georgia O'Keefe, Marsden Hartley, Stuart Davis, John Sloan, and John Marin.

Nearly two thousand artifacts illustrate the contributions of the Plains Indians, the Spanish, and the Anglo settlers to the history of the Southwest in the **Rogers Aston Collection of American Indian and Western Art.** On display are outstanding examples of Indian

quill and beadwork, Spanish arms and armor, and Western artifacts and firearms.

The **Peter Hurd Collection** focuses on the art of Roswell's most
famous artist, who was born here in 1904 and lived most of his life
on a ranch about fifty miles west of town in the Hondo River Valley. A selection of his paintings from the 108 works in the museum
collection is always on display and is the most popular permanent
exhibit at the museum.

The **Native American and Hispanic Collection** offers fine examples of Indian pottery, baskets, textile arts, carvings, silverwork,
and paintings. Hispanic arts are represented in the Rogers Aston
Gallery and in the Permanent Collection Gallery.

One of most unusual exhibits at the Roswell Museum and Art
Center is the **Robert H. Goddard Collection.** Often called the
"Father of Modern Rocketry," Goddard successfully tested the
world's first liquid fuel rocket in 1926 in Roswell and then worked
for twelve years perfecting his propulsion system. A special
memorial wing of the museum displays the actual engines, rocket
assemblies, and personal memorabilia left behind by this rocketry
genius. Included in the wing is a special display commemorating
the Apollo XVII Moon Flight, along with the spacesuit worn by
New Mexico's astronaut, Dr. Harrison H. Schmidt. The wing also
has a planetarium.

The museum is open 9 a.m.–5 p.m. on weekdays and 1 p.m. to
5 p.m. on Sundays and holidays. Admission is free. More information may be obtained by calling 624-6744. There are two other
interesting museums in Roswell. A visit to the **Chaves County Historical Museum,** 200 N. Lea at the corner of Lea and Second Street,
is like taking a trip back to the turn of the century. The former
mansion of the James Phelps White family has been painstakingly
restored to its former glory and features Victorian antiques and
artifacts donated by Chaves County residents. The kitchen has
been re-created down to the smallest detail, including a wood- and
gas-burning cookstove, a pie safe, an ice box, and hundreds of the
utensils of the day.

Upstairs is a gallery of changing exhibits including the History of
American Fashions and displays of early business machines. The
third floor houses the archives of the Chaves County Historical
Society, and this collection includes rare books and photographs,
as well as business and family records from Roswell and southeastern New Mexico.

This museum is open 1 to 4 p.m. on Fridays, Saturdays, and Sundays for a small admission fee. Special tours may be arranged by
calling the museum at 622-8333.

The **General Douglas L. McBride Museum,** located on the campus of New Mexico Military Institute, College Boulevard off North Main Street, is a million-dollar facility designed to highlight the history of NMMI cadets from 1890 to the present. There are interesting displays of uniforms, weaponry, and awards here, plus instructive exhibits that tell about the exploits of the alumni in the various conflicts and wars in which they have served. For information on visiting the museum and the campus of the institute, contact NMMI at 622-6250, extension 409. Open 9 a.m.–4 p.m. Mon.–Fri.

★ ★
LODGING

Although Roswell cannot offer any historic inns or bed and breakfast places, the city does have some nice motels. Perhaps the finest is the **Sally Port Inn,** so named because of the "sally port" at nearby New Mexico Military Institute, through which graduates "sally forth" to their military careers. Sally Port Best Western Inn, 2000 N. Main Street (622-6430 or 1-800-528-1234), has 124 rooms, an atrium landscaped with tropical plants, an indoor swimming pool, tennis courts, Jacuzzis, saunas, a restaurant, a lounge, and a game room. Each guest room has a refrigerator and complementary movies.

Among the other recommended motels that have swimming pools, restaurants, and lounges, as well as nice rooms, the **Days Inn,** 1310 N. Main (623-4021); the **Roswell Inn,** 1815 N. Main (623-4920 or 1-800-426-3052); and **Best Western El Rancho,** 2205 N. Main (622-2721 or 1-800-528-1234).

★ ★
DINING

Roswell is still in the heart of cattle country, so steaks and prime rib dominate the local menus. Fortunately, some excellent **New Mexican** restaurants balance the steak houses. These include **El Toro Bravo,** 102 S. Main (622-9280), open 11 a.m.–2:30 p.m. and 5 p.m.–9 p.m. Mon.–Fri., Saturday, 11 a.m.–9 p.m., closed Sunday; **Los Ranchos,** 911 E. Second (622-9545), open 11 a.m.–9 p.m. Mon.–Sat., closed Sunday.

Recommended restaurants featuring **Steak and Seafood** are: **Cattleman's Steakhouse,** 2010 S. Main (623-8950), open Mon.–Fri. 11 a.m.–2 p.m., 5 p.m.–10 p.m. Sat. 5 p.m.–10 p.m. Sun. 11:30 a.m.–9 p.m.; the **Cattle Baron,** 12th and Main streets

(622-2465), open 11 a.m.–9:30 daily, until 10:30 p.m. on week-ends; **The Establishment,** 118 E. Third (623-5006 or 625-9901), open 11 a.m.–2 p.m., and 5 p.m.–9 p.m. Mon.–Sat., bar stays open later, closed Sunday; **The Claim,** 1310 N. Main (623-4021), with quail, lamb, and trout dishes also on the menu, open 11 a.m.–2 p.m., and 5 p.m.–10 p.m. on Mon.–Fri., 5 p.m.–10 p.m. Sat., closed Sunday; and **The Club House,** nine miles west of town on US Hwy. 70/380 (622-1158), which serves fresh seafood and oyster in addition to steaks and ribs. It is open 5 p.m.–10 p.m. Mon.–Thurs., and until 11 on weekends, but is closed Sunday.

Other recommended restaurants include **Hunan Restaurant,** 2609$^{1}/_{2}$ N. Main (623-8630) serving hot and spicy Hunan and **Szechuan** cuisine, open 11 a.m.–2:30 p.m. and 4:30 p.m.–9 p.m. daily.

★ ★
SPECIAL EVENTS

The two biggest events in Roswell are the **Eastern New Mexico State Fair,** held at the Chaves County Fairgrounds south of town in September, and the **Spectacular Air Show New Mexico** in early May at the Roswell Industrial Air Center on South Main Street. For additional information on these events or about Roswell in general, contact the Roswell Convention and Visitors Bureau at 623-5695 or 623-5906.

★ ★
THE GREAT OUTDOORS

Because of its location in the Pecos River Valley, Roswell has a number of parks and wildlife facilities that were created by the artesian water in the region. Within the city limits, the **Spring River Park and Zoo** on E. College Blvd. (624-6760), offers a fishing pond and a small zoo with a prairie dog colony. There are picnicking facilities here, along with an antique carousel and a miniature train. Outside of town, there are several additional interesting recreational facilities.

BOTTOMLESS LAKES STATE PARK
Located twelve miles southeast of Roswell via US Hwy. 380E and then right three miles on NM Hwy. 409, these lakes are not really bottomless, but who would want to change the name at this late date? The bottomless legend stems from the fact that the lakes were

created by underground rivers that created sinkholes in the limestone formations.

Early New Mexico cowboys who visited the seven small lakes
here attempted to compute the depths of the lakes by using their
lariats and discovered that even two ropes tied together apparently
did not touch the bottom — hence the handle "bottomless." But since
the deepest lake is really only 96 feet deep, we can safely assume
that the ropes were being carried by the strong currents which
prevented them from sinking to the bottom.

This state park was New Mexico's first and it offers extensive
interpretive displays and a network of trails at the park headquarters at **Cottonwood Lake**. At **Lea Lake**, there is a concession
building with a cafe and paddleboat rentals. Swimming is permitted in Lea Lake, and because of the clarity of its waters, the lake
is a popular destination for scuba divers, who don't have many
places to dive in southeastern New Mexico.

Some of the lakes are stocked with trout, and camping facilities
with showers and rest rooms are available. For more information,
call the state park at 624-6058.

BITTER LAKE NATIONAL WILDLIFE REFUGE

This large wildlife sanctuary is about twelve miles northeast of
Roswell just off both US Hwys. 380 and 70 and is a major wintering
area for migrating waterfowl. The refuge, established in 1937, consists of two separate units, each about 23,000 acres. The south unit
has seven small lakes, including **Bitter Lake**, and a self-guided car
tour of about eight miles. The loop tour has picnic tables and
numbered instructional markers that are explained in a tour leaflet.
A nature trail winds along an old oxbow of the Pecos River.
Seasonal fishing is permitted on the lakes but camping and boating
are not.

The north unit of the wildlife refuge is the **Salt Creek Wilderness
Area**, which may be entered only on foot or by horseback. The
Bitter Lake refuge is the most important waterfowl refuge in eastern
New Mexico and peak populations of more than 100,000 ducks and
up to 10,000 geese stop here. Waterfowl species include sandhill
cranes, Canada geese, pintails, mallards, mergansers, and teals.

More than 280 species of birds have been sighted at the refuge,
and an additional 38 species have been sighted but are considered
to be out of their normal range. Amateur ornithologists will be excited to learn that they may spot warblers, larks, orioles, avocets,
snowy plovers, sandpipers, and the endangered least terns during
their visit to Bitter Lake. Additional information on the refuge may
be obtained by calling 622-6755.

DEXTER NATIONAL FISH HATCHERY

Seventeen miles south of Roswell on US Hwy. 285 or NM Hwy. 2 and about a mile east of Dexter on State Road 190 is a facility which is devoted to the preservation of endangered fish in case of a catastrophic loss in the wild. In fact, the Dexter National Fish Hatchery is the only hatchery in the nation devoted exclusively to saving America's threatened fish.

The hatchery has 35 ponds and seventeen concrete tanks containing seventeen separate species of fish. Four of these fish — the beautiful shiner, the Gila topminnow, the Colorado squawfish, and the razorback sucker — were extinct in New Mexico. But the hatchery has been restocking the sucker in the San Juan River and reintroducing the squawfish into the Colorado River.

The squawfish is particularly interesting because it is the largest member of the minnow family in North America, reaching unminnow-like lengths of four to six feet! It was once so prevalent in the Southwest that early settlers called it the "Salmon of the Colorado." The squawfish was wiped out by over-fishing but the scientists at Dexter are working hard to bring back its population.

Visitors are welcome at the hatchery, but it's best to call 734-5910 for directions. The Visitors Center is open April through October, but visitors are welcome all year round. The hatchery is open 7 a.m.–4 p.m. daily.

CLOVIS AND PORTALES

These twin cities on the **Llano Estacado** ("staked plains") of New Mexico make up the agricultural center of eastern New Mexico and have a combined population exceeding 50,000. A mere eighteen miles apart on US Hwy. 70, the two towns maintain separate identities but share the same market area. The known history of the region extends back to the time of the paleo-Indians.

In 1932, the reign of Folsom Man as the oldest American ended when spearpoints were discovered in Blackwater Draw, located in what is now **Oasis State Park** between Clovis and Portales. The points of Clovis Man were found by Edgar Howard of the University of Pennsylvania after he received a tip from an amateur archaeologist. Howard's discovery led to more extensive excavations in the 1950s, which proved conclusively that there were paleo-Indians older than Folsom Man. The Blackwater Draw site was ravaged by fossil collectors until the El Llano Amateur Archaeological Society began excavations. Eventually the site was turned over to Dr. George Agogino of the anthropology department at Eastern New Mexico University.

The digs in this ancient lake bed revealed a Folsom layer in association with extinct bison. But below that was another layer containing the bones of mammoths, horses, and camels, plus flint points larger than those of Folsom Man. Radiocarbon dating of these Clovis deposits placed them in a time range of 11,000 to 12,000 years ago, or about a thousand years earlier than Folsom Man. Clovis Man turned out to be quite a wanderer: His points have been found all over North and South America, from Nova Scotia to Tierra del Fuego, which could mean that Clovis Man was the primary paleo-Indian settler of the New World. As is true of Folsom Man, no bones of Clovis Man have ever been found, just his artifacts.

In more recent history, the eastern plains of New Mexico were the home of the Comanches and the Kiowas, who often raided central New Mexico after they learned how to ride the horses imported by the first Spanish explorers. The earliest settlement of the region occurred in the early 1800s when buffalo hunters and cowboys driving cattle stopped at Portales Springs, where the cave openings resembled porch (*portal* in Spanish) arches. Portales itself was originally a construction camp for workers on the Pecos Valley and Northern Railroad. Clovis was called Riley Switch and was a siding on the Santa Fe Railroad until 1907, when it was renamed Clovis after the King of the Franks.

Both towns depend on farming and ranching for much of their income base, but there are several other large employers in the area. Major employers in Clovis are the Santa Fe Railroad and Cannon Air Force Base, while Portales has Eastern New Mexico University, founded in 1934, an institution with an enrollment of nearly four thousand students. Neither town is particularly famous as a center of tourism, but there are many interesting attractions, particularly the museums.

MUSEUMS

The **Blackwater Draw Museum,** located between Clovis and Portales on US Hwy. 70, commemorates the discovery of Clovis Man on this site in 1932. It has displays of five main areas of interest: the evolution of the world before man, the history and development of the Blackwater Draw site, a re-creation of the Blackwater Draw region (complete with fossils), the paleo-Indian and his way of life, and replicas of the Blackwater Draw artifacts.

The Blackwater Draw Museum is one of the few in the country devoted to a single site, and it is managed by the department of anthropology at Eastern New Mexico State University. It is open

Tues.–Sun. from 12 p.m.–5 p.m. For additional information, call 562-2254.

There are three other museums located on the campus of Eastern New Mexico University. The **Natural History Museum** (562-2723, Science Dept. office) in Roosevelt Hall has wildlife exhibits, aquariums, and a bee colony. The **Miles Collection** (by appointment only, 562-2498) features rare stones and minerals of the collection of former rock hound Fred Miles, and is a private collection used primarily for research. The **Roosevelt County Museum** (562-2840) is affiliated with the Museum of New Mexico. In addition to traveling exhibits from Santa Fe, this museum displays nineteenth- and early twentieth-century artifacts that figured prominently in the culture of Roosevelt and Curry Counties. Included in the museum's displays are tools, utensils, firearms, antiques and an original 1896 Sears Catalog.

★ ★
LODGING AND DINING

Standard motels comprise the lodging facilties of both Clovis and Portales. Recommended in Clovis are the **Holiday Inn,** 2700 E. Mabry Dr. (762-4491 or 1-800-238-8000) with an indoor pool, a restaurant, and a racquetball court; **Sands Motel,** 1400 E. Mabry Dr. (763-3439), with an outdoor heated pool; and **La Vista Best Western Inn,** 1516 E. Mabry Dr. (762-3808), which also has a swimming pool. In Portales, try the **Dunes Motel** on the Roswell Highway (US Hwy. 70) (356-6668), or the **Portales Inn,** 218 W. 3rd Street (359-1208).

Recommended **New Mexican** restaurants include **Guadalajara Restaurant,** 916 W. First Street in Clovis (769-9965), open 11 a.m.–2 p.m., 5 p.m.–9 p.m. Mon.–Fri, 5 p.m.–9 p.m. on Sat., and closed Sunday; **Juanitos Restaurant,** 1608 Mabry Dr. in Clovis (762-7822), open 11 a.m.–9 p.m. Tues.–Sat., 11 a.m.–2 p.m. Sunday, but closed Monday; **El Monterrey,** 118 Mitchell in Clovis (763-4031), serving spicy food since 1934, open 11 a.m.–2 p.m. and 4:30 p.m.–8:30 p.m., closed Sunday; and **La Hacienda,** 909 N. Avenue K in Portales (359-0280), open 11 a.m.–8 p.m. Mon.–Sat., 11 a.m.–7 p.m. Sunday.

Other suggested restaurants in Clovis and Portales are **Poor Boy's Steak House,** 2115 N. Prince in Clovis (763-5222), open 11 a.m.–9 p.m. Sunday–Thurs. and 11 a.m.–10 p.m. Fri. and Sat.; and the **Cattle Baron,** 1600 S. Avenue D in Portales (356-5587), serving steaks and seafood, open 11 a.m.–9 p.m. daily, until 10 p.m. on weekends.

OTHER ATTRACTIONS

The **Hillcrest Park Zoo,** located at Hillcrest Park on Sycamore Street in Clovis (762-1101), is a 22-acre zoological park with more than two hundred species of birds and animals on display. Hours are 9 to 6 Tuesday through Sunday and admission is $1 adults, and $.50 for children. **Greene Acres Park,** at 21st and Main streets in Clovis has a lake stocked with bass and trout. **Ned Houk Park,** ten miles north of Clovis on NM Hwy. 18, also has a fishing pond, plus picnic areas, a playground, and a small museum.

   Grulla National Wildlife Refuge (806-946-3341, Muleshoe Refuge headquarters), twenty miles east of Portales on NM Hwy. 88, is, with 3231 acres, the smallest wildlife refuge in the state. It is primarily a refuge for the lesser sandhill crane and there are no public facilities here, just wildlife. Muleshoe Refuge oversees the Grulla Refuge and is located twenty miles south of Muleshoe, TX on FM 214.

   Oasis State Park, eighteen miles southwest of Clovis via US Hwy. 70 and NM Hwy. 467, is literally an oasis of cottonwoods set amongst sand dunes. The park offers picnicking, camping facilities with utility hookups, rest rooms with showers, and a small fishing lake stocked with rainbow trout. For more information, call the park at 356-5331.

   The **Clovis Stockyards,** 504 S. Hull Street (762-4422), are among the largest in the country, with cattle auctions held weekly and horse auctions held in Mar., May, Aug., and Nov. Spectators enjoy the action even if they don't buy a Charolais bull to take home with them.

SPECIAL EVENTS

Clovis Pioneer Days at Monte Patrol Arena is celebrated during the first week in June each year with a parade, rodeo, balloon fiesta, and pageants that honor the first settlers, and commercial exhibits. The **Curry County Fair** happens in mid-August in Clovis at the Curry County Fairgrounds, and the **Peanut Valley Festival** is held

every late October on the ENMU campus in Portales. It features
(no kidding) the Peanut Olympics, with peanut-related competi-
tions for all ages. For additional information on these events and
the Clovis-Portales area, contact the Roosevelt County/Portales
Chamber of Commerce in Portales (356-8541) or the Clovis Chamber of Commerce (763-3435).

★ ★
NEARBY ATTRACTIONS

FORT SUMNER
Virtually every part of eastern and southern New Mexico proclaims
itself to be "Billy the Kid Country," regardless of reality. The Kid
played a very minor role in the history of the state and this is particularly true for Fort Sumner, a small community town of about
1500 located 62 miles west of Clovis on US Hwy. 60/84. Although
Billy was shot and buried near here, he was more influential in Lincoln, and so his mythology is described in detail under the Lincoln
listing, below.

Fort Sumner was built in 1862 to guard Navajo and Mescalero
Apache captives who were imprisoned at Bosque Redondo along
the Pecos River. It was abandoned in 1869 but was purchased by
Lucian Maxwell, the famed land grant king, who retired there and
remodeled the fort to become his ranch headquarters. It was here
that Billy the Kid was shot by Pat Garrett in 1881.

Today the town named after the fort is a quiet ranching and
retirement community that attracts occasional tourists, though it
certainly is not a center of tourism. Lodging and dining facilities are
quite limited and most visitors stay overnight in Clovis or Santa
Rosa.

Probably the best time to visit Fort Sumner is during the second
week in June, when the town's annual **Old Fort Days Celebration**
is in full swing. In addition to a parade, a country music show, and
a large barbecue, Fort Sumner sponsors the **World's Richest Tombstone Race.** During this amusing competition, which was inspired
by the recurrent theft of Billy the Kid's tombstone, contestants carry eighty-pound tombstone replicas over an obstacle course to win
a $1000 purse. For information, call the DeBaca County Chamber
of Commerce (355-7705).

FORT SUMNER STATE MONUMENT
During 1862 and 1863, the U.S. Army sought to end the Indian
wars and dispatched Kit Carson to invade the homeland of the

Navajos and Mescalero Apaches. Carson's soldiers destroyed Indian homes, crops, and livestock and literally starved the Indians into submission with this scorched-earth policy. The captives — about five hundred Apaches and nine thousand Navajos — were forced to march nearly four hundred miles to the Bosque Redondo along the Pecos River, which was guarded by Fort Sumner, built specifically for that purpose. This journey was called "the long walk."

This internment was a disaster, one of the worst in the sorry history of the U.S. government's treatment of Native American people. There was never enough food, wood, or potable water, and crops were ravaged by insects, drought, and hail. Hundreds of Indians died of disease and malnutrition before General William Tecumseh Sherman ended the "reservation experiment" in 1868.

The renovated fort was declared a State Monument one century later and was listed on the National Register of Historic Places. A visitor center at the former fort site contains exhibits that detail the living — and dying — conditions at Bosque Redondo, and rangers are on hand each weekend to answer questions and to present living history demonstrations.

Fort Sumner State Monument is located eight miles southeast of Fort Sumner via US Hwy. 60/84, and right three miles on NM Hwy. 212. Hours are 8 a.m.–5 p.m. Thurs.–Mon. Closed Tuesday and Wednesday. For information call the monument at 355-2573. Near the State Monument is the **Old Fort Sumner Museum**, which contains artifacts, pictures, and documents relating to the fort and to Billy the Kid, whose grave is behind the museum. Another privately owned museum is the **Billy the Kid Museum** on US Hwy. 60/84 two miles east of downtown Fort Sumner. This museum and curio shop contains more than 60,000 relics of the old west and two classic cars collected by the late Ed Sweet.

The **Bosque Redondo Recreation Area,** located south of town on Real Wind Road, is a popular fishing and picnicking spot. Overnight camping is allowed, but there are no hookups or rest rooms. North of Fort Sumner is **Sumner Lake State Park**, which is described in the Santa Rosa listing.

For more information about Fort Sumner, which county promoters have dubbed the "International Billy the Kid Capital," call the De Baca County Chamber of Commerce at 355-7705.

ESTANCIA AND MOUNTAINAIR

These two towns on the east side of the Manzano Mountains are located in what is called the Estancia Basin. This valley without an outlet was once a huge Pleistocene lake that was created by heavy rainfall and (some say) melting glaciers in the Manzanos. Eventually the prehistoric Lake Estancia evaporated and only the salt lakes, **Laguna del Perro**, located on US Hwy. 60 about 20 miles east of Mountainair, remain today. There are no recreational facilities here, just the series of brackish marshes named *salinas* by the Spanish which supplied salt for Indians living in nearby pueblos. These three Salinas Pueblos are now **Salinas National Monument** (see below).

The Spanish recognized the value of the salt here and used Indian slaves to mine it and load it upon *carretas*, mule-drawn wagons. The salt was transported to the mines in Chihuahua, a two-month trip. When there is heavy rain in the Estancia Basin, Laguna del Perro is transformed from a marsh into a small lake, and sometime waterfowl are in evidence there.

Neither Estancia (at the intersection of NM Hwy. 41 and NM Hwy. 55) nor Mountainair (US Hwy. 60 and NM Hwy. 55) are tourist towns, so lodging and dining facilities are basic. However, they are adjacent to the Manzano Mountains and **Cibola National Forest**, which offer numerous camping areas off NM Hwy. 14, including **Fourth of July** and **Tajique** near Tajique and **Red Canyon** and **New Canyon** near Manzano. For more information on these campsites, call the Cibola National Forest ranger station at Mountainair, 847-2990.

SALINAS NATIONAL MONUMENT

A few years ago, this three-unit national monument consisting of the ruins of the Saline Pueblos was two state monuments, Abo and Quarai, and one national monument, Gran Quivira. A name change and unification into Salinas National Monument made sense for several reasons. First, since the pueblos were regionally related, they could be better managed and preserved by one government agency rather than two. Second, the name "Gran Quivira" was confusing and misleading because it conjured up images of Quivira, the mythical land for which Coronado was searching when he went on that wild goose chase into Kansas (see listing for Coronado State Monument).

At the time of the earliest Spanish settlements in New Mexico, one of the Saline Pueblos, Tabira, was reputed to be the headquarters for a huge gold and silver mining operation in the Manzano Mountains. The Franciscan order began building what would become the largest church in North America at Tabira in 1628, and rumor had them utilizing Indian slave labor to mine the gold, which supposedly was stashed in tunnels below the church. During the 1680 Pueblo Revolt, the story went, the friars carved a map to the treasure on a large stone, and then abandoned the pueblo and escaped south to El Paso.

Such were the first innocuous connections between Tabira and Quivira: their names rhymed, they were vaguely located somewhere on the eastern plains, and a tale of treasure accompanied both places. Adolph Bandelier speculated that it was simply a matter of semantic confusion. After the Pueblo Revolt, he wrote, Tabira "had lain in ruins . . . but its treasures were supposed to be buried in the neighborhood, for it was said there had once been a wealthy mission there, and the priests had buried and hidden the vessels of the church. Thus the Indian kingdom known as Quivira was metamorphosed in the course of two centuries into an opulent Indian mission."

Evidently, some time in the late 1700s, New Mexicans and others decided that Coronado's Quivira had moved from Kansas to the abandoned pueblo of Tabira. A scenario for the totally inaccurate appellation of Gran Quivira to Tabira was proposed in 1915 by L. Bradford Prince, president of the Historical Society of New Mexico: "It is not at all unlikely that when some party from the Rio Grande Valley, in search of game or gold, crossed the mountains and the wilderness lying to the east, and was suddenly amazed by the apparition of a dead city, silent and tenantless, but bearing the evidences of large populations, of vast resources, of architectural knowledge, mechanical skill, and wonderful energy, they should have associated it with the stories heard from childhood of the mythical center of riches and power, and called the new-found wonder the Gran Quivira."

The **Gran Quivira Unit** of Salinas National Monument is located 25 miles south of Mountainair on NM Hwy. 55. Not only was it once called Tabira, at least two other names have been ascribed to it: Pueblo de las Humanas, and Pueblo of Cueloze. Audio-visual presentations and artifacts highlight the visitor center and a trail leads visitors through the 21 pueblo ruins on the six hundred acres of the monument. Gran Quivira was the largest pueblo on the eastern plains in the 1500s and evidence of this fact is the large plaza and ruins, and the remains of the massive church, San Buenaventura.

In 1853, Major James Henry Carleton triggered a resurgence of interest in Gran Quivira and its legendary treasure. His expedition diary retold through hearsay the treasure story of the pueblo, and published an account from an Indian (supposedly a descendant of the pueblo *cacique*, or chief) that described the location of the treasure as a cellar three hundred yards from the parish church cemetery.

His report prompted a horde of treasure hunters to descend upon the ruins of the pueblo. Treasure maps, claimed to be from the original inhabitants of Tabira, proliferated. By 1893, according to historian Charles Lummis, "Scarce a month goes by in which the territorial newspapers do not print some new fable or allusion to the old; and even as I write, an expedition is fitting out in Albuquerque to seek the 'buried treasure.' " Many of these treasure hunters sank deep shafts in an effort to find the gold and silver, but none were ever successful. All such treasure hunting ended in 1933 when the federal government took control of Gran Quivira after Congress made it a national monument.

The **Abo Unit**, located about ten miles west of Mountainair along US Hwy. 60, has the ruins of the San Gregorio Mission, one of the most beautiful mission churches built in New Mexico. It was constructed of red sandstone, which contrasts with the older adobe of the original pueblo walls. Because of Apache and Comanche raids, the mission was abandoned in the 1670s.

The **Quarai Unit**, about eight miles north of Mountainair just off NM Hwy. 55, features the ruins of the mission church La Purisima Concepcion, which was built sometime between 1629 and 1639. There is a small museum here, along with interpretive trails and a picnic area. Like the church at Gran Quivira, this one was also huge: the walls were forty feet high and five feet thick.

Quarai was the first of the Saline Pueblos to be abandoned. Evidence indicates that Apaches raided the pueblo in 1674, killing most of the native residents and driving off the Franciscan friars. Together, the pueblos of Salinas National Monument are often called "the cities that died of fear" because of the manner in which they succumbed to the fierce attacks by hostile Apaches.

For additional information about the three units of Gran Quivira National Monument, call the National Park Service at 847-2585, or write P.O. Box 496, Mountainair, NM 87036.

CARRIZOZO

This small town at the intersection of US Hwy. 54 and US Hwy. 380 has had a larger influence on local history than its size would indicate. It did not even exist until 1899, when the El Paso and Northeastern Railway extended its rails to this point and a settlement sprang up around the terminal. It was named Carrizozo after the *carrizo*, or reed grass that grows in the area.

The coming of the railroad led to the demise of one boom town, White Oaks (see below) and the creation of another. Many railroad employees decided to homestead the surrounding rangeland, receiving 640 acres of land if they could live on it for three years.

Carrizozo's population boomed in the first two decades of this century, and by 1920 the town boasted of more than two thousand citizens.

The townsite was laid out by railroad man Charles B. Eddy, who specified in his plan that only certain lots could sell liquor. One of these locations was directly across from the railway depot so that the officials could determine which of their employees was spending too much time in the saloon.

In 1909 Carrizozo became the seat of Lincoln County, which at one time was the largest county in the country—25,000 square miles, three times the size of the state of New Jersey. Several counties were carved out of Lincoln, and its present size of 4859 square miles makes it about as large as Connecticut.

A railroad strike in 1923 and the modernization of the railway machinery took its toll on Carrizozo, and the population declined to about half of what it was during the boom times. Today the town has stabilized at about 1200, and the residents earn their living by ranching, working for Lincoln National Forest, or from commercial enterprises.

★ ★
LODGING AND DINING

Tourist facilities in Carrizozo are limited and basic. The **Four Winds Motel**, at the intersection of US Hwy. 54 and US Hwy. 380 (648-2356), has 22 rooms. The **Four Winds Restaurant** and lounge are just up the street. Green chile cheeseburgers are the specialty of the **Outpost Bar, Grill, and Laundry** at 415 Central (648-9994), open 10 a.m.–2 a.m. daily. Another restaurant is the **Coffee Cup Cafe** on US Hwy. 54 (648-2832), which specializes in burgers and New Mexican food. It is open 11 a.m.–1:30 p.m., and 5 p.m.–6:30 p.m. Mon.–Fri.

★ ★
NEARBY ATTRACTIONS

For visitors who delight in historical artifacts, **My House of Old Things** should not be missed. This former railroad depot is located three miles east of Ancho off US Hwy. 54 about 24 miles north of Carrizozo. It is a private museum crammed full of thousands upon thousands of items collected over a fifty-year period by Mrs. Jackie Silvers, former postmaster of Ancho. My House of Old Things is open daily May through October 15, from 8 to 6. Admission is adults $1.50, children $.50.

WHITE OAKS

Located eleven miles northeast of Carrizozo via US Hwy. 54 and NM Hwy. 349, White Oaks is a semi-ghost town, which means that although it is mostly deserted, a few families still live here. "Rip Van Winkle," "Old Abe," and "Little Hill" were the names of some of the area's mines that produced nearly $3 million worth of gold and silver between 1879 and 1906.

During the boom, White Oak's population topped four thousand, Billy the Kid was a frequent visitor, and casinos, saloons, and an opera house sprang up. The town was so prosperous that the citizens were certain that the railroad connecting Santa Rosa to El Paso would pass through the town. Greedy landowners refused to donate right-of-way, holding out for substantial payments. But the El Paso and Northeastern Railway bypassed White Oaks and created Carrizozo. After the ores played out, the town of White Oaks faded.

Today many of the town's larger structures still stand and others are being restored. One of the more interesting buildings is "Hoyle's Folly," a large Victorian mansion built at a cost of $42,000 in 1887 by Matthew Hoyle, a wealthy gold mine foreman. Hoyle built his "castle" as a lure for his girlfriend back east, hoping she would move to White Oaks. But she rejected him and Hoyle disappeared, leaving his folly to the bank which held the mortgage. Local legend says the mansion is haunted.

VALLEY OF FIRES STATE PARK

Located three miles west of Carrizozo on US Hwy. 380 is the second-largest lava flow in New Mexico, called Valley of Fires. It is one of the youngest flows in the United States, about 1500 years old. The lava poured out of a vent in Little Black Peak at the northern end of the Tularosa Valley and flowed south for 44 miles, eventually covering an area of 127 square miles. In some places the lava flow is five miles wide and up to 162 feet deep.

As with the McCarty's Flow (see Grants listing), blown-in dirt and sand amidst the lava have allowed vegetation to grow, which in turn has attracted a surprising variety of wildlife. Petroglyphs and pottery sherds found in the *malpais* indicate that the area was utilized by the Indians of the Jornada branch of the Mogollon culture until about 1400.

A 463-acre tract of this huge flow was declared a state park in 1966. Facilities here include campsites with electrical hookups, picnic tables, a playground, and rest rooms. Visitors may wander along an interpretive nature trail that twists and turns through the folded lava formations.

THREE RIVERS INDIAN PETROGLYPH SITE

This fascinating attraction should not be missed. Located about thirty miles south of Carrizozo via US Hwy. 54, Three Rivers contains more than five thousand rock carvings—making it one of the largest prehistoric petroglyph locations in the Southwest. The same Indians that utilized the Valley of Fires—the Jornada branch of the Mogollon culture—carved these designs, which resemble the Mimbres style (see Silver City listing). They were descended from nomadic tribesmen who lived in south-central New Mexico from about 5000 B.C. to A.D. 900 and established several villages in the Three Rivers areas. A severe drought near the end of the thirteenth century is thought to be the cause of the abandonment of the region by the Jornada Mogollons, who migrated north.

But before they left, the Indians created elaborate carvings of animals, human figures, and geometric designs on the rock outcroppings that overlook the Tularosa Valley. The selection of these particular rocks has much in common with the Albuquerque petroglyph site (see Albuquerque listing). It is a good lookout point, and the view in all directions is breathtaking. To the northwest, the Valley of Fires lava flow is visible; the rolling dunes of the White Sands invade the valley from the south and meet the lava. The towering peak of Sierra Blanca (12,003 feet), sacred mountain of the Mescalero Apaches, rises above the petroglyph site and is snowcapped most of the year. Perhaps petroglyph sites such as this one are celebrations of the surrounding environment, nature books carved into the rocks and inspired by such spectacular vistas.

The petroglyphs here were probably inscribed by the inhabitants of a partially excavated Indian pithouse village which is several hundred yards south of the rock outcroppings. There is a pithouse replica for public inspection, and a trail about a two-thirds of a mile long wanders through the rock carvings. Visitors should be warned that defacement or removal of any rocks on this site can lead to a term in federal prison.

The adjacent picnic area has six shelters with tables and barbecue grills. Overnight camping is permitted (no hookups) and there are rest rooms on-site. For more information, contact the Bureau of Land Management in Las Cruces at 525-8228.

SMOKEY BEAR HISTORICAL STATE PARK

One of the most famous citizens ever to emerge from New Mexico was Smokey the Bear, beloved symbol of forest fire prevention. Smokey was rescued from a disastrous fire in Lincoln National Forest near Capitan in 1950, and then was sent to Washington, D.C., where he lived at the National Zoo until his death in 1975. Smokey has since been replaced at the zoo by another orphaned black bear from New Mexico.

The people of Capitan led the campaign for a museum and monument to Smokey—and succeeded in 1974, when state and federal funds were allocated for a state park. The new museum building opened in 1979 and has historical exhibits about the history of Smokey, whose grave is located on the grounds. A nature trail outside the museum provides an introduction to native New Mexico plants.

Smokey Bear Historical State Park is located in Capitan, twenty miles southeast of Carrizozo on US Hwy. 380. Picnicking facilities are available here, but no camping is allowed. For more information, call the park at 354-2748.

Four miles southeast of Capitan just off US Hwy. 380 is Fort Stanton and **Fort Stanton Historical Museum.** Fort Stanton was established in 1855 to control the Apaches and was briefly occupied by Confederate forces in 1861. Reoccupied by Union forces the next year, Fort Stanton was rebuilt and lasted until 1896 when it became a Merchant Marine hospital for the treatment of tuberculosis. After a brief stint as a German prisoner of war camp during World War II, the fort became a state tuberculosis hospital, and later, in 1966, a National Historic Landmark. Displays at the small museum tell the story of Fort Stanton.

LINCOLN
The seat of Lincoln County before Carrizozo was this tiny town of Lincoln, named for President Abraham Lincoln. Today it is mostly a state monument on US Hwy. 380 between Carrizozo and Roswell, but back in 1876 it was the location of a bloody conflict which has become known as the Lincoln County War. This feud arose out of a conflict between two factions in Lincoln County. One faction was aligned with Lawrence Murphy, the "dictator" of the county, and the other was led by Alexander McSween and John Tunstall, both backed by Texas cattleman John Chisholm.

The dispute was centered upon lucrative beef contracts and financial control of the county. Murphy, who would tolerate no interference in his domain, sent gunmen to ambush Tunstall in 1878. McSween retaliated by hiring a gang called "The Regulators," one member of which was a hired gun named Henry McCarty, alias Billy the Kid. The Regulators avenged the murder of Tunstall by killing four of Murphy's men, including the sheriff and his deputy.

Murphy, however, had friends in high places, namely the "Santa Fe Ring," a group of powerful politicians in Santa Fe. They provided a new sheriff and promised military protection for Murphy. The war culminated in July, 1878, with a shootout in Lincoln at the Tunstall store. During this three-day battle, Murphy's men were assisted by a detachment of soldiers from Fort Stanton. The force surrounded McSween's house, set it ablaze, and proceeded to shoot the men as they ran to escape the fire. McSween was killed (along with four of his men), but Billy the Kid escaped.

The situation in Lincoln became so terrible that President Hayes removed the Territorial Governor, Samuel Axtell, and replaced him with Lew Wallace, who later became famous as the author of the novel, *Ben-Hur*. Wallace gained presidential permission for the use of troops to subdue further violence.

Billy the Kid continued his life of crime and became, despite the minor role he played in history, "America's immortal legend" and the central hero of the frontier West. How and why The Kid gained such mythological stature is a puzzle that has perplexed scholars and started a verbal range war among historians, who wish to separate truth from legend, and mythologists, who wish to understand the meaning of the legend of Billy the Kid.

In reality, not much is known about the facts of Billy the Kid's life. His given name was Henry McCarty but no one really knows where he was born. The name William Bonney was an alias he adopted to protect his family name, but he used it so often that it stuck. Between the time he left home in Silver City and the day he was killed, Billy the Kid was a horse thief, a cattle rustler, and a hired gunman. He was well-liked by a great number of people who knew him, and The Kid was not regarded as particularly evil — except later, when the press wrote about him and created the more negative image.

After his involvement in the Lincoln County War, The Kid was captured by Pat Garrett at the quaintly named Stinking Springs. The Kid escaped from the Lincoln County jail, killing two guards in the process. He was tracked down and ambushed at night at the Maxwell ranch in Fort Sumner by Pat Garrett: This event set up the classic good versus evil confrontation so typical of romantic literature.

And just how evil was The Kid? All of his murders involved fights, escapes, or the capture of enemies, so he appears to be neither a calculating, cold-blooded killer nor a raging maniac. Folklore generally attributes 21 murders to The Kid, one for each year of his life, but the true score is four unassisted killings plus five killings in which he was possibly an accomplice. None of the killings were committed in the course of a robbery or rustling. There is no evidence that he ever killed an Indian or an Hispanic, and eight out of nine of the killings were directly related to the Lincoln County War. The other killing was a shooting that terminated a physical attack upon The Kid.

Interestingly enough, despite the fact that The Kid played "a trivial, even meaningless" role in history (according to Kid-scholar Stephen Tatum), the American people have re-created their own Billy the Kid as every possible type of hero—from outlaw hero to romantic hero to tragic hero, and finally, to an ironic, absurdist hero. And unlike most legends, the Billy the Kid mythology has been thoroughly documented as it occurred, giving mythologists a living example of the mythmaking process as it evolved from history. Today there are many more than one thousand citations of works concerning Billy the Kid, everything from dime novels to motion pictures to scholarly treatises to ballets. Twenty-three Billy the Kid movies were made between 1940 and 1943 alone, and another Kid movie, ''Young Guns,'' was shown in New Mexico in 1988.

A chronological study of these citations shows how the myth evolved, but it is far too complicated to detail here. The most important point to remember about Billy the Kid is that The Kid of legend has transcended The Kid of history. If it were not for such mythology, The Kid would not have become a universal hero, but would have remained just another semi-obscure gunman, forgotten except by historians.

Many of the buildings in Lincoln have been rebuilt or restored and are managed as part of **Lincoln State Monument.** One is the **Tunstall Store Museum** on Main Street, which was built as Tunstall Mercantile in 1877 and today is preserved as a virtually unchanged museum containing much of its original stock. The **Lincoln County Courthouse,** on the west end of Main Street at the other end of town, was built in 1874 and served as the **Murphy-Dolan Store.** It is now a museum, but in 1881 Billy the Kid made his daring escape from its jail, and soon had Sheriff Pat Garrett hot on his trail. This event is re-created the first weekend in August during **Old Lincoln Days,** when the seventy residents of Lincoln don Western duds and play the roles of their favorite characters in the Lincoln County War. Also presented during this celebration is "The Last Escape of Billy the Kid," a pageant staged on an outdoor set. Evidently, the legend of Billy the Kid will never fade in New Mexico. As writer Eugene Cunningham described the worship of The Kid: "He will continue to ride—so long as all of us thrill to the tales of those who unwittingly followed the Nietzschean admonition, had lived, lived dangerously, and lived daringly. . . .''

The only lodging in Lincoln is provided by the **Wortley Hotel** (653-4500), which burned to the ground in the 1930s but which was reconstructed on its original foundations thirty years later. The hotel, which also houses a restaurant, is owned and managed by the Lincoln County Heritage Trust. The Lincoln Pageant and Festival Corporation stages the Billy the Kid show. This hostelry has eight rooms furnished with antiques and can sleep a maximum of eighteen people. It is closed during winter season, but opens March 1; admission is $4 to all museums.

For information regarding any part of Lincoln State Monument, stop at the Historical Center, or call 653-4372.

RUIDOSO AND MESCALERO

These two towns are perfectly situated to cater to thousands upon thousands of Texans hungry for mountain recreation that is unavailable in the Lone Star state. Consequently, this scenic region surrounded by Lincoln National Forest is one of the most popular resort areas in New Mexico and features virtually every form of outdoor sport.

Ruidoso, located on US Hwy. 70 at the foot of Sierra Blanca, gets its name from the *ruidoso* or "noisy stream" that runs through town. The town got its start with Dowlin's Mill, a grist mill along the river which was built in the early 1880s. The town grew quite slowly until tourism began to attract businesses and residents to the area in the 1930s.

Mescalero, fifteen miles southwest of Ruidoso on US Hwy. 70, is the center of the 460,000-acre Mescalero Apache reservation. This reservation was established in the early 1870s near the original home of the Mescaleros after decades of fighting among the Apaches and the Mexicans and Americans. The Mescaleros survived military campaigns, starvation, and internment at Bosque Redondo to become a progressive tribe with a variety of recreational enterprises that are now quite profitable.

The origin of the name Mescalero, or "one who uses the *mescal*," is often debated because there are at least three different mescals (*mezcal* in Spanish) that grow in the Southwest. First is the *agave*, or century plant, which the Mescaleros prepared for food by roasting the fleshy leaves in underground pits. Second is the mescal bean, the hallucinogenic (and highly toxic) seed of a species of locust called the mountain laurel. The name mescal is also given to the tops of the peyote cactus, which are called "mescal buttons."

Although it is possible that the Mescaleros utilized all three plants at various times, the most likely explanation for their name comes from the agave, a principal food of the Mescaleros before the advent of ranching and farming.

★ ★
TOURIST INFORMATION

RUIDOSO CHAMBER OF COMMERCE
P.O. Box 698, Ruidoso, NM 88345 (257-7395)

★ ★
RECREATIONAL FACILITIES

SKI APACHE
It's not very often skiers have a chance to ski the slopes of a 35 million-year-old volcano that is also a sacred mountain. But at Ski Apache, the opportunity arises at the 11,500 foot skiing summit of Sierra Blanca, the highest mountain in the United States south of the latitude of Mount Whitney in California, and the southern-most mountain in the country where the artic life zone occurs. It is also called "Old Baldy" because of the tree-less arctic conditions on the peak.

The Mescaleros, who revered Sierra Blanca as a sacred moun-tain, have constructed an excellent ski area on its slopes, complete with 39 trails, of which forty per cent are advanced (one trail runs eight thousand feet), eight chair lifts, and snowmaking on one-third of the area. There are on-slope bars, restaurants, and snack bars, and lodging is available in Mescalero or in Ruidoso. The resort has a complete rental shop, skiing lessons, and ski races.

Ski Apache receives an average of 190 inches of snow per year. It is reached via NM Hwy. 48 north to Alto and then NM Hwy. 532. For additional information, contact Ski Apache Resort at 257-9001 for a ski report.

RUIDOSO DOWNS
During the summer racing season mid-May through Labor Day, about 300,000 horse racing fans flock to Ruidoso for seventy days of racing and some of the largest purses in the world. Among the most famous races here are the Kansas Futurity, the Rainbow Futurity, and the richest quarterhorse race in the world, the All American Futurity with an estimated purse of $2,530,000 ($1 mil-lion to the winner). Additionally, some of the most expensive horses in the world are sold at the All American Sales Arena at the track during the summer.

The track has a Jockey Club, the All American Turf Club, and a grassy forecourt area where visitors can relax in their own lawn chairs. It is located one mile from town on US Hwy. 70 east of Ruidoso and can be reached by calling 378-4431.

INN OF THE MOUNTAIN GODS
Located three miles from Ruidoso via US Hwy. 70 and Carrizo Canyon Rd. and perhaps the finest resort in New Mexico, the Inn of the Mountain Gods has been described as "serene, secluded, and spectacular" by Wendell Chino, president of the Mescalero Apache Tribe, which built and manages the resort. The inn offers 230 deluxe rooms, ten mini-suites, and ten parlors with either a lakeside or mountain view.

Within the resort complex are three restaurants, including the **Dan Li Ka Dining Room,** which is highly recommended. Also, the inn has three lounges and several snack bars including the **Apache Tee,** adjacent to the golf course.

Recreational facilities at the Inn of the Mountain Gods are numerous. The eighteen-hole championship golf course has a resident PGA professional and staff, club rental, lessons, and is regarded as one of the best mountain courses in the world. Horseback riding through the nearby forests is provided by the inn's stables. Year-round tennis is available on six outdoor and two indoor courts, with lessons available from the resident USPTA professional.

Hunting and fishing are available through the Mescalero tribe's programs that cater to the sportsman. A hunting coordinator arranges trips for trophy-sized deer, elk, bear, and other game. There is also a trap and skeet range at the inn. Because the inn is situated beside a fully stocked trout lake, fishing is easy from dockside or from boats that are available for rent. Canoes and sailboats are also available.

Other amenities at the Inn of the Mountain Gods include a swimming pool, gift shops, a game room, bicycle rentals, a jogging track, whirlpools, saunas, bus service to Ruidoso Downs or Ski Apache, and a conference center. For reservations, contact the inn at (257-5141 or 1-800-545-9011) or write P.O. Box 269, Mescalero, NM 88340 for more information.

LODGING

The Ruidoso area has more than eighty lodging firms providing more than three thousand beds as well as more than 55 restaurants, so finding places to sleep and eat shouldn't be a problem.

CARRIZO LODGE
Because it is a large complex with 117 one-, two-, and three-bedroom units, the Carrizo is perfect for families. Both the lodge and the restaurant are on the National Register of Historic Places, and guests can utilize an outdoor pool, whirlpool and sauna, or take art classes. The Carrizo is located about four miles southwest of Ruidoso on Carrizo Canyon Road (257-9131).

INN AT PINE SPRINGS CANYON
This 96-room facility is directly across the street from Ruidoso Downs on East US Hwy. 70. It offers four luxury suites and whirlpool and saunas. Call 378-8100.

MONJEAU SHADOWS
This Victorian-style farmhouse (built in the 1980s) is a bed and breakfast country inn with private baths and fireplaces, and a large entertainment room. It is located on NM Hwy. 48 in Alto (336-4191 or 648-2392).

SWISS CHALET BEST WESTERN
As we saw in Red River, some lodging developers are determined to transport Switzerland to New Mexico. Despite its out-of-place appearance, the Swiss Chalet is a comfortable, 82-room motel atop Alto Crest overlooking the Ruidoso Valley. It is the closest lodging to Ski Apache and offers a restaurant, lounge, and some rooms with steam bath. The Swiss Chalet is located on NM Hwy. 48 North, take Sudderth exit, then right on Mechem (258-3333 or 1-800-47-SWISS).

SIERRA BLANCA CABINS
This resort features rustic log cabins set among tall pines along the "noisy" Rio Ruidoso. Amenitites include kitchenettes, cable TV, a children's playground, and picnic areas. The cabins are two miles west of US Hwy. 70/NM Hwy. 48, then right on Country Club Dr. past the bridge—cabins are on the left (257-2103).

SIERRA MESA LODGE
A small bed-and-breakfast inn, Sierra Mesa has five guest rooms decorated with brass and four-poster beds, plus a hot tub spa and living room with a fireplace. The lodge is in Alto on Fort Stanton Road (336-4515). From Ruidoso, take NM Hwy. 48 north (Mechem

Dr.) six miles past Sudderth intersection. Turn right on Fort Stanton Rd., then left at the fork in the road, lodge is 1.9 miles farther on left.

STORY BOOK CABINS
Another group of log cabins set in the pines along the Rio Ruidoso, Story Book has one, two, and three bedroom units with kitchenettes, cable TV, and stone fireplaces. These cabins are on Upper Canyon Rd. (257-2115), the most preferred area in Ruidoso. Located on the west side of Ruidoso, off Sudderth (US Hwy. 70).

VILLAGE LODGE AT INNSBROOK
Located two miles north of town on NM Hwy. 48 at Innsbrook Dr. (258-5441), the Village Lodge has one-bedroom suites with kitchenettes and fireplaces. Other amenities include a trout pond, two tennis courts, an outdoor swimming pool, a supper club, and a par-three golf course.

Other recommended facilities are **Ruidoso Inn,** on East US Hwy. 70 in town (378-4051); **A-Frame Cabins,** NM Hwy. 48, two miles north of ski area (258-5656); **High Country Lodge,** on NM Hwy. 48 north in Alto (336-4321) and **Shadow Mountain Lodge,** off NM Hwy. 8 on Upper Canyon Rd. (257-4886).

★ ★
ECLECTIC LODGING NEAR RUIDOSO

Try the **Casa de Patron,** a historic B&B in the Rio Bonito Valley near Lincoln (653-4676), or the **Village Lodge,** which offers 32 suites next to a golf course in Ruidoso (800-722-8779). The **High Country Lodge** has 30-plus cabins next to Alto Lake (800-845-7265) and **Dan Dee Cabins** is a cottage resort on the winding Ruidoso River (800-345-4848). The **Sierra Mesa Lodge** features guest rooms and an indoor spa on a wooded hillside (366-4515).

★ ★
DINING

As befitting a major resort town, Ruidoso has restaurants catering to all tastes. Many of them are located on NM Hwy. 48 north, also known as Mechem Dr.

NEW MEXICAN

The **Casa Blanca,** 501 Mechem Dr. (257-2495), has the usual enchiladas and *chiles rellenos* plus burgers and live entertainment on weekends. Open daily 11 a.m.–10 p.m.

CONTINENTAL

La Lorraine, 2523 Sudderth (257-2954) is one of the more sophisticated restaurants in town, serving mostly French cuisine with an emphasis on unusual poultry dishes using quail, pheasant, and duck. Veal and seafood are also presented very professionally. Open 11:30 a.m.–2 p.m. Mon., and Wed–Sat. 4:30 p.m.–9:30. Reservations are necessary on weekends. The **Swiss Chalet,** in the motel of the same name (see above), bakes its own pastries and serves a variety of Continental dishes. **Delphi-Gyros,** 2415 Sudderth (257-5175) specializes in Greek sandwiches and pastries. Open 10 a.m.–5 p.m. daily.

STEAK AND SEAFOOD

Quite a few Ruidoso restaurants specialize in beef and seafood, with a little New Mexican cuisine thrown in for good measure. The **Bull Ring of Ruidoso,** 1200 Mechem Dr. (258-3555) is a perfect example of such an establishment. Open 11 a.m.–10 p.m. daily. Bar open 'til 2 a.m. Its large lounge has a fireplace in-the-round and live entertainment. "All you can eat ribs" is the specialty of the **Cattle Baron Steak House,** 657 Sudderth (257-9355), which also has excellent prime rib and steaks that are cut daily on the premises. Open 11 a.m.–9:30 p.m. daily. The **Inncredible Restaurant and Saloon,** NM Hwy. 48 north at Ski Run Road (336-4312), serves steaks, ribs, chicken, fish, veal, and pastas in several dining rooms, including a large greenhouse sun (or moon) room. Open 11:30 a.m.–10:30 p.m. daily, evening dinners from 5 p.m.

It's well worth the 25-mile drive east on US Hwy. 70 to visit **Tinnie's Silver Dollar Restaurant** in the lovely Hondo Valley at tiny Tinnie, New Mexico (653-4425). The Silver Dollar features steak and lobster but also prepares excellent continental dishes in an atmosphere enhanced by Victorian antiques and stained glass. The restored, historic mercantile building houses the restaurant and a gift shop. Open Wed.–Fri., 5 p.m.–10 p.m.; 11:30 a.m.–4:30 p.m. for lunch on Saturday and Sunday, and 5 p.m.–10 p.m. for dinner. It is closed Monday and Tuesday.

SPECIALTIES

For fiery Chinese food, scale the **Great Wall of China,** 2913 Sudderth (257-2522), and find Szechuan and Hunan dishes. Open 11:30 a.m.–9 p.m. daily, except closed Mon.

And perhaps the award for Best Scenic View at a Ruidoso Restaurant should go to the **Cree Meadows Restaurant,** 301 Country Club Dr. (257-2733), which offers prime rib and lobster and a breathtaking vista of Sierra Blanca. Open for breakfast Saturday and Sunday 7 a.m.–2 p.m., dinner Friday and Saturday 6 p.m.–10 p.m. Lunch is served Tuesday–Sunday from 11 a.m.–2 p.m. Closed Monday.

GALLERIES

Ruidoso is the art center of the southern half of New Mexico. Art lovers should be sure to visit **Crucis Art Bronze and Foundry,** 524 Sudderth (257-7186), which offers sculpture and jewelry; **Mountain Arts,** 2530 Sudderth (257-9748) sells rugs, pottery, weavings, prints, and lithographs. A complete list of Ruidoso galleries is available at the Chamber of Commerce Office at 720 Sudderth Dr.

JUST FOR THE FUN OF IT

FLYING J RANCH
This operation features a western village, pony rides, a stage show with the "Flying J Wranglers," gold panning, a gift shop, and a pistol shoot for kids. The Chuckwagon Suppers are pretty basic, but filling. The Flying J is located on NM Hwy 48 north of town, a mile and a half beyond Ski Apache Road. Reservations are suggested (336-4330). Open Memorial Day until Labor Day, except Sundays.

BINGO
Gambling buffs will enjoy betting on letter and number combinations at the new Bingo of Mescalero facility located near the skeet range at the Inn of the Mountain Gods. Bingo is played Wednesday through Monday nights. Players have a chance to win up to $30,000 on just seven numbers. Reach Bingo of Mescalero by calling 257-9268.

ASPENFEST

Ruidoso's biggest celebration lasts two months. It starts Labor Day Weekend with the All American Futurity at Ruidoso Downs, and ends in mid October. In between are mule races, fishing and golf tournaments, a motorcycle rally, street dances, and a hot rod run. Perhaps the biggest event is the Aspen Festival, held the first weekend in October, which features a parade, street festival, arts and crafts fair, a bicycle race, and the New Mexico State Open Chili Cookoff. The **Cowboy Symposium** is held the second weekend in October. Cowboy poets, artists, writers, and musicians gather to share their talents and participate in fiddling contests, trail rides, and a chuckwagon cookoff. For additional information, contact the Ruidoso Chamber of Commerce at 257-7395.

LINCOLN NATIONAL FOREST

Facilities for camping, hunting, and fishing are plentiful in the national forest that surrounds Ruidoso. Principal campgrounds are **South Fork**, fourteen miles northwest of town off NM Hwy. 48 with sixty spaces and stream and lake fishing at **Bonito Lake; Oak Grove**, five miles northwest of town off NM Hwy. 48 with twenty-nine camping spaces but no water; **Cedar Creek**, also off NM Hwy. 48; and **Nogal Lake**, between NM Hwy. 37 and Capitan along NM Hwy. 48. Fishing is also available at **Eagle Lakes** and **Alto Lakes**, both off NM Hwy. 48.

For detailed information on recreational facilities in Lincoln National Forest, contact the office of the forest supervisor in Alamogordo at 437-6030 or the Smokey Bear Ranger Station in Ruidoso at 257-4095.

Mescalero Apache Tribal Campgrounds include: **Ruidoso Recreation Campground, Eagle Creek**, and **Silver Lake**. For directions and fee information, contact the Mescalero Tribal Offices at 671-4427.

ALAMOGORDO

This small city of about 30,000 people has been transformed in the past eighty years from a ranching and farming community into one of the high tech centers of New Mexico. It all started in 1898, when railroad magnate Charles B. Eddy purchased Alamo Ranch from Oliver M. Lee, one of the pioneer ranchers in southeastern New Mexico. Eddy envisioned his own planned community, and established a division point at the ranch for his El Paso and Northeastern Railroad. In 1899, Alamogordo, which means "fat cottonwood tree" in Spanish, was selected as the seat of Otero County, which had been carved out of Lincoln and Doña Ana counties. Large cattle and sheep ranches on nearby flats and mesas, apple and cherry orchards in the mountains, and lumbering provided most of the economic base.

With the coming of the railroad, Alamogordo boomed and by 1902, four thousand people lived there. After Eddy moved his railroad shops to Carrizozo, the town's growth slowed a bit, but was revived during World War II when Holloman Air Force Base and White Sands Proving Ground (now Missile Range) were established. The first atomic bomb was exploded at Trinity Site just sixty miles north of town in July, 1945.

Today, both the air force base and the missile range provide the largest part of Alamogordo's economic base. Both guided missles and pilotless aircraft are tested in the area, and White Sands Missile Range is the backup landing strip for the space shuttle flights. Most of the high-tech testing at these facilities is top-secret, so visitors may not enter without permission from the base commander. However, special tours of Holloman Air Force Base for fifteen to thirty persons can be arranged by calling the public information office at 479-5406. In September the base conducts an open house complete with aircraft displays, and sometimes, a flyover by the famous Thunderbirds.

★ ★
TOURIST INFORMATION

ALAMOGORDO CHAMBER OF COMMERCE
1301 S. White Sands Blvd., Alamogordo, NM 88310 (437-6120)

★ ★
LODGING AND DINING

Alamogordo's lodging facilities are limited to standard chain motels, but there are some interesting older hotels in nearby Cloudcroft (see listing below). Recommended motels in Alamogordo, both of which have a swimming pool, restaurant, and lounge, are **Desert Aire Best Western,** 1021 S. White Sands Blvd. (437-2110 or 1-800-848-5405); and the nearby **Holiday Inn,** 1401 S. White Sands Blvd. (437-7100 or 1-800-465-4329).

For New Mexican specialties, **Ramona's Restaurant,** 2913 N. White Sands Blvd. (437-7616) serves great *chimichangas*, an un-

translatable word for a stuffed, deep-fried burrito. It is open
6 a.m.–10 p.m. daily. **Me and Tex,** 10th Street and Oregon (437-
9749) also has chimichangas and the usual chile-hot foods. This
establishment is open 6 a.m.–9 p.m. Mon.–Fri., 11 a.m.–9 p.m.
Sat., and 11 a.m.–8 p.m. Sun.

Steaks and burgers are the name of the game at **Cattleman's
Steak House,** 2904 N. White Sands Blvd. (434-5252), open
4:30 p.m.–9:30 p.m. daily, **Furgi's Pub,** 10th Street and Scenic
(434-1540), open 11 a.m.–2 a.m. Mon.–Sat., US Hwy. 82 in Mountain Park (682-9929). The restaurant is open daily 5 p.m.–9 p.m.

Alamogordans love their barbecue, as is evidenced by the
popularity of **Mr. C's Pit Barbecue,** 323 New York Avenue
(437-7587), with great soul food by Warner Coleman.

NEARBY ATTRACTIONS

ALAMEDA PARK AND ZOO
Located at 10th Street and US Hwy. 70, this small, free zoo is the
oldest in the Southwest and has a duck pond and a collection of
American and African animals. Nearby is the Chamber of Commerce building at 1301 White Sands Blvd. (437-6120 or 1-800-
545-4021), which houses the **Tularosa Basin Historical Museum**
with local history exhibits and Indian artifacts. The museum is
open 10 a.m.–4 p.m. daily.

THE SPACE CENTER
This futuristic complex located at Indian Wells Rd. and Scenic Dr.
is the pride of Alamogordo. It is the only facility in the world that
honors the men and women who have risked their lives for space
research. The **International Space Hall of Fame** is housed in a five-
story concrete and glass "golden cube" where visitors can relive the
history of space exploration. Exhibits include moon rocks, a lunar
rover, satellites, rockets, and the fascinating Space Station 2001,
with visitor-operated controls.

The **Tombaugh Space Instruction Center** is a combination planetarium and Omnimax Theater. Named after Clyde W. Tombaugh,
discoverer of the planet Pluto, the center provides a dramatic ren-
dering of the universe — and the wonders of planet Earth. The

Omnimax Theatre, one of only a few in the world, has a forty-foot-high, wrap-around screen that shows 70 mm film, plus a six-channel audio system. Watching a film in this theatre is so realistic that the experience can be dizzying or even disconcerting for the faint of heart. The theater is also the site of laser light concerts daily during the summer and on weekends during the winter.

The planetarium has a Spitz 512 projector capable of producing more than two thousand stars, the Milky Way, and all of the visible planets, and it can duplicate the sky as it would be seen from any vantage point on earth on any day on the year. Also at the Space Center is the grave of Ham the Astro-Chimp. Ham was the first chimpanzee to be rocketed into space—on January 3, 1961. He died of old age, not as a result of the space flight.

The Space Center is open daily 9 a.m.–6 p.m. Admission fee for a combination visit of both the theater and space hall is $5 for adults and $3.50 for children. For additional information, call 437-2840.

WHITE SANDS NATIONAL MONUMENT

By far the harshest desert environment in New Mexico is this beach without an ocean—White Sands, a vast area of dunes where three ancient seas evaporated long ago. Here is the ultimate extreme of a desert: a combination of aridity, high temperatures, and harsh chemicals. Despite such a foreboding description, an astonishing variety of flora and fauna have adapted to this hostile environment. As one naturalist put it, "In this strange gypsum desert, living creatures have found a harsh, forbidding, and inhospitable environment. Nevertheless, during past centuries, species of both plants and animals have adapted to the unusual habitat and have developed ways and means to survive and reproduce, even under the unique conditions presented by this sea of sand.

Most interesting are the dunes themselves, which consist not of the usual silica sand, but of gypsum, or calcium sulfate, the principal ingredient of plaster of Paris. This gypsum was deposited during the Permian period of about two hundred million years ago, and, over the intervening millennia, it washed out of the mountains and into prehistoric Lake Otero, which covered most of the Tularosa Basin.

As Lake Otero evaporated over the past 20,000 years to form present-day Lake Lucero, the gypsum crystalized and was blown into dunes. During spring runoff, when the water table is high, the chemical exists in solution in the shallow waters of Lake Lucero. As this lake dries up during the summer, prevailing southwest winds continue to pile the gypsum crystals into dunes up to one hundred feet high. Currently the white sands cover an area of about three hundred square miles, though only about three-quarters of that area is included in White Sands National Monument. The area is so vast that on weather satellite photos it's often mistaken for snow. One source makes a brave estimate that there is enough gypsum in these dunes to fill 214 million freight cars — enough freight cars to circle the earth 57 times!

How is it possible for trees to survive amidst these dunes? Of the 228 species of plants found in the Tularosa Basin, only 62 species can exist in the high concentrations of calcium sulfate. Of those 62, only six perennials can actually resist the action of the dunes by growing above them: These plants extend their stems below the dunes and into the solid ground. Soaptree yuccas with stems as long as thirty feet have been found, and spectacular pillars of gypsum have formed around the trunks of cottonwoods and sumacs as they are alternately covered and uncovered by the dunes. The roots of these trees penetrate into the soil beneath the blown-in sand and extend into the water table, which is only about six feet below the ground.

Most of these trees are found on the edges of the dunes, where they can resist the smothering action of the sand for a while. But eventually, the inorganic triumphs over the organic. In the vast center of this gypsum beach, no life at all can survive and the visitor might as well be visiting another planet.

The principal area of life is found in the interdunal flats, that zone of conflict between the organic and inorganic. One of the animal survival methods is a form of protective coloration called "color matching." Because darker animals stand out so prominently against the stark white sands, most inhabitants of the interdunal zone have evolved into forms much lighter than their normal colors. Snout and tiger beetles are very pale, and the white camel cricket is so close to transparent that its internal organs are clearly visible. The crickets are preyed upon by a very pale form of northern scorpion, so in this scenario in the dunes, survival is a matter of the invisible escaping from the camouflaged.

Lizards have adapted well to the gypsum dunes. The Cowle's prairie lizard and the bleached earless lizard are almost pure white, and the latter has the chameleon-like ability to change color according the darkness of the background. Lizards chase the insects that make up their diets mostly during the cooler morning hours during the summer; they would quickly fry if they lounged about on the hot sand for any length of time during midday.

The Apache pocket mouse has evolved to total whiteness in the dunes, unlike its cousins who live just north in the Valley of the Fires lava flow—they have become jet black to match the lava. When the white pocket mice remain motionless against the sands, they are nearly invisible to their primary threats, hawks and owls. These pocket mice and their cousins, the kangaroo rats, do not drink water to survive. The moisture they need is produced during the process of digesting the seeds they eat, and this fluid is recycled by the mouse's kidneys instead of being passed as urine.

Such specialized creatures often can be seen during the early morning hours at White Sands National Monument. A walk along the **Big Dune Trail,** a one-mile, one-hour course that reveals by interpretive signs the fascinating ecology and geology of the gypsum dunes.

Visitors not wishing to expend so much energy can examine the displays in the visitor center, which retell the story of the formation of the dunes and the evolution of its denizens, and they can take the sixteen-mile loop drive and watch for signposts that correspond to informative paragraphs in the monument's brochure. Picnic facilities and rest rooms are provided here; campers should stop at commercial campgrounds in Alamogordo. White Sands National Monument is located fifteen miles southwest of Alamogordo on US Hwy. 70. For more information, call the monument at 437-1058.

OLIVER LEE MEMORIAL STATE PARK

This unique park, eight miles south of Alamagordo via US Hwy. 54, then two miles east on County Rd. 16, is nestled at the foot of the Sacramento Mountains at the mouth of Dog Canyon. Natural springs seep out of the mountains at this point and support a variety of rare and endangered plant species. Dog Canyon, a classic box canyon, has been a camping spot for paleo-Indian hunters, an Apache Indian stronghold, and the site of the homestead of Oliver Lee's vast ranching operation. The canyon got its name in the 1860s when ranchers chased a band of Mescaleros into the canyon. Somehow, the Indians disappeared and the ranchers found only a dog in the box canyon.

The visitor center has displays that describe the natural and cultural history of the site, and a mile south of the center is the ranch house that was Oliver Lee's headquarters. It has been restored and turned into a museum to give visitors a glimpse of turn-of-the century ranch life in southern New Mexico.

The 180-acre park is an oasis in the desert and has picnicking and camping sites with utility hookups, hiking trails, and rest rooms with showers. The visitor center is open from 9 to 4 daily and can be contacted by calling 437-8284.

LA LUZ
Located eight miles northeast of Alamogordo via US Hwy. 70 and NM Hwy. 545, La Luz, founded in 1705, is the oldest settlement in the Tularosa Basin. It is now an arts and crafts colony with art galleries and studios featuring the work of weavers, potters, and jewelers.

TULAROSA
Located just twelve miles north of Alamogordo along US Hwy. 70/82, this town of about five thousand inhabitants was founded in 1863 when about a hundred families from the flooded lower Rio Grande Valley moved to the Rio Tularosa and began homesteading. Tularosa is known as the City of the Roses, and a Rose Fiesta each May celebrates this flower with pageantry and an arts and crafts exhibit. The **Tularosa Village Museum,** 301 Central Ave. (585-2057) has exhibits of pioneer life as well as interesting artifacts.

CLOUDCROFT
The highway from Alamogordo to Cloudcroft (US Hwy. 82) rises six thousand feet in just 27 miles and is perhaps the steepest roadway in the state. It roughly parallels the tracks of the former El Paso and Northeastern cog railway to the logging camps in Russia Canyon built in the years 1898–99. Near Mountain Park the road passes through the only highway tunnel in the state, and the view of the Tularosa Basin is spectacular all along the way to Cloudcroft.

Cloudcroft began its existence as a logging camp for the railroad, which was cutting timbers for cross-ties. The railroad built a lodge at the camp as a summer retreat for its officers and other El Pasoans, and soon a mountain resort village began to take shape at an altitude of 8640 feet.

★ ★
TOURIST INFORMATION

CLOUDCROFT CHAMBER OF COMMERCE
P.O. Box 125, Cloudcroft, NM 88317 (682-2733)

LOCAL ATTRACTIONS

Located on US Hwy. 82 across from the Chamber of Commerce, the **Sacramento Mountains Historical Museum** (682-2958 or 682-2932) illustrates local history with photographs, antiques, and artifacts. The museum is open weekdays during the summer from 1 p.m.–4 p.m., Saturdays 10 a.m.–4 p.m., and weekends 1 p.m.–4 p.m. during the winter.

    Sacramento Peak Observatory at Sunspot is one of the largest solar observatories in the world and features live television close-ups of the sun and all its spots. There are guided tours of the facility on Saturdays at 2 p.m., May through October. To reach Sunspot, take NM Hwy. 130 south from Cloudcroft two miles to the junction of Forest Rd. 245 and turn right. This paved road leads to the **Nelson Canyon Vista Trail**, which has beautiful views of the Tularosa Basin and White Sands. The Forest Road ends at Sunspot, which also offers spectacular vistas of the surrounding landscape. For more information, call Sacramento Peak at 434-1390.

SKI CLOUDCROFT
This facility is the southernmost ski area in the U.S. and is located two and one-half miles east of town on US Hwy. 82. It features 26 trails that descend from a maximum altitude of 9400 feet. There is one chairlift here, two tows, and snow-making equipment on sixty percent of the slopes. Ski Cloudcroft has a snack bar on location, but lodging is available only in Cloudcroft. The area receives about ninety inches of snow a year, and 36 percent of the trails are reserved for beginner skiers. Night skiing is available Friday and Saturday, 5 p.m.–10 p.m. Cross-country skiing is available at The Lodge, below. Open Friday through Sunday during the season, Ski Cloudcroft can be reached at 682-2333.

LINCOLN NATIONAL FOREST
Campgrounds are plentiful in the Cloudcroft area and include **Fir Recreation Area,** three miles northeast of town on NM Hwy. 130, with 89 camping sites, rest rooms, fireplaces and botanical trails; **Pines Campground,** two miles northeast of town on NM Hwy. 130, has 49 units; **Sleepy Grass Campground,** two miles east of town on US Hwy. 82 with 43 units; and **Deerhead Campground,** a mile south on NM Hwy. 130, offers 35 units.

    Fishing is available with state or tribal license along the **Peñasco River** at Mayhill and at **Silver Lake** on the Mescalero Reservation, eight miles north of town on NM Hwy. 130. Three commercial enterprises offer trout fishing with no license required; however, most charge $.50 per person and fish are $.30 an inch. They are **Mountain Park Trout Farm** (682-2698) at mile marker 11 along US Hwy. 82 in Mountain Park; **Silver Springs Recreational Campground** (682-2803), five miles north of town on NM Hwy. 244; and **Runyan Trout Farm,** 687-3542 near mile post 56 on US Hwy. 82.

Hiking enthusiasts can choose between the **Rim Trail,** a thirteen-mile walk, or **Osha Trail,** an easy two-and-one-half-mile jaunt. Maps are available at the Cloudcroft Ranger Station or the Chamber of Commerce. Another interesting trail is **La Parada Encantada** ("enchanted walk"), a self-guided loop nature trail from the **Sleepy Grass Campground** (see above). For additional information on Lincoln National Forest, contact the ranger station in Cloudcroft at 682-2551.

OTHER RECREATIONAL FACILITIES

Considering its small resident population of 550, Cloudcroft has a surprising number of private recreational facilities. The **Ponderosa Pines Golf Course** is a new nine-hole course nine miles south of town on NM Hwy. 130 in Cox Canyon (682-2995). **Triple M's Snowplay Area** (682-2205) offers snowmobile rentals, innertubing, and ice skating and is located four and one-half miles south of town on Sunspot Highway. Bull riding enthusiasts will enjoy the **Wimsatt Rodeo Arena,** seven miles east of town on US Hwy. 82 (682-2457), which offers NMRA-sanctioned rodeos during late May and early October. Horseback riding is available at **Chippeway Stables and Restaurant** (682-2565) during the summer. Free tennis courts are found at **Frazer Courts** next to the Chamber of Commerce.

★ ★
LODGING

The Lodge, off NM Hwy. 82 on Corona Street (682-2566), is far and away the most interesting place to stay in Cloudcroft. This turn-of-the century European-style facility is a state landmark that has offered lodging to such notables as Pancho Villa, Clark Gable, and Judy Garland. In addition to its nicely restored rooms (try the Governor's Suite), The Lodge has many amenities including a tower with a panoramic view of the Sacramento Mountains, a nine-hole golf course with the highest altitude (9200 feet) in the

country, cross-country skiing with ski rentals on premises, an outdoor pool, whirlpool and sauna, and restaurants and a nightclub
(see listing below). Also available is The Lodge's **Summer Pavilion,**
a bed and breakfast inn.

Other recommended lodging facilities are **Buckhorn Cabins**
(682-2421) off US Hwy. 82 near Village Center; **Silver Top Cabins**
(682-2396) just off US Hwy. 82 behind the chamber of commerce
building, with a restaurant and skating pond; and the **Summit Inn**
(682-2814) just off US Hwy. 82 near Village Center.

★ ★
DINING AND ENTERTAINMENT

The finest restaurant in Cloudcroft is **Rebecca's,** the main dining
room at The Lodge (682-2566). Named after a friendly female ghost
who reputedly haunts The Lodge off US Hwy. 82 at Corona Street,
Rebecca's features continental cuisine in a nicely decorated room
with a great view of the mountains. There is a lounge here along
with a nightclub called the **Red Dog Saloon** which offers live entertainment on weekends.

Cloudcroft has two "western-style" entertainment complexes.
The **Flying J Ranch** (336-4330) has a western village, chuckwagon
suppers, and what a brochure describes as a "foot-stompin' stage
show." The **Chippeway Park and Stables,** six miles southeast of
town on NM Hwy. 130 (682-2565) features beef barbecued over
oak wood and a western stage show put on by the entire Fuller
family, which owns the facility.

Other recommended restaurants are the **Texas Pit Barbecue** on
Burro Avenue (682-2307), with hickory-smoked meats and chili
con carne served cafeteria-style; and **Ray's Western Cafe,** also
on Burro Avenue (682-2817). Ray's is open 7 a.m.–10 p.m., Ray's
hours vary.

★ ★
SHOPPING

Burro Avenue, which runs parallel to and just north of US Hwy.
82, is the main shopping area. Here the visitor will find gift shops
and arts and crafts galleries. Stop by **The Copper Butterfly,**
(682-2765); **Sleepyeye Trading Company,** (682-2270); and **Klingler
Gallery,** call for directions, 682-2988.

More information on Cloudcroft is available from the Chamber
of Commerce at 682-2733.

ARTESIA

From Cloudcroft, US Hwy. 82 East descends from the Sacramento Mountains through a lonely but beautiful stretch of New Mexico until it reaches the eastern plains and the town of Artesia, which is located between Roswell and Carlsbad along US Hwy. 285. Artesia was named for the vast Artesian Basin beneath Eddy County, but it wasn't the water that first drew settlers to the region.

The first settler of Artesia was Union soldier John Truitt, who homesteaded at Chisholm Springs Camp along the Chisholm Trail, which was located about three blocks from Artesia's main business district. The arrival of the Pecos River Railroad caused the town to adopt the name of Miller's Siding, but the name was later changed to Stegman, after its first postmaster.

In 1903, the drilling of an 830-foot-deep well, then the deepest in the world, provided irrigation water and caused another change in the town's name — and this time, the name stuck: Artesia. Twenty years later, another well was sunk, but this one yielded oil, not water. It was the first producing oil well in New Mexico and only the third in the petroleum-rich Permian Basin, and it started an oil and gas boom in the southeast part of the state.

Today Artesia depends upon oil and gas as well as farming and ranching for most of its income base. This town of about 12,000 is not known for tourism, but there are some interesting sights.

★ ★
TOURIST INFORMATION

ARTESIA CHAMBER OF COMMERCE
P.O. Box 99, Artesia, NM 88210 (746-2744)

★ ★
LOCAL ATTRACTIONS

Artesia is proud of its museum, the **Artesia Historical Museum and Art Center,** 505 W. Richardson Ave. (748-2390). It is located in the Moore-Ward Cobblestone House, which was built in 1904 of cobblestones hauled from the bed of the nearby Rio Peñasco. The museum specializes in local history and has displays of frontier life from about 1800 to the present. It is open Tuesday through Saturday from 10 a.m.–noon and 1 p.m.–5 p.m., and admission is free.

An offbeat attraction in Artesia is, believe it or not, **Abo Elementary School** at 18th and Center streets. This facility is often called

the "bomb shelter school" because it was built completely underground in the early 1960s as a fallout shelter for two thousand people. The play area for recess is located atop the school's concrete
roof. Fortunately for us all, the school has never been used as a fallout shelter.

Lodging in Artesia is provided by fairly basic motels, the best
of which are the **Best Western Pecos Inn,** 2209 W. Main Street
(748-3324 or 1-800-676-7481); **West Winds Motel,** 1820 S. First
Street (746-9801) with a swimming pool; and **Starlite Motel** 1018
S. First Street (746-9834).

For dining, New Mexican specialties can be found at **La Fonda,**
210 W. Main Street (746-9377), open Mon.–Thur. 11 a.m.–2 p.m.
and 5 p.m.–9 p.m.; Fri., Sat., and Sunday open 11 a.m.–9 p.m.
,For oriental food, the **Kwan Den** 2209 W. Main Street (inside the
Pecos Inn) is the answer (746-9851). It is open 6 a.m.–10 a.m. for
breakfast, 11 a.m.–2 p.m. for lunch, and 5 p.m.–9 p.m. for dinner,
Monday through Saturday. Open Sunday from 5 p.m.–8 p.m.

CARLSBAD

Like Roswell, Carlsbad's early fortunes depended on cattle. In
1866, two Texas cattlemen — Charles Goodnight and Oliver Loving
— established a trail from San Angelo, Texas, north along the Pecos
River to Fort Sumner, and then further north into Colorado,
Wyoming, and Montana. Along this trail they drove huge herds of
longhorn cattle, which they sold to the military, to miners, and to
other Western ranchers who needed to replenish their herds.

The Goodnight-Loving Trail crossed to the east side of the Pecos
at the present site of Carlsbad, which in 1888 was originally called
Eddy after John and Charles Eddy, two ranchers who settled in the
area and helped develop the town. In 1899 the name of the town
was changed to Carlsbad because a hot spring north of town resembled the famous spa of Karlsbad in Czechoslovakia.

Ranching and farming were Carlsbad's major businesses until
1925, when potash deposits were discovered east of town. Commercial mining of these deposits commenced in 1931. Potash is used
in the manufacture of commercial fertilizers and is expensive to
ship, so the profitability of mining it has fluctuated greatly over the
years and the mines open, close, and reopen periodically.

The proximity of Carlsbad Caverns National Park (see the listing
below) has helped Carlsbad become a major tourism center in the
last few decades. This small city of about 30,000 has also become
a popular retirement center because of its mild climate, relaxed
lifestyle, and recreational facilities.

★ ★
TOURIST INFORMATION

CARLSBAD CHAMBER OF COMMERCE
P.O. Box 910, Carlsbad, NM 88220 (887-6516)

★ ★
CITY SIGHTSEEING

Carlsbad has an interesting mix of sights within the city limits as
well as the spectacular national parks nearby. The **Carlsbad Museum and Art Center,** 418 W. Fox Street (887-0276), is a combination
natural history, art, and historical museum. It has exhibits on the
formation of the solar system, the unique geology of the Pecos
River, fossils from the Permian reefs, and artifacts of pre-Clovis
paleo-Indians dated to 20,000 years ago (this date is disputed by
many archaeologists). The museum's art exhibits feature paintings
by members of the Taos Society of Artists, including Fremont Ellis
and Ernest Blumenschein, and there are displays of local history as
well. The museum is open 10 to 6 daily except Sundays.

The **National Parks Visitor and Information Center,** 3225 National Parks Hwy. (US Hwy. 62/180) (785-2232) can provide details
about the two national parks in the area, Carlsbad and Guadalupe Mountains (see listing below).

LIVING DESERT STATE PARK
Undoubtedly, this state park is one of the most interesting in New
Mexico. Located just north of town off US Hwy. 285 and atop the
Ocotillo Hills, the park is a combination zoo, botanical garden,
and museum that concentrates on the flora, fauna, and ecology of
the Chihuahuan Desert. Within its 1120 acres are sixty species of
birds, mammals, and reptiles, and a thousand varieties of desert
plants. A large Desert Arboretum also contains hundreds of species
of cacti and succulents from desert areas all over the world, including those of South America and Africa.

The visitor center has displays that provide a good introduction
to the region's geology, archaeology, local history, and the unique
environment to which the plants and animals have adapted. A gift
shop with an excellent bookstore is also located at the visitor
center.

Outside, a paved, self-guiding trail leads the visitor through sand
dunes, desert uplands, and gypsum soils that support a surprising
variety of plant life. Among the interesting plants are yuccas,

agaves, mesquite, bird of paradise, acacia, locust, and many species of cacti.

Living Desert is not a zoo in the traditional sense of housing animals captured or bred for display purposes. All caged animals and birds in the park are there because they were found sick or injured and could no longer survive in the wild. Additionally, many species of wild birds, mammals, and reptiles live on the grounds because it is their natural habitat.

The trail leads the visitor through an arroyo exhibit featuring javelinas, enclosures with bison, elk, and deer, an aviary with hawks and owls, and a nocturnal exhibit that features kangaroo rats, kit foxes, and ringtails. Along the way, one might encounter many other species of desert animals, including black bears, bobcats, prairie dogs, pronghorns, and the rare Mexican wolf.

One of the greatest myths of the West is that its deserts are barren, lifeless places. Living Desert State Park dramatically disproves that idea, and children seem to find it particularly interesting. The park is open daily except for Christmas. Hours are 9 a.m.–5 p.m. during the winter and 8 a.m.–6:30 p.m. in the summer; admission is $3 per person, but children six and under can get in free. For more information, call the park at 887-5516.

LAKE CARLSBAD RECREATION AREA

A dam on the Pecos River has created a lake three miles long in the center of town and this body of water is used by locals and visitors alike for swimming, boating, fishing, waterskiing, and windsurfing. On the west side of the lake is **Lake Carlsbad Park,** at the end of Church Street, with a boat ramp, docks, a beach, tennis courts, and a picnic area. The east side of the lake has **President's Park** on Muscatel Avenue (887-0512), complete with a municipal campground, golf course, and playground. Also at President's Park is an amusement center, a narrow-gauge railway, and an old-fashioned paddlewheeler named "George Washington," which carries passengers between the two parks. Below Lake Carlsbad is **Bataan Recreation Area,** a smaller lake reserved for sailboating, canoeing, fishing, and picnicking.

★ ★
LODGING AND DINING

Large chain motels make up the only lodging choice in Carlsbad, which has about 1200 rooms available. All of the following are recommended and have swimming pools, restaurants, and lounges:

Best Western Motel Stevens, 1829 S. Canal (887-2851 or 1-800-528-1234), the largest in town with 181 rooms; **Carlsbad Inn,** 601 S. Canal (887-3541); and the **Rodeway Inn,** 3804 National Parks Hwy. (887-5535).

Recommended restaurants in Carlsbad include **Cortez,** 506 S. Canal (885-4747), open 11:30 a.m.–1:30 p.m., 4:30 p.m.–8:30 p.m. Weds.–Sun., closed Monday and Tuesday; and **Golden China,** 509 S. Canal (885-2953) featuring fiery Szechuan and Hunan food. Golden China is open 11 a.m.–2 p.m. and 5 p.m.–9 p.m.; closed Sunday.

For additional information on Carlsbad and the surrounding area, contact the Chamber of Commerce at 887-6516. The Chamber sponsors a "fun phone," 885-CAVE, which highlights current events and attractions.

★ ★
NEARBY ATTRACTIONS

CARLSBAD CAVERN NATIONAL PARK
In 1901, James White, a Carlsbad-area cowboy, was intrigued by a huge flock of bats that seemed to fly right out of the ground. After further investigation, White discovered a cave opening, which he promptly explored with the aid of a kerosene torch. Such was the modest beginning of the exploration of Carlsbad Caverns, one of the largest and most spectacular caverns in the world.

Curiously, it wasn't the beautiful cave formations that first interested the early explorers, but rather it was the bats—or specifically, the bats' guano, which was valuable as a fertilizer. Guano mining operations began about 1904 and the fertilizer was shipped to the orange groves of southern California. Although the mining lasted twenty years and produced more than 100,000 tons of guano, high shipping costs prevented the efforts from being profitable. The guano operation experienced problems much like the difficulties other miners experienced with another fertilizer ingredient of the region, potash.

James White worked for the various guano-mining companies and in his spare time, descended deeper and deeper into the caverns. His tales of fantastic formations caught the attention of public land officials who assigned federal geologists to explore Carlsbad Caverns. The reports filed by these geologists impressed President Calvin Coolidge, who declared the caverns a National Monument in 1923. The following year, White led a National Geographic expedition into the caverns, and the subsequent publicity— including an on-location radio broadcast by "Believe It Or Not" reporter Robert Ripley—made the caverns so famous that they were declared a National Park in 1930.

In the late 1920s, the caverns were scouted as a possible location for Hell by filmmaker Henry Otto, who was making the film *Dante's Inferno* for the Fox Film Company. Unable to find a suitable location in California realistic enough to "satisfy the fundamentalists," Otto toured Carlsbad Caverns but came away disappointed. According to one witness, "One look at the vast interior of the cave convinced Mr. Otto that here was no place to shoot the Inferno. This didn't look like Hell. Why if he made his film in this fairyland, it would be nothing less than a clever bit of propaganda for Hades, and everybody would want to go there."

The vast caverns began as an organic reef complex in the inland sea which covered southern New Mexico during the Permian period about 240 million years ago. This reef was covered by the sediment of subsequent seas for millennia and then about sixty million years ago, earth movements caused an uplift that fractured the reef, which was now buried beneath surface of the earth. This fracture allowed water to filter down through the reef and dissolve parts of the limestone. Over millions and millions of years, the water created crevices, then pockets, and finally the huge rooms we see today. Then, about three million years ago, the uplift that created the Guadalupe Mountains (also a reef), lowered the water table and the water drained out of the caverns and was replaced by air.

Rainwater and melting snow seeped into the caverns and filtered into the underground chambers, dissolving more limestone as it went. As soon as this water was exposed to the air, it evaporated, leaving the crystalline forms of limestone, calcite, and aragonite. Over many centuries, this process produced an incredible number and variety of stalactites, which develop from the ceiling of the chambers. Water that reached the floor of the chambers before evaporating created stalagmites, and when joined together, the two formations make columns or pillars. The brown, red, and yellow colors of these formations are the result of small amounts of minerals, such as iron oxide, in the limestone.

Visitors have a choice of how they would like to enter the caverns. On the Red Tour, an elevator at the visitor center descends directly to Underground Lunchroom 750 feet below, where a tour of the Big Room begins. But far more interesting is the Blue Tour, a one-and-three-quarter-mile walk into the caverns along a trail through the Main Corridor, which takes the visitor on a spectacular, convoluted tour to 830 feet below the surface. This trail also ends up at the Big Room, which is large enough to engulf fourteen football fields and a 22-story building.

The caverns contain many beautiful formations with imaginative names such as Whale's Mouth, Temple of the Sun, the Queen's Chamber, and the Hall of Giants. Visitors should bring a camera equipped with a flash attachment and plenty of color film. Temperature inside the caverns is a steady 56 degrees and humidity is ninety per cent, so warm clothing is suggested even in the summer. Fees are charged for both the elevator and walk-in tours, both of which are self-guided. From Nov. to Jan. there are guided tours during the week in the main corridor only. Lunch is served underground for a nominal fee, or visitors may bring their own food. All food must be consumed in the lunchroom and not along the trail.

More adventurous visitors may make reservations for the two-hour New Cave Tour in ominously named Slaughter Canyon. This tour is a rugged visit to a newer section of the park that has opened recently. Visitors must carry their own water and flashlights and be prepared for a long climb to the cave mouth, and then a one-mile hike through the cave. Rangers guide 25 people at a time on this tour, and it is by reservation only.

There is no camping permitted at the park, but there are commercial campgrounds nearby at White's City. Picnicking is permitted at the Rattlesnake Springs and Walnut Canyon Road turnouts, where visitors may explore the fascinating desert environment. At the visitor center are informative displays regarding the geology, history, and ecology of the caverns, plus a well-stocked gift shop and bookstore. Since this park attracts more than 700,000 visitors per year, there is sometimes a long wait for the tours and elevators. The best time to arrive at the caverns during the summer is when the park opens in the morning, 9 a.m.

One particularly fascinating aspect of the caverns is the flight of the colony of Mexican freetail bats. Each evening during the summer, some 300,000 bats leave the mouth of the caverns in a counter-clockwise spiral at the rate of about five thousand bats per minute. This flight is eagerly watched by visitors who assemble in the outdoor amphitheater while park rangers explain that the bats are leaving on their nightly feeding mission. In the morning, they return to feed their young, which are hanging upside down on the ceilings inside the caverns.

The National Park Service conducts an annual "Bat Breakfast," which is quite popular. In 1988, more than six hundred bat enthusiasts ate breakfast while watching these beasties, who themselves were returning from their own breakfast feast of flies, moths, and other insects.

Carlsbad Caverns National Park is located 27 miles southwest of Carlsbad via US Hwy. 62/180. For additional information, call the park information center at 785-2232.

WHITE'S CITY

This commercial community, named after the early cavern explorer James White, has the lodging and dining facilities closest to Carlsbad Caverns. White's City is located just off US Hwy. 62/180 27 miles southwest of Carlsbad and has filling stations, an amusement park, RV park, and numerous curio and gift shops. The information center and post office has details about visiting the caverns.

The **Cavern Inn** on Hwy. 80 (785-2291 or 1-800-528-1234) is a Best Western motel with 131 rooms and two pools and is the most convenient place to stay while visiting the national park. The **Million Dollar Museum,** across the street, has twelve rooms packed with 30,000 collectibles including European dollhouses, guns, antique cars, and believe it or not, a 6000-year-old mummified Indian.

GUADALUPE MOUNTAINS NATIONAL PARK

The Guadalupe Mountains are part of the Capitan reef system that includes Carlsbad Caverns. The mountains run roughly north and south and straddle the New Mexico–Texas border, with the portion of the range in New Mexico part of Lincoln National Forest and the portion in Texas designated Guadalupe Mountains National Park. The Guadalupes have the four highest peaks in Texas, including Guadalupe Peak (8749 feet) and the magnificent escarpment, El Capitan Peak, which tops out at 8078 feet, three thousand feet above the surrounding desert.

From the highway (US Hwy. 62/180) that runs southwest along the Guadalupes from Carlsbad Caverns, the mountains appear to have the same environment as the surrounding desert. But the Guadalupes are deceptive because of the numerous deep canyons that support a surpising variety of plant and animal life — 255 species of birds, 67 mammals, and 58 reptiles and amphibians. **McKittrick Canyon,** accessible by a paved road off the highway, has high, sheer walls, a running stream, and many species of non-desert trees such as maple, oak, and walnut. Two self-guiding, round-trip hiking trails lead from the canyon to **Pratt Cabin** and to the **Grotto Picnic Area.**

Vehicle campgrounds are available at **Pine Springs** and **Dog Canyon.** Backcountry camping is available in designated sites, and an eighty-mile trail system makes the park accessible by foot, but the going is often rough.

The **Frijole Visitor Center,** 55 miles southwest of Carlsbad on US Hwy. 62/180 (915-828-3307 or 915-828-3251), has all the necessary information about exploring the Guadalupes. Nearby and accessible by four-wheel drive vehicles are the **Butterfield Stage Line Station,** the ruins of the "Pinery" station built in 1858, and **Williams Ranch Historic Site.**

LINCOLN NATIONAL FOREST
The New Mexico portion of the Guadalupes, encompassing 285,000 acres, can be visited most easily by NM Hwy. 137, which leaves US Hwy. 285 just north of the Living Desert State Park. Forest Road 276 leads to **Sitting Bull Falls Picnic Area,** which features a waterfall pouring over a spectacular canyon wall. The water originates from a spring on the flat bluff above, falls one hundred feet in three streams, collects in a pool deep enough for swimming, and then disappears back into the rocks. The falls are a day-use picnic area only, with rest rooms but no camping allowed. There are nature trails that wind through the nearby piñon and juniper forest.

Legend holds that a posse pursued Chief Sitting Bull and his braves to this waterfall in 1881 after they stole horses and cattle, but a simple check of historical sources proves that the Sioux chief was in Canada at the time. The falls were the location for the shooting of the movie *King Solomon's Mines* in the 1950s.

Further along on NM Hwy. 137, Forest Road 540 takes the visitor to **Five Points Vista,** an overlook with a breathtaking view of the desert below. For more information on the Guadalupe Ranger District of Lincoln National Forest, contact the Carlsbad office at 885-4181.

BRANTLEY DAM STATE PARK
One of New Mexico's newer state parks is located twelve miles north of Carlsbad just off US Hwy. 285 and was created by Brantley Dam on the Pecos River. Facilities include picnicking and camping sites with hookups, rest rooms, and a boat ramp. Boating and fishing are the major recreational activities at this state park.

HOBBS

The second-largest city (38,000) in the southeastern part of New Mexico was founded because of a chance meeting between two covered wagons. In early 1907, James Hobbs and his family were crossing the **Llano Estacado** ("staked plain") that covers much of the eastern section of New Mexico and West Texas. The Hobbs family was headed to Alpine, Texas, when they met an eastbound wagon of settlers returning from that very town. They told the Hobbs family that it was impossible to make a living in Alpine, so Mr. Hobbs

turned north and built a dugout house at the location of the city
that would eventually bear his name.

Hobbs was a tiny farming and ranching community, completely
dependent upon cotton and cattle for the livelihood of the few
dozen families that were attracted by the promise of free land in
what was then the New Mexico Territory. Some of the nearby
ranches were gigantic: the Hat Ranch, for example, measured 35
miles wide and 150 miles long. The town of Hobbs remained in the
agrarian mode for about twenty years, and then the "Black Gold
Rush" transformed Hobbs into one of this state's biggest boom
towns ever.

On November 8, 1928, Midwest Refining Company — now Amoco
— struck oil in Hobbs and began producing seven hundred barrels
of "Black Gold" or "Texas Tea" per day. The population of the town
was between fifty and 100 persons. Two years later, the population
had soared to 12,000 during the first stage of the boom. People
poured into Hobbs from all over the country, arriving by car,
truck, bus, airplane and even on foot. These new settlers lived in
tents, crude shacks, and hastily erected metal sheds as more wells
were drilled.

In January, 1930, the second stage of the first boom began when
Humble Oil Company's Bowers Number 1-A rig began to pump
9720 barrels of crude a day. Soon electricity and the railroad arrived, and many of the temporary buildings were replaced with
wood and brick structures. However, the boom was short-lived because the Great Depression reduced oil revenues from $1.05 per
barrel to about fifty cents. By the middle of 1931, one-fourth of all
the buildings in Hobbs were vacant.

The town then turned to other enterprises to keep the money
flowing. Despite Prohibition, there were numerous taverns in town
that were disguised as roller-skating rinks by day. Brothels, pool
halls, and gambling parlors were also in evidence, but even profitable vice could not defeat the economic situation. The price of oil
dropped until it reached ten cents per barrel and soon three-
quarters of the population abandoned the boom town to seek better
fortunes elsewhere.

Hobbs's turnaround began in 1934 when the price of oil rose
enough to make drilling profitable again. The second boom began
slowly as the town recovered, and by 1940 about 14,000 people
again inhabited Hobbs. During World War II, Hobbs became the
site of an Army base which trained soldiers to operated B-17 and
B-24 bombers. After the war, the city purchased the old air base
and renamed it Hobbs Industrial Air Park. This was the beginning
of a diversification of industry that made Hobbs the commercial

center for West Texas and the southeastern corner of New Mexico.

Such diversification has helped Hobbs to survive recent crashes in oil and gas prices in the U.S. New Mexicans by now know to take steps to avoid the boom and bust cycles that have turned so many cities into ghost towns. By learning from past mistakes, mineral or energy-oriented towns like Grants, Carlsbad, Farmington, and Hobbs are broadening their income base to include a balance of mining, commercial development, farming, ranching, and in some cases, tourism.

★ ★

TOURIST INFORMATION

HOBBS CHAMBER OF COMMERCE
400 N. Marland, Hobbs, NM 88240 (397-3202)

★ ★

NEARBY ATTRACTIONS

Lea County Cowboy Hall of Fame and Western Heritage Center, 5317 Lovington Highway on the campus of New Mexico Junior College, is a combination commemorative hall and museum. Each year, no more than three men or women receive the coveted "Bronze Cowboy Award" for outstanding contributions to ranching and rodeoing. They are then inducted into the Hall of Fame and their memorabilia goes on display. Displays at the Heritage Center are arranged chronologically to depict the history of Lea County from earliest times to the present day. These exhibits consist of Indian artifacts, tools, and equipment from early ranching operations, and Southwestern wildlife dioramas. Hours of operation are Mon.–Thurs. 8 a.m.–5 p.m. and Friday 8 a.m.–3 p.m. For more information, call the Hall of Fame at 392-5518.

Thelma A. Webber Southwest Heritage Room (392-6561), located in Scarborough Memorial Library on the campus of the College of the Southwest just off Turner Street north of town, has an interesting collection of artifacts ranging from those of prehistoric Indians to those of ranching to some pieces from early oil field times. There is also a collection of about four thousand books on the Southwest here. Hours of the heritage room are Mon.–Thurs. 8 a.m.–9 p.m., Friday 9 a.m.–5 p.m. Visitors who are aircraft aficionados should visit the **Confederate Air Force Museum** (392-5342), located at the Hobbs-Lea County Airport on US Hwy. 62/180 west of town. This museum is open 9 a.m.–4 p.m. daily and has some fascinating aircraft on display, including a Ryan PT-22, a Stinson L-5, and a Japanese VAL.

★ ★
LODGING AND DINING

Recommended motel accommodations in Hobbs are the **Hobbs Motor Inn,** Seminole Highway (397-3251); **Woodleaf Executive Suites,** 3320 N. Dal Paso (392-2106); **Best Western Leawood Motel,** 1301 E. Broadway (393-4101 or 1-800-528-1234); the **Executive Inn,** 211 N. Marland (397-6541). All are fairly standard chain establishments except for Woodleaf Executive Suites, which offers suites for weekly and monthly rates.

Dining in Hobbs offers many possibilities. For New Mexico cuisine, try **La Fiesta,** 604 E. Broadway (397-1235), open 11 a.m.–2 p.m. and 5 p.m.–9 p.m. Mon.–Sat., closed Sunday. Hamburger aficionados will be pleased with **W.R. Snappy's,** 4006 N. Grimes (392-8511), open 10:30 a.m.–9 p.m. daily, and **Casey's,** 209 W. Broadway (393-0308), open 7 a.m.–5 p.m. daily and Sundays 7 a.m.–4 p.m.

★ ★
RECREATION

Hobbs has good reason to proclaim itself the "Soaring Capital of the United States." The city is blessed with weather patterns providing terrific thermals—uplifting winds—that are perfect for gliders. Also, the Industrial Air Park provides excellent runways and hangars for aircraft. Hence the skies over Hobbs are constantly filled with soaring enthusiasts who take advantage of the good weather and favorable winds. Hobbs hosted the World Soaring Championships in 1983 and in 1991. More information on soaring in Hobbs is available from the National Soaring Foundation at 392-1177.

Harry McAdams State Park, four miles north of town via NM Hwy. 18 (392-5845), is an intensely landscaped 37-acre park with two small duck ponds. Facilities include picnicking and camping sites, rest rooms with showers, utility hookups, a playground, sports facilities, and exhibits describing the natural and human history of the southeast corner of New Mexico. Another nearby facility is **Green Meadow Lake** on the north edge of town off Turner Street, which is well-stocked but really more a pond than a lake.

Index